Indiana Barn Quilt
Coloring Book Two
John H. Lettau

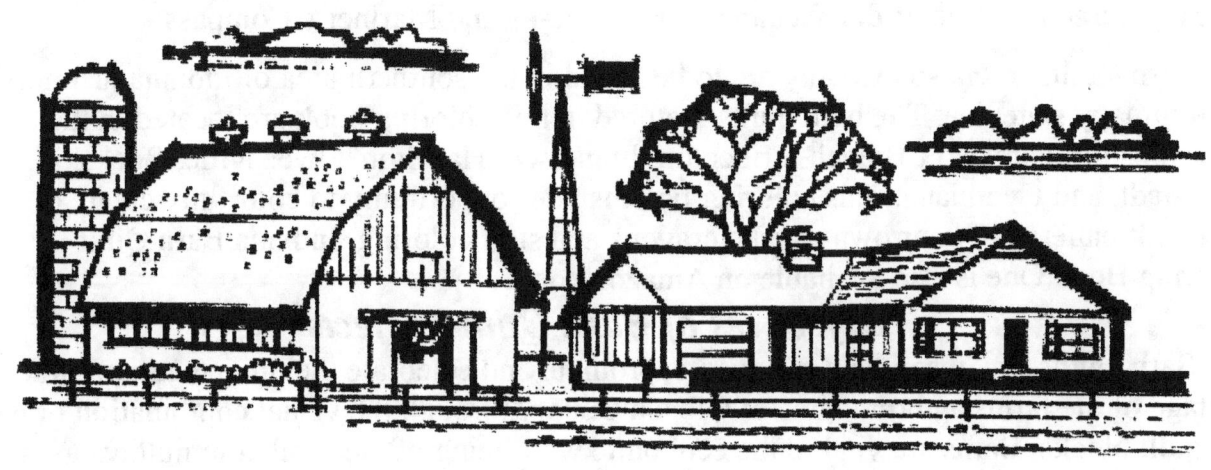

Barn Quilts of Gibson County, Indiana

Cover Barn Quilts

Wheel of Fortune
Compass Star
Bob's Pinwheel
Summer Dayz

Gibson County Indiana Barn Quilt Coloring Book Two

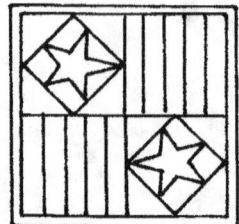 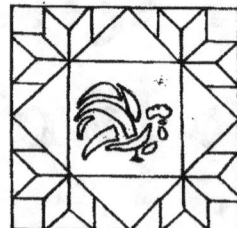 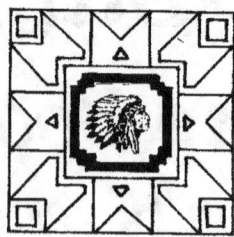 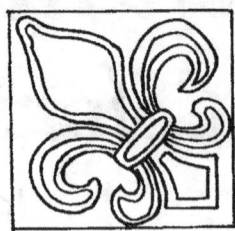 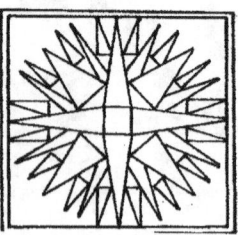

A drive through Gibson County, Indiana is very colorful today because many brilliant "quilt blocks," called barn quilts, are displayed on barns and other buildings throughout the rural area. Five sample barns quilt patterns located in Gibson County are pictured above...Stars & Bars, Chicken Scratch, Home of the Kickapoos, Fleur-de-lis and Mariner's Compass.

The Barn Quilts of Gibson County are to be found in the southern area of Indiana just north of the Kentucky state line. The barn quilts featured in this coloring book are located in the townships of...Patoka, Ft Branch, Princeton, Francisco, Hazelton, Owensville, Buckskin, Haubstadt, and Cynthiana. This coloring book is your opportunity to colorfully create different barn quilt patterns of your own so take crayons and start coloring. Indiana Barn Quilt Coloring Book One is also available on Amazon.com.

Objectives of Barn Quilt Projects

The Barn Quilts of Gibson help to educate, promote and celebrate the unique agricultural heritage of the farms and rural area of Gibson County through the visual combination of barns and quilt blocks. Barns are vital to the economic well-being of the rural community, and the comfort of hand-made quilts provided warmth, beauty, and an outlet for individual artistic expression.

Making a barn quilt allows individuals and volunteer groups the opportunity to create and paint their own quilt block, The design that is chosen may represent a family patterrn from a loved family quilt or perhaps a new pattern meaningful to the individual creator(s).

What is a Barn Quilt?

A barn quilt is made by painting a barn quilt pattern on two 4' by 8' sheets of ¾ inch plywood then mounting them on barn to form an eight foot square. Two coats of primer are applied to both sides of the boards and the edges. After the pattern is drawn out Frog (painter's) tape is applied. Three coats of each color are applied, with each coat being allowed to dry overnight. After the quilt is finished, it is allowed to dry for at least two weeks before it is put upon a barn.

Barn Quilts of Gibson County Information

Gibson County Visitors & Tourism Bureau
702 West Broadway Princeton, Indiana 47670
888-390-5825   812-385-0999   Fax 812-385-0545
www.giboncounty.org

Book Two Barn Quilts of Gibson County Indiana

Folded Star	E SR 64	Francisco, Indiana
Horn of Plenty	E 200 N	Princeton, Indiana
Star	E Brummitt	Owensville, Indiana
IU Nine Block	E 100 N	Princeton, Indiana
Windmill	S Center	Francisco, Indiana
Skip To My Lou Nine Patch	S 650 E	Princeton, Indiana
Indian Trail	S 650 E	Francisco, Indiana
Drunken Path	S 650 E	Francisco, Indiana
Fleur-de-lis	S 100 E	Princeton, Indiana
Red, White and Blue Star	W Main	Francisco, Indiana
Sky Rocket	S 653 E	Francisco, Indiana
Indian Trails	Outer Lake Rd	Princeton, Indiana
Sunflower	E 550 S	Princeton, Indiana
Double Wedding Ring	E 100 N	Princeton, Indiana
Tennessee	S 450 E	Francisco, Indiana
Seven Sisters	E 350 S	Francisco, Indiana
Star Burst	E SR 56	Hazelton, Indiana
Church of God Flames	E 350N	Francisco, Indiana
Toad In The Pond	N Frog Pond Rd	Hazelton, Indiana
Stripes and Nine	E 900 S	Buckskin, Indiana
Stars and Bars	S 1500 W	Owensville, Indiana
Liberty Star	N 825 W	Hazelton, Indiana
Compass Star	E 350 N	Francisco, Indiana
Flying Kite	W 225 N	Patoka, Indiana
Lucky Star #2	E SR 64	Princeton, Indiana
Fleur-de-lis 2	2400 Taylor Ave	Princeton, Indiana
Heaven's Ablaze	W Grave	Patoka, Indiana
County Fair	E Embree St	Princeton, Indiana
Tree and Tulips	N McCreary	Ft Branch, Indiana
Checkered Popcorn	E 750 S	Ft Branch, Indiana
Patriot	W Brummitt	Owensville, Indiana
Bob's Pinwheel	Poplar St	Patoka, Indiana
Chicken Scratch	S 150 E	Haubstadt, Indiana
Home of the Kickapoos	S SR 65	Owensville, Indiana
Ohio Star	E Hasenour Dr	Ft Branch, Indiana
Farmer's Wife	W 950 S	Owensville, Indiana
Contemporary Cross	E Spring St	Patoka, Indiana
Star Bound	S 200 W	Haubstadt, Indiana
Potted Flowers	S Prince	Princeton, Indiana
Grandma's Flower Garden	N SR 65	Patoka, Indiana
Moon & Stars Over the Mts	W 225 N	Princeton, Indiana
Summer Dayz	N 75 E	Patoka, Indiana
Dora's Delight	Old Hwy 41	Hazelton, Indiana
Wheel of Fortune	Mary Lee Dr	Princeton, Indiana
The Flag	N Hart St	Princeton, Indiana
Posie Whirl	S 40 W	Haustadt, Indiana
Mariner's Compass	10th St	Princeton, Indiana
Black Eyed Susan	S 100 W	Princeton, Indiana
Hunter's Star	S 450 W	Cynthiana, Indiana
Nine Patch	S Mohican Dr	Patoka, Indiana

Folded Star

Gibson County Indiana Barn Quilt

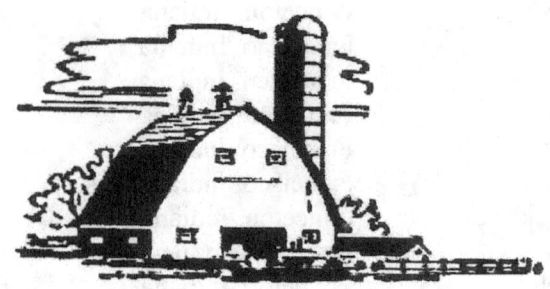

Barn Location
E ER
Francisco, Indiana

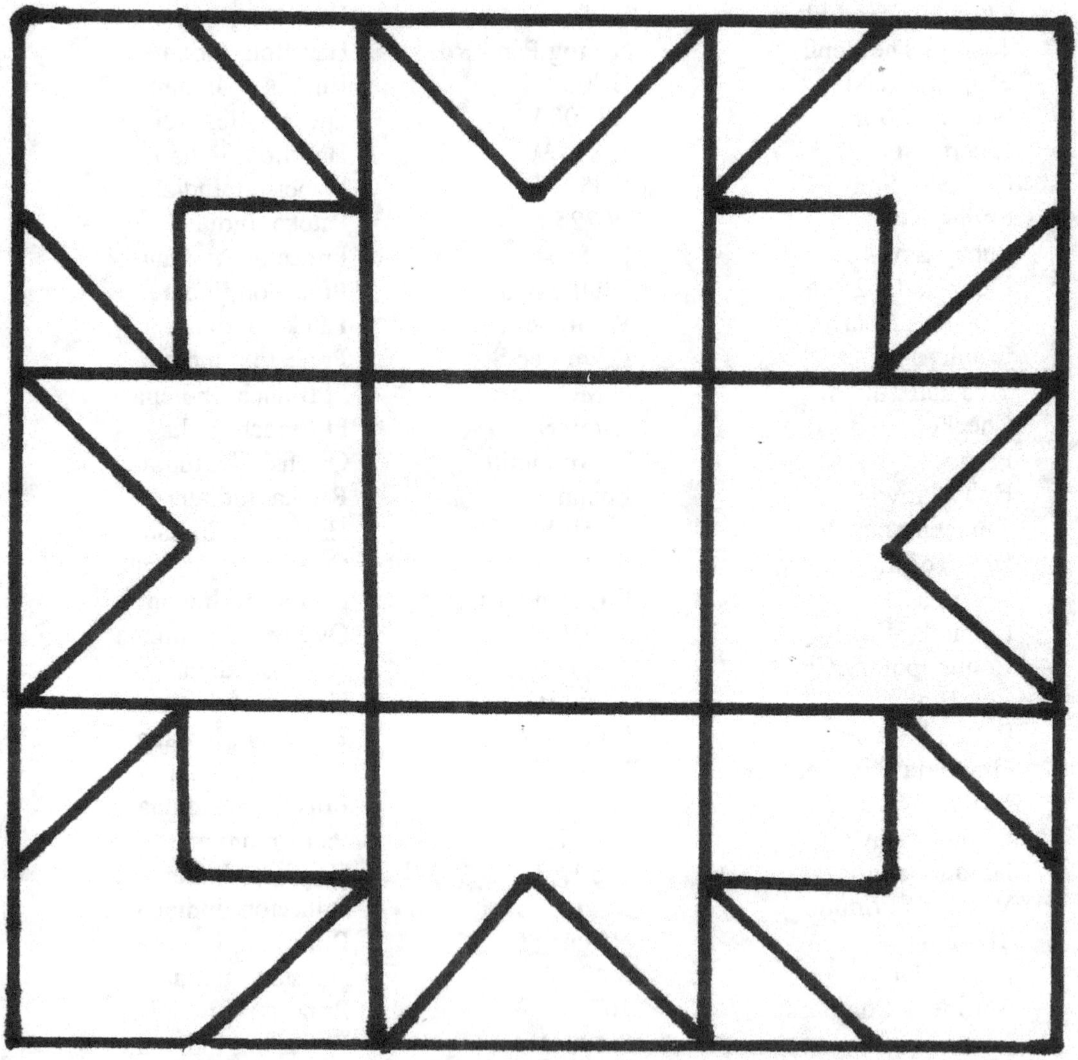

Gibson County Barn Quilt Folded Star

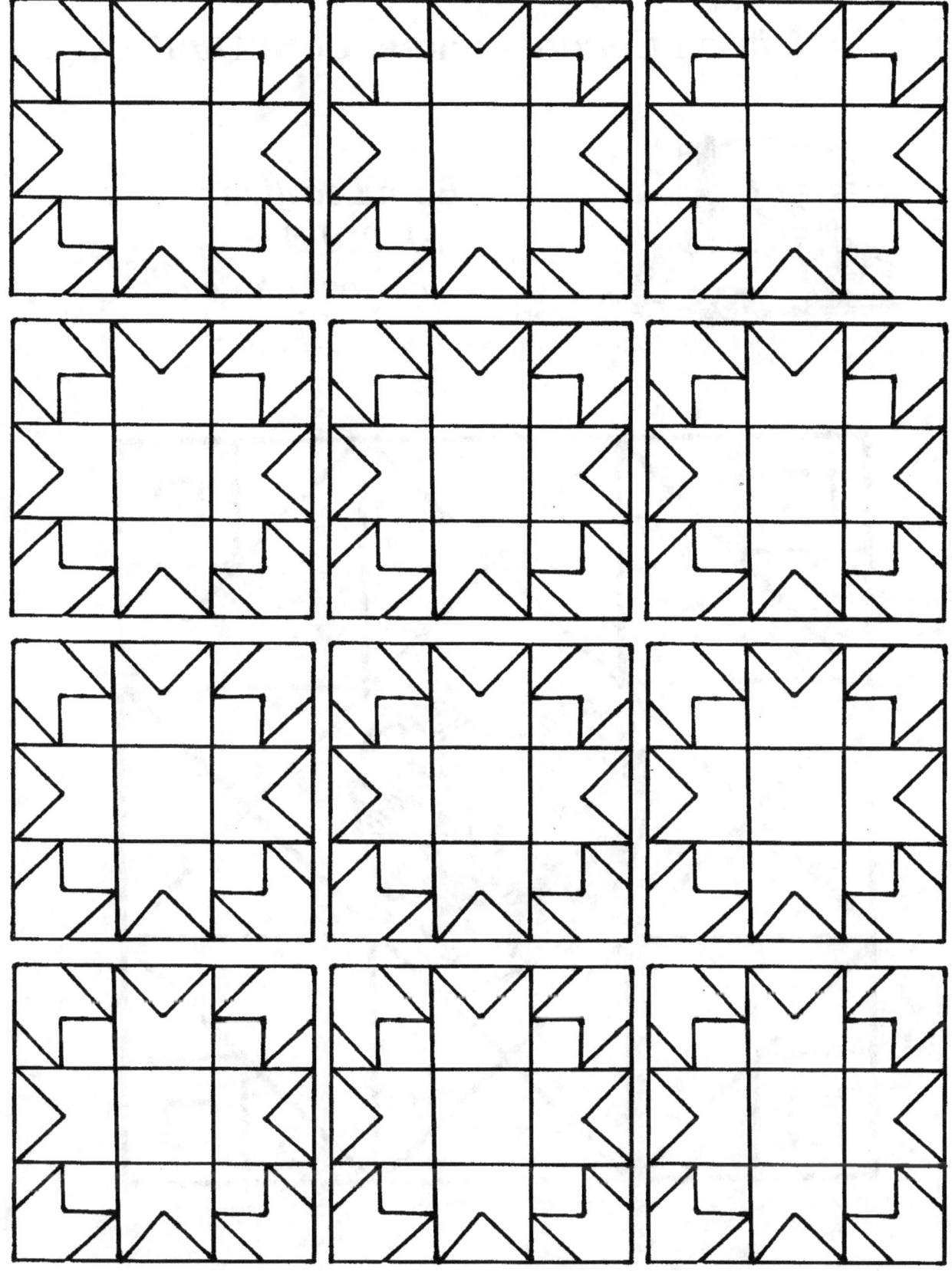

Horn of Plenty
Gibson County Indiana Barn Quilt

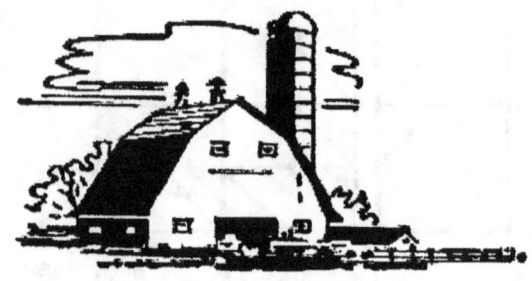

Barn Location
E 200 N
Princeton, Indiana

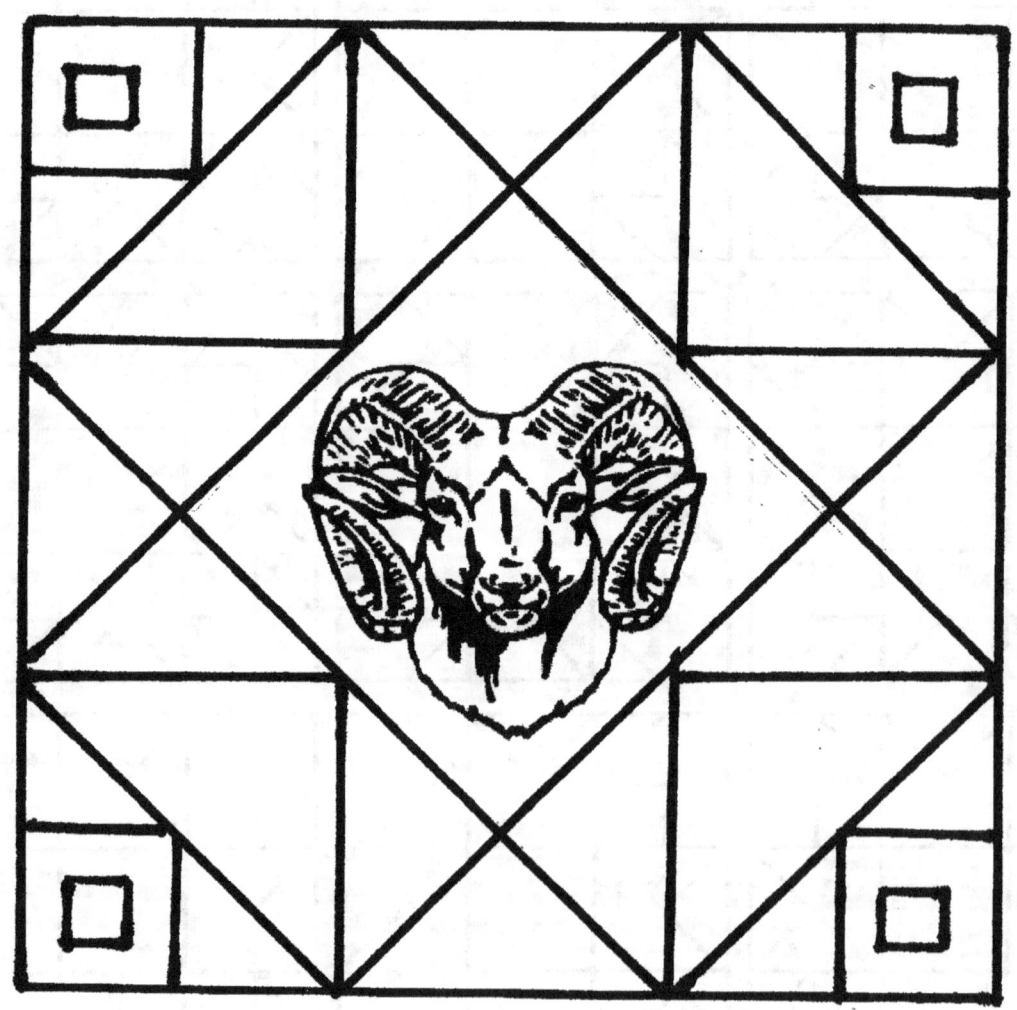

Gibson County Barn Quilt Horn of Plenty

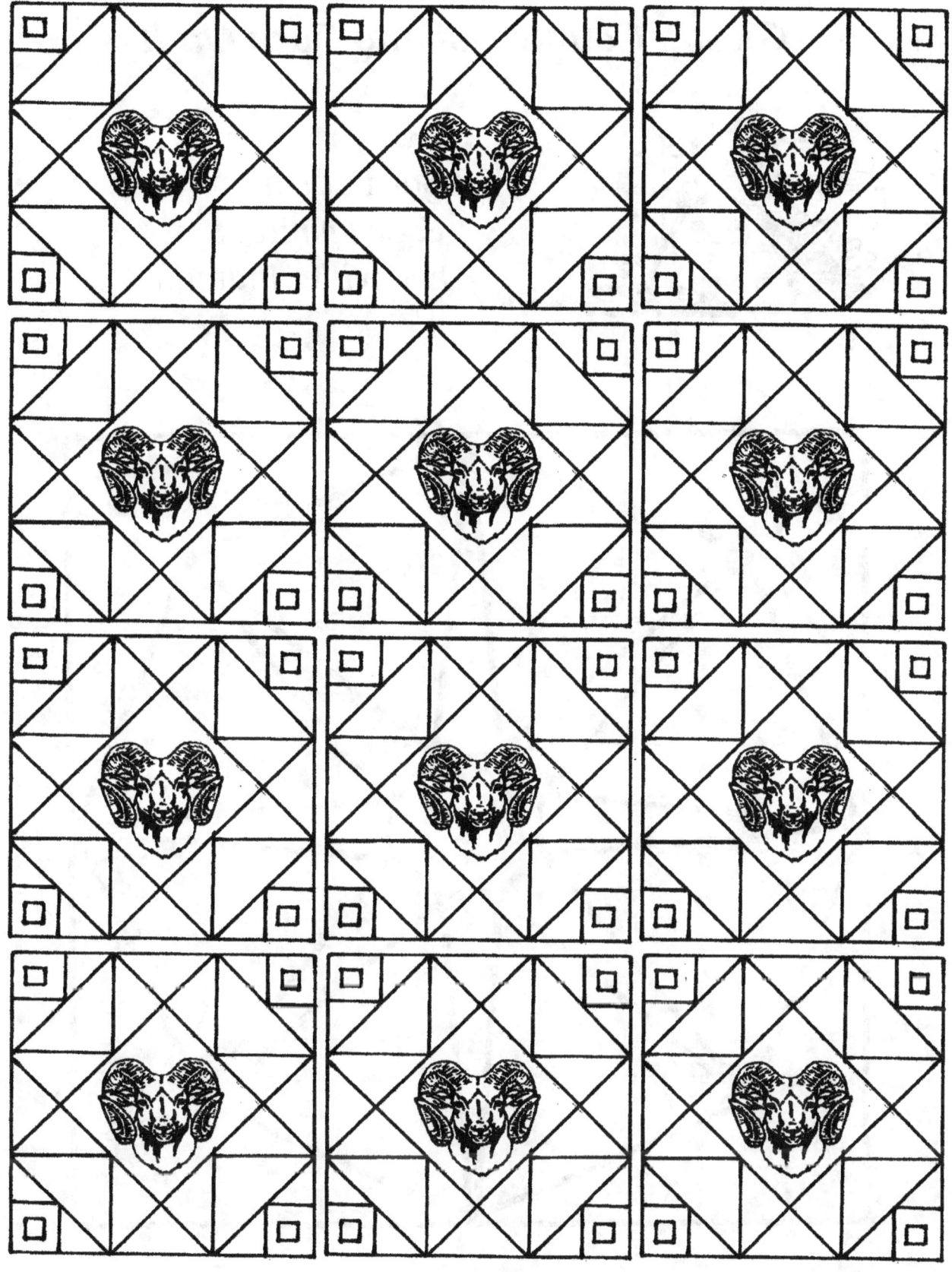

Star
Gibson County Indiana Barn Quilt

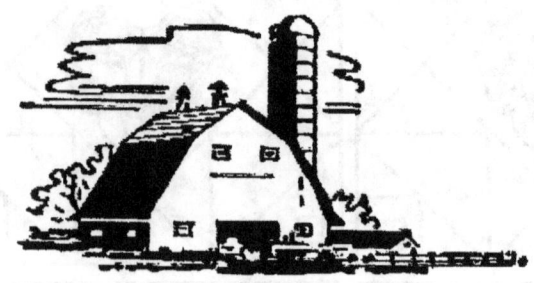

Barn Location
E Brummitt St
Owenville, Indiana

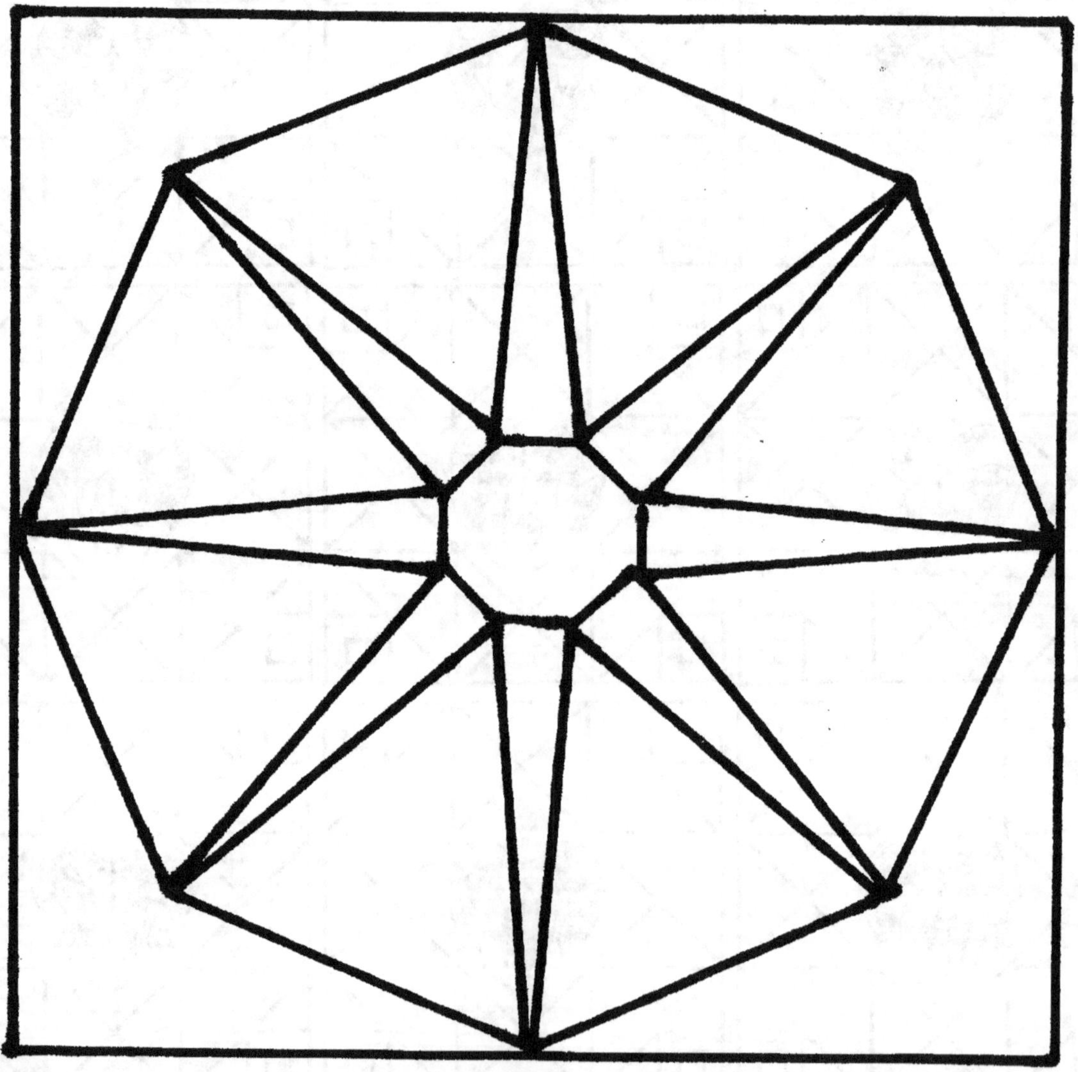

Gibson County Barn Quilt Star

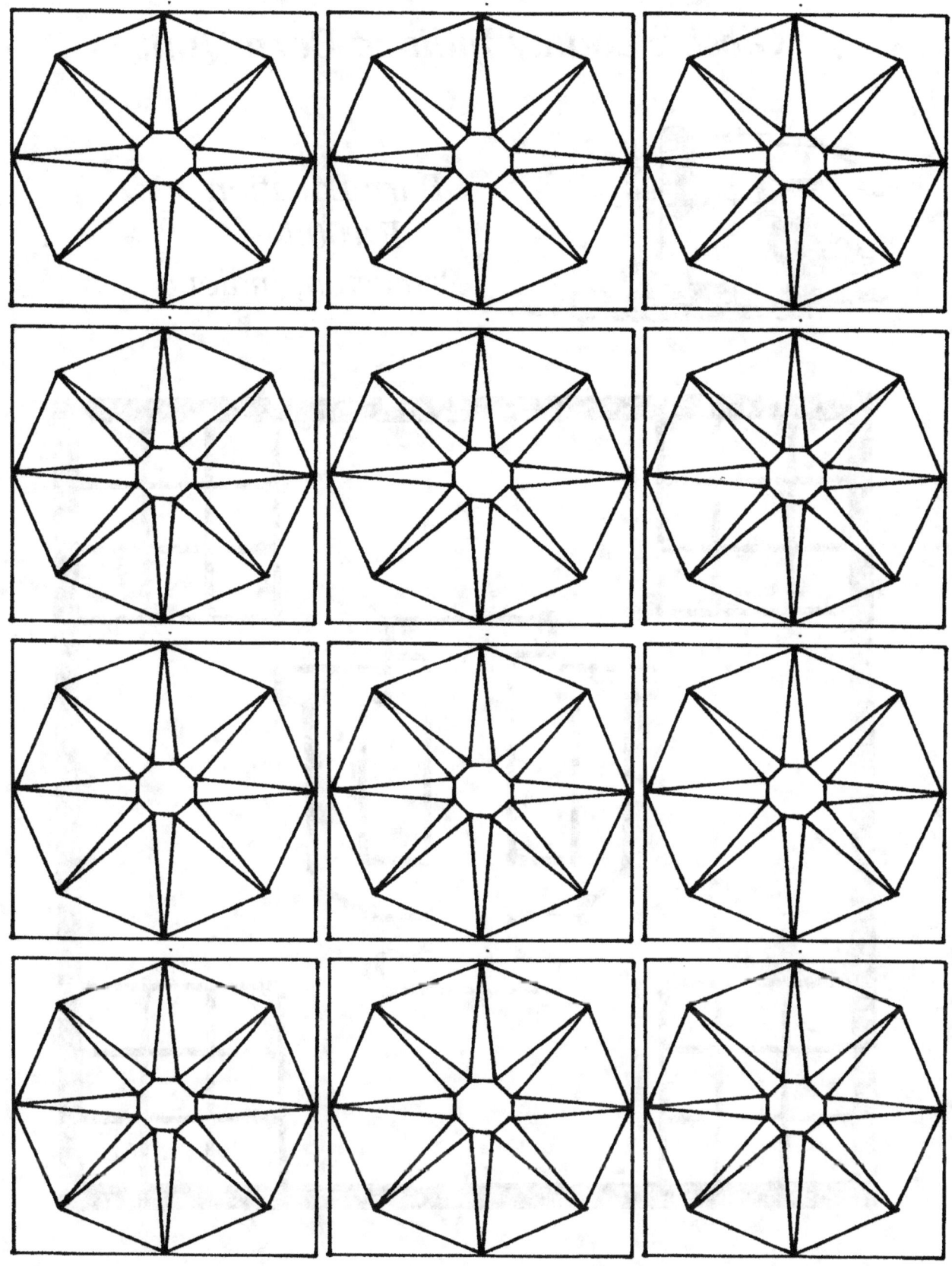

IU Nine Blocks
Gibson County Indiana Barn Quilt

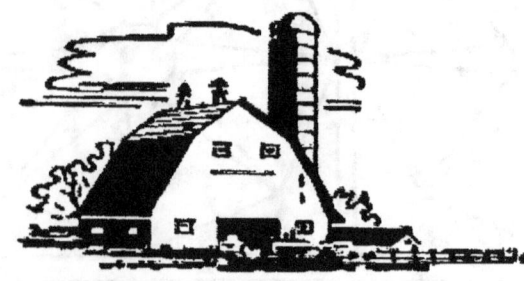

Barn Location
E 100 N
Princeton, Indiana

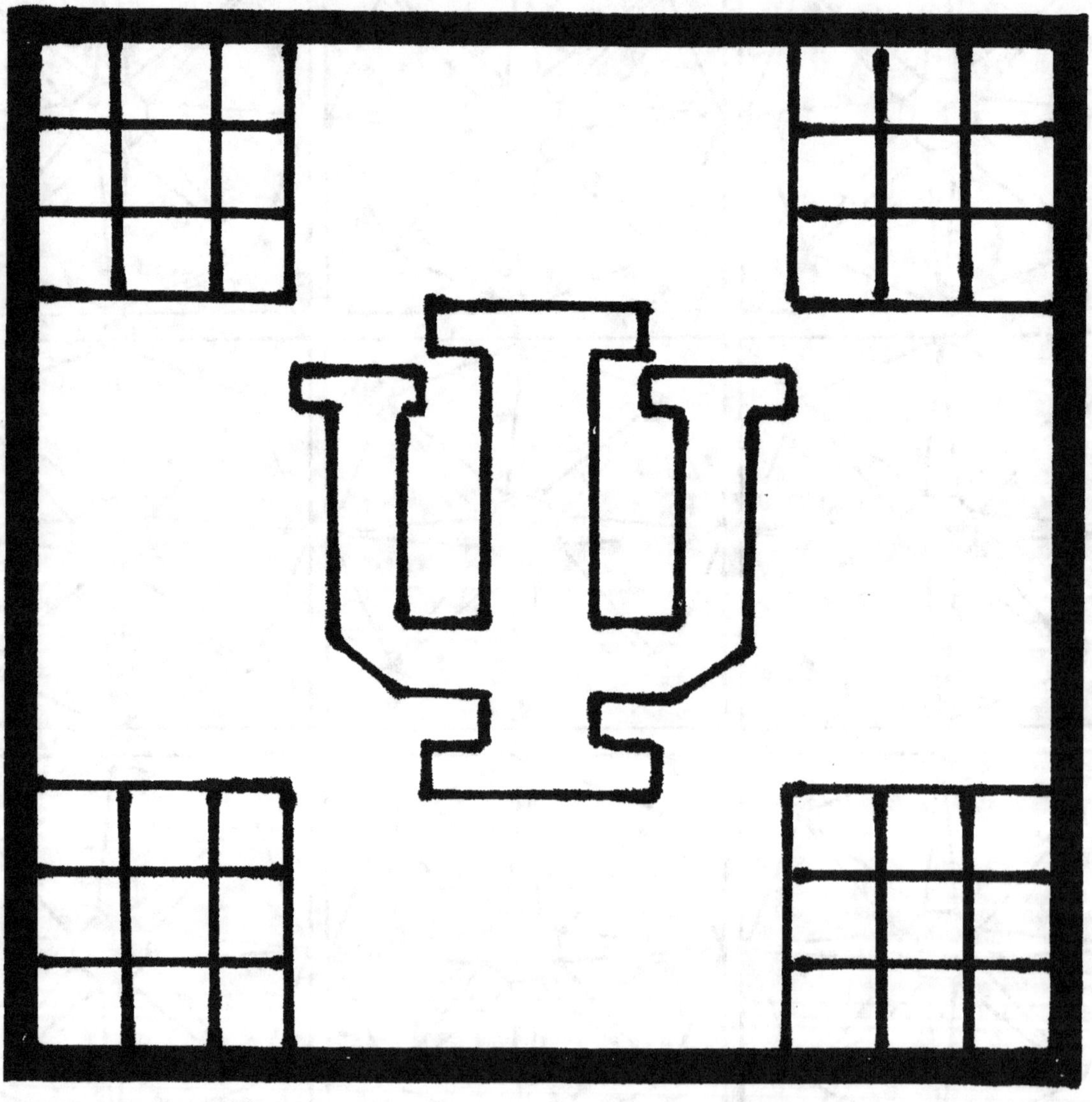

Gibson County Barn Quilt IU Nine Patch

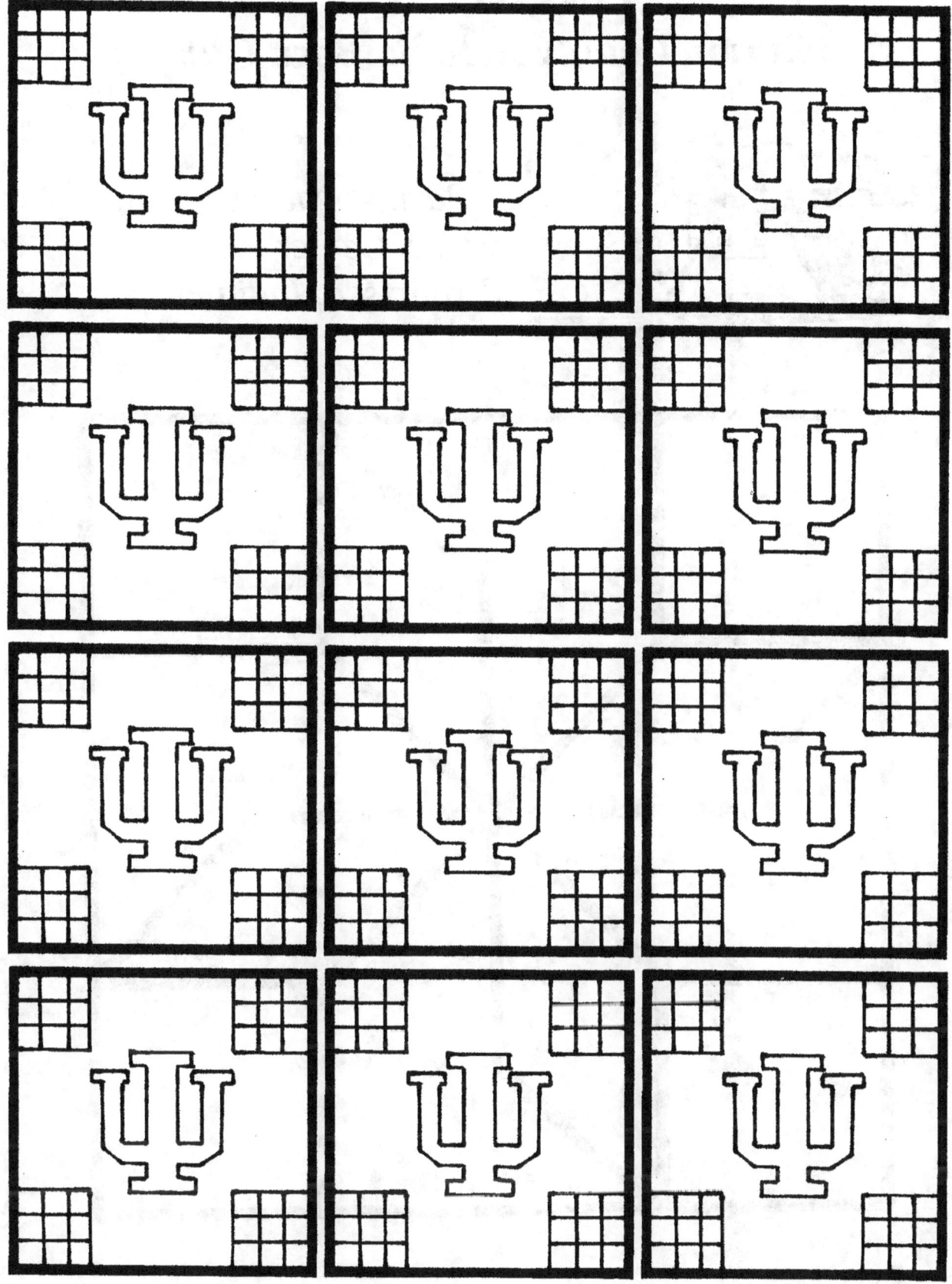

Windmill
Gibson County Indiana Barn Quilt

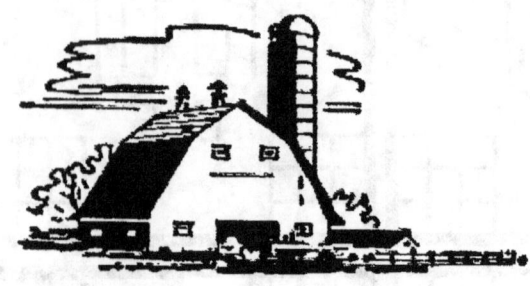

Barn Location
S Center
Francisco, Indiana

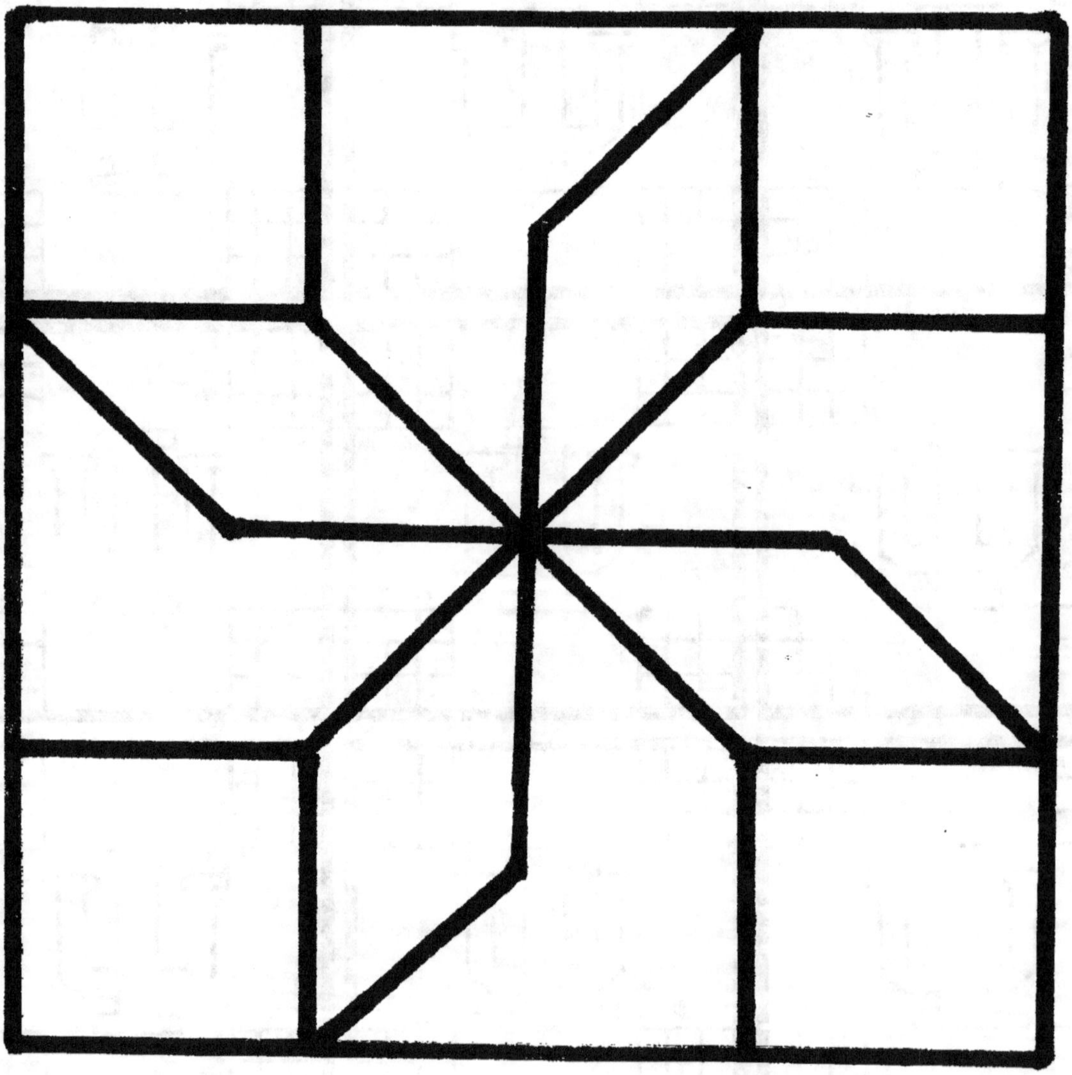

Gibson County Barn Quilt Windmill

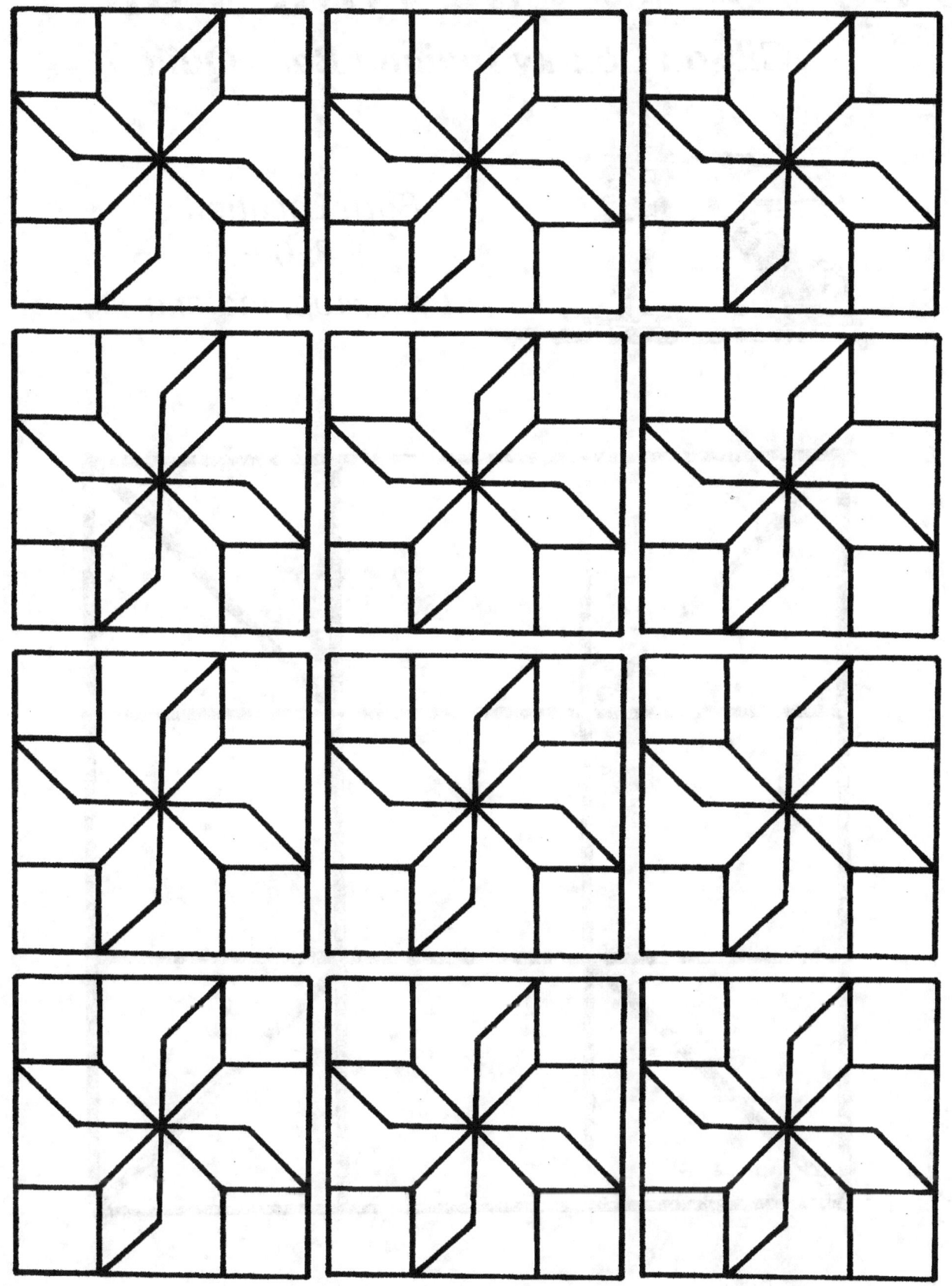

Skip To My Lou Nine Patch

Gibson County Indiana Barn Quilt

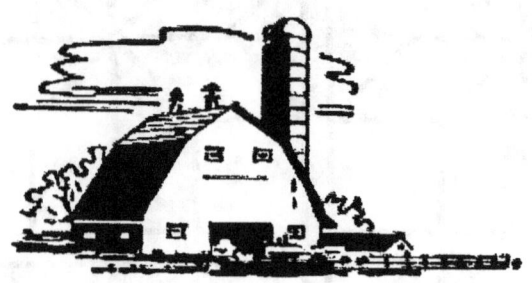

Barn Location
S 650 E
Princeton, Indiana

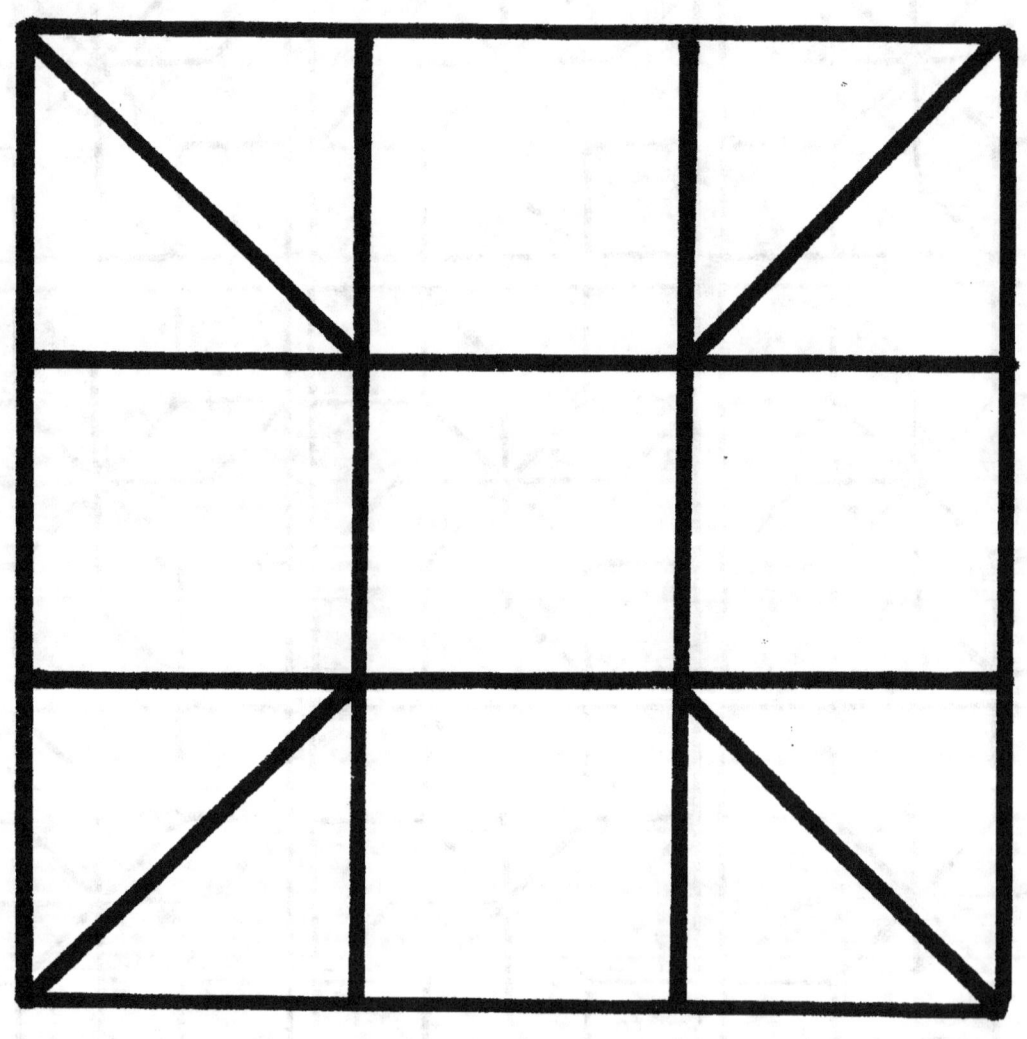

Gibson County Barn Quilt Skip To My Lou Nine Patch

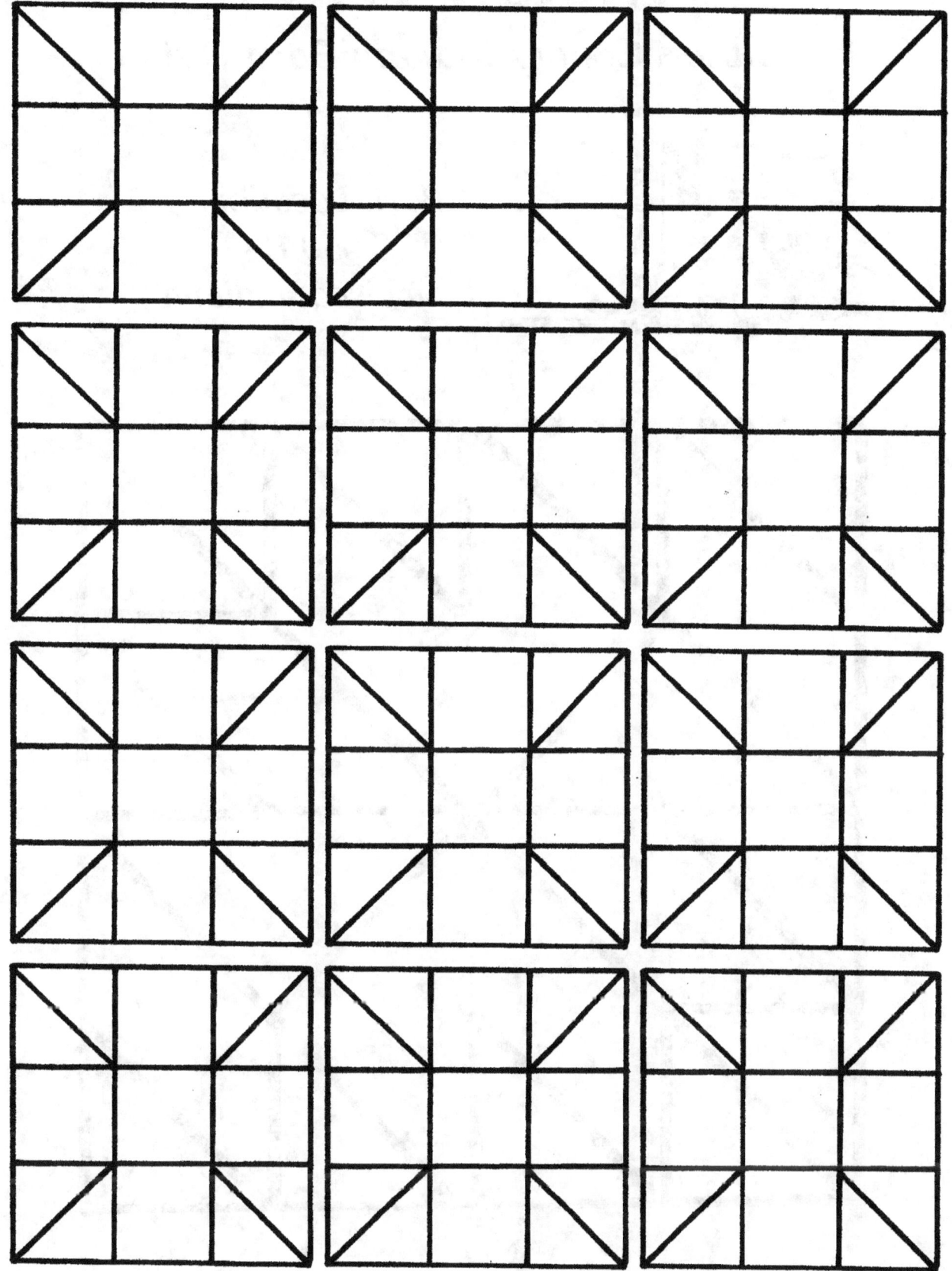

Indian Trail
Gibson County Indiana Barn Quilt

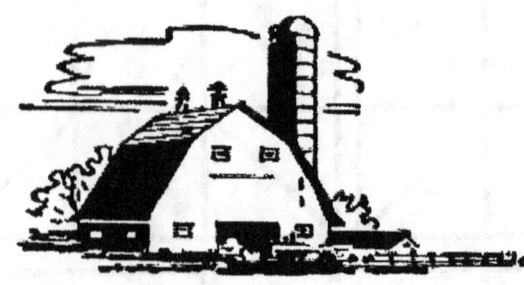

Barn Location
S 650 E
Francisco, Indiana

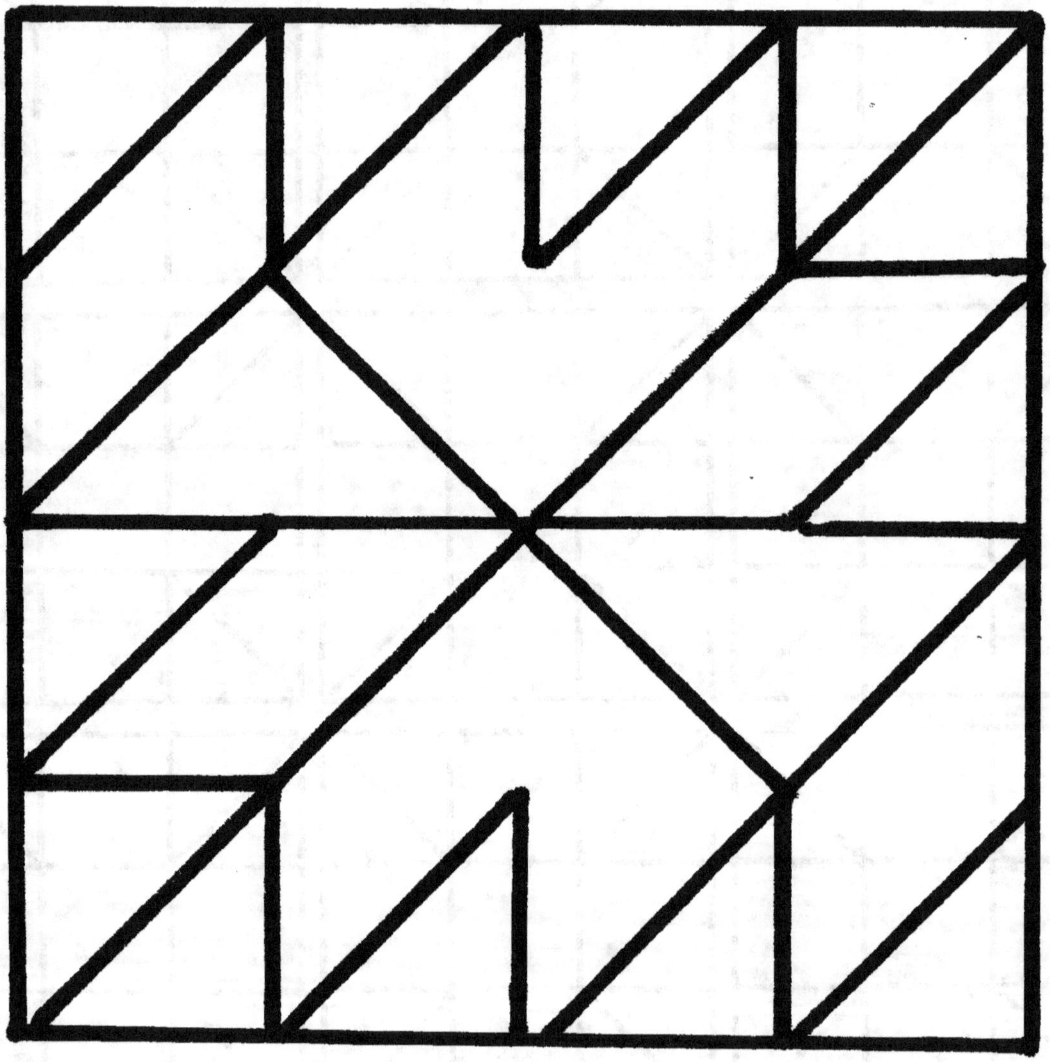

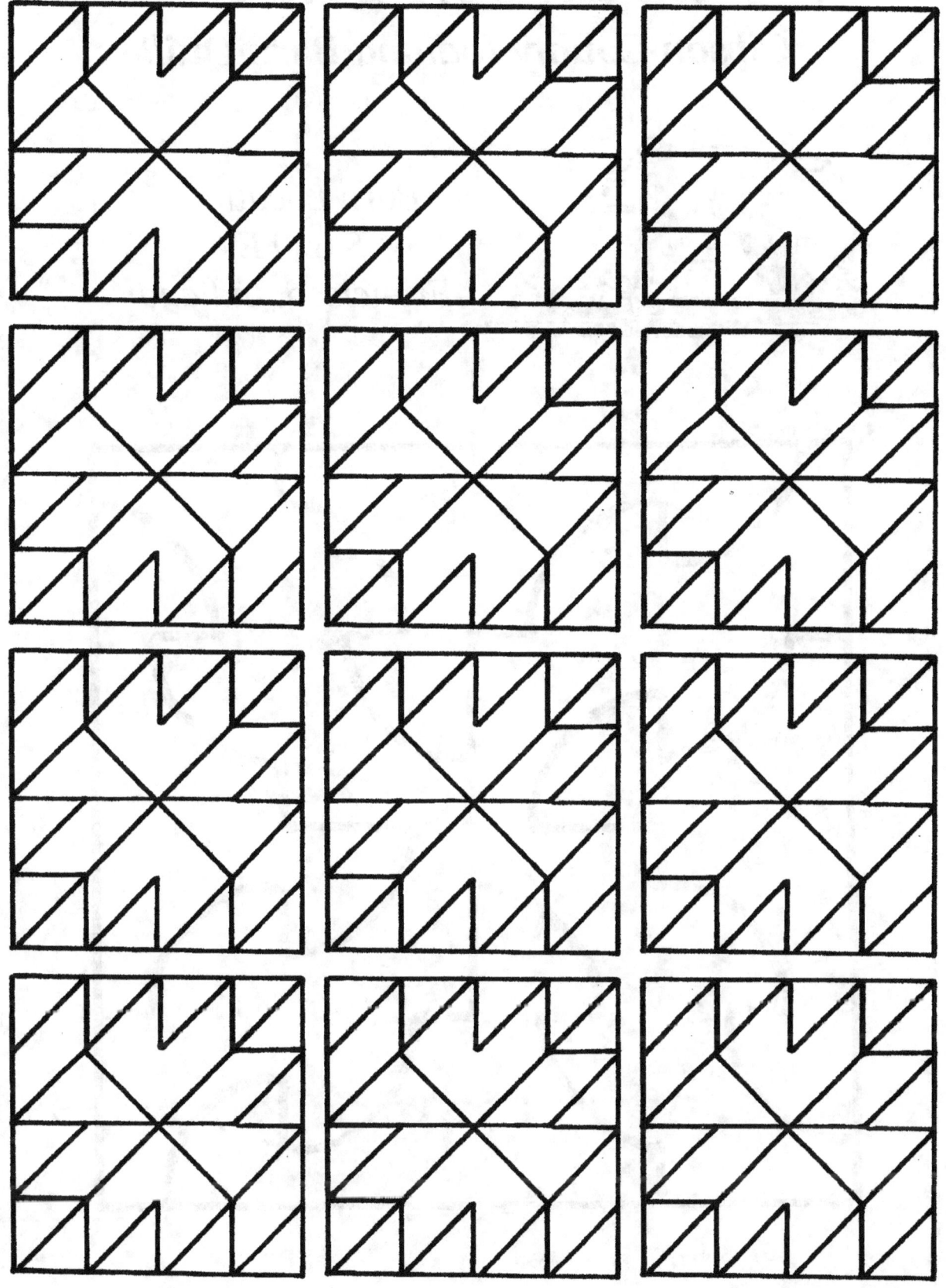

Drunken Path

Gibson County Indiana Barn Quilt

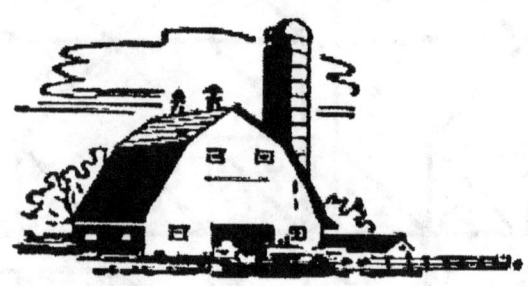

Barn Location
S 650 E
Francisco, Indiana

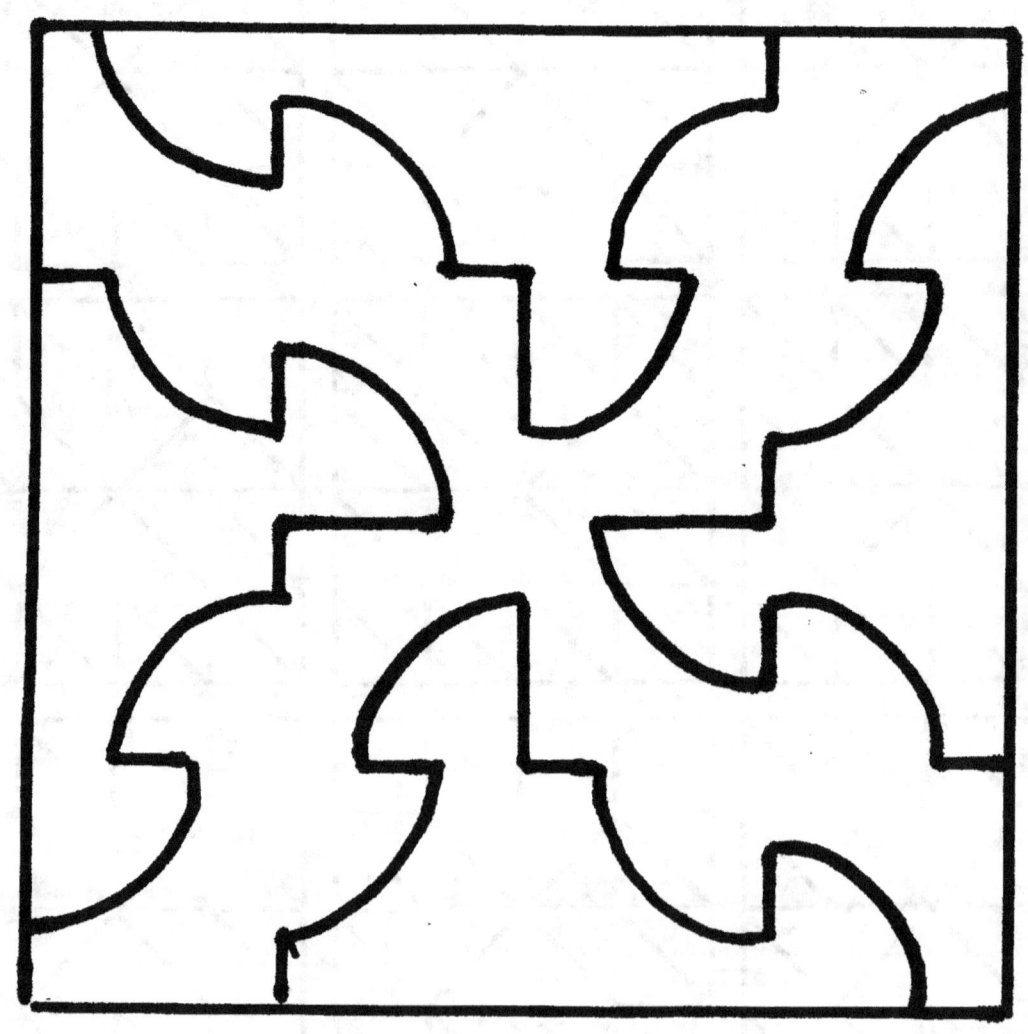

Gibson County Barn Quilt Drunken Path

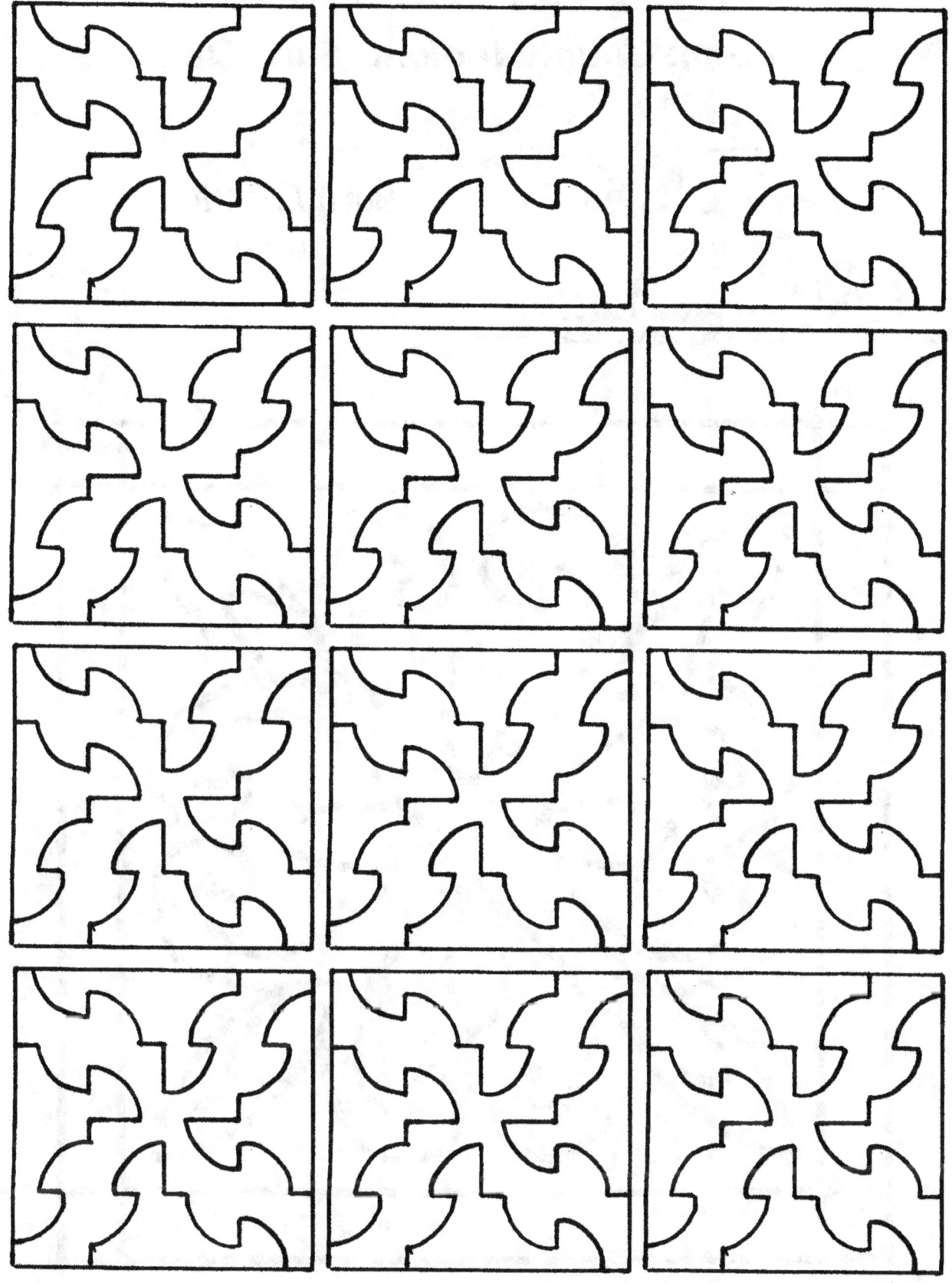

Fleur-de-lis
Gibson County Indiana Barn Quilt

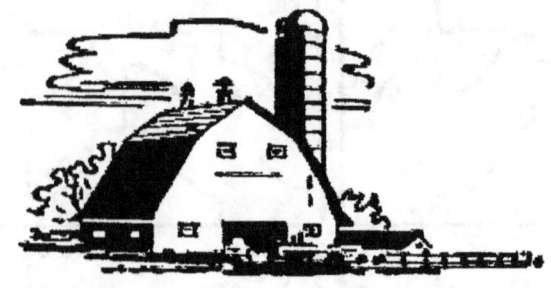

Barn Location
S 100 E
Princeton, Indiana

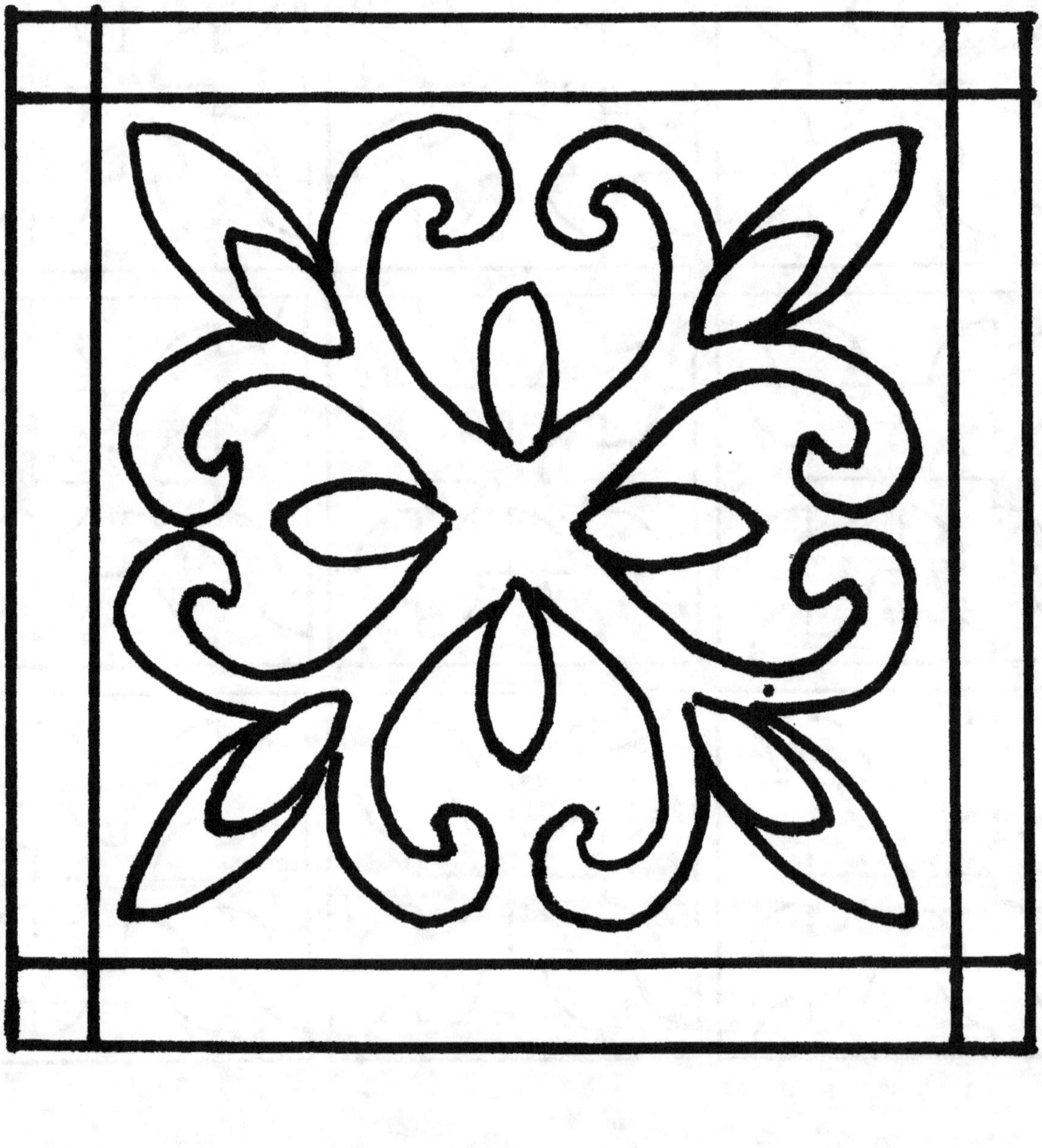

Gibson County Barn Quilt Fleur-de-lis

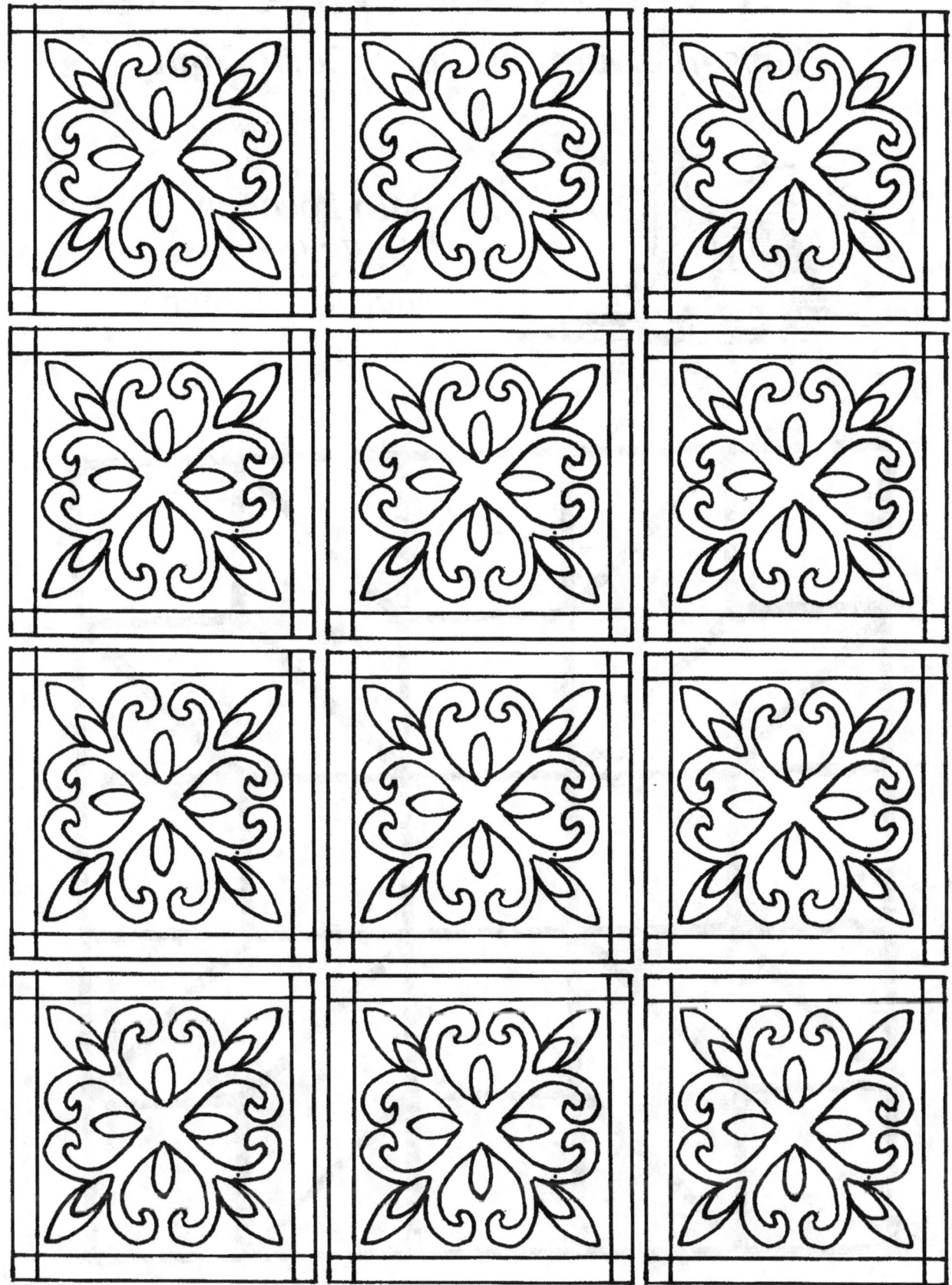

Red, White & Blue Star
Gibson County Indiana Barn Quilt

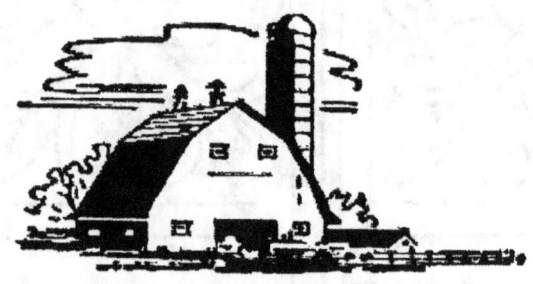

Barn Location
W Main
Francisco, Indiana

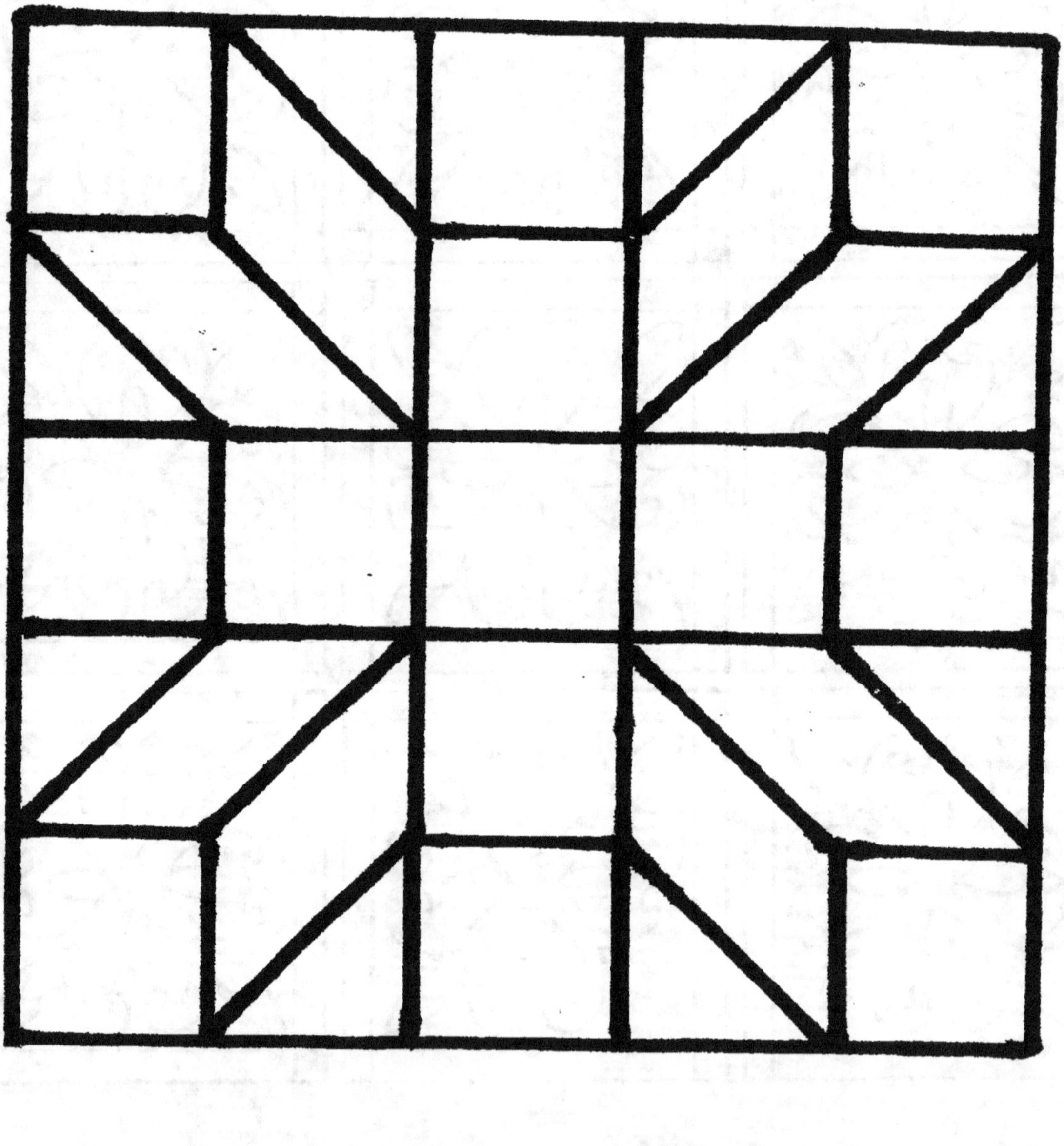

Gibson County Barn Quilt Red, White & Blue Star

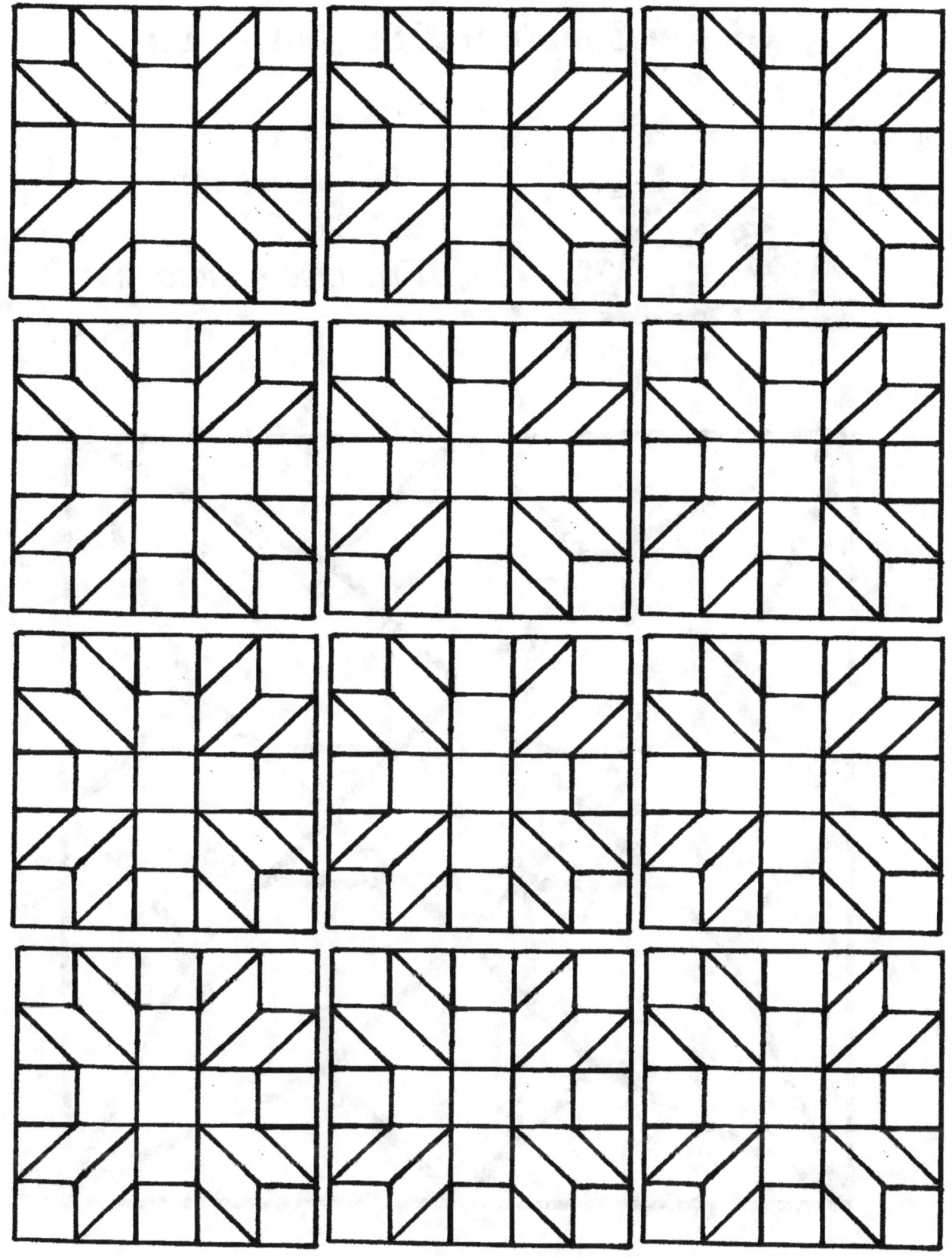

Sky Rocket
Gibson County Indiana Barn Quilt

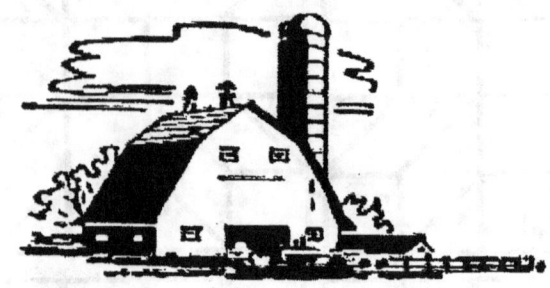

Barn Location
S 650 E
Francisco, Indiana

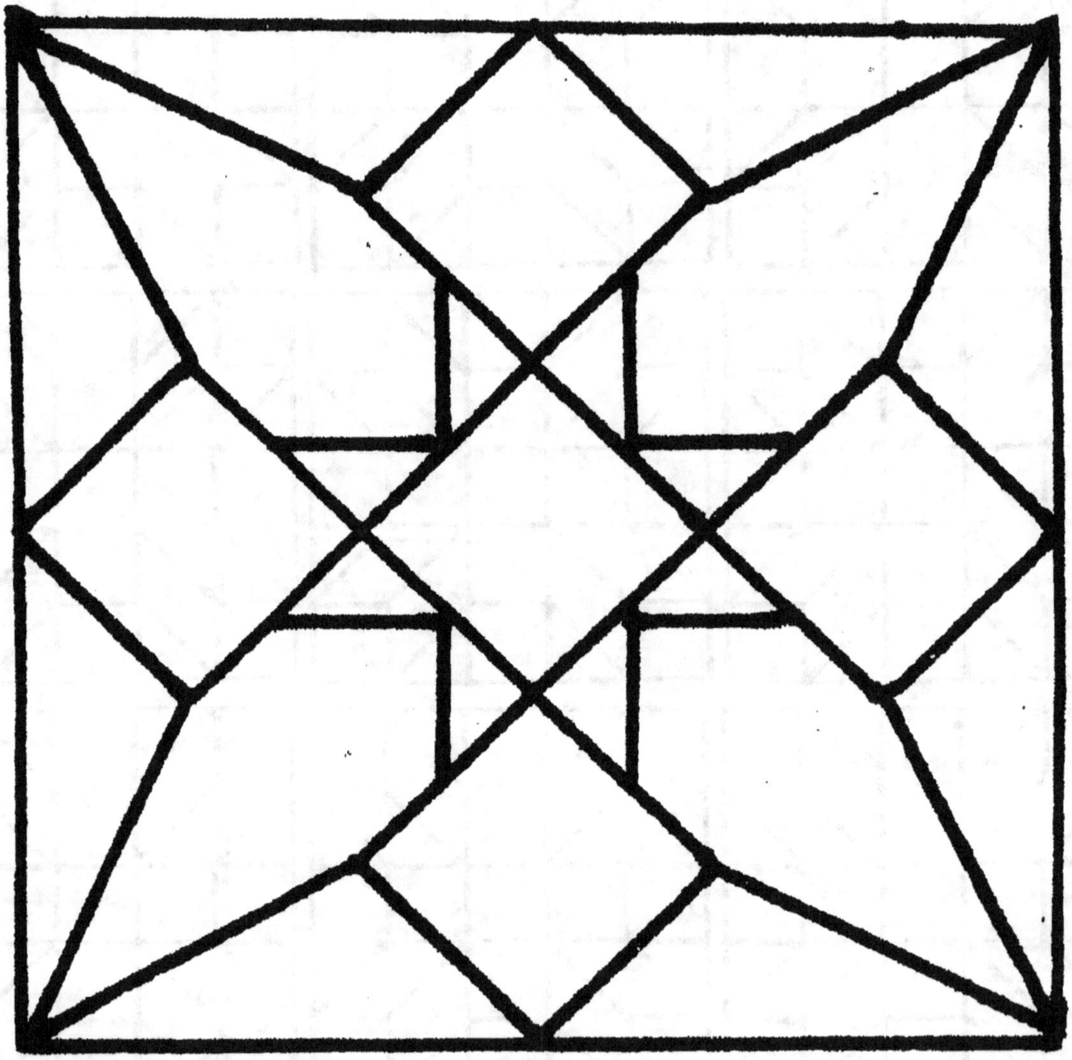

Gibson County Barn Quilt Sky Rocket

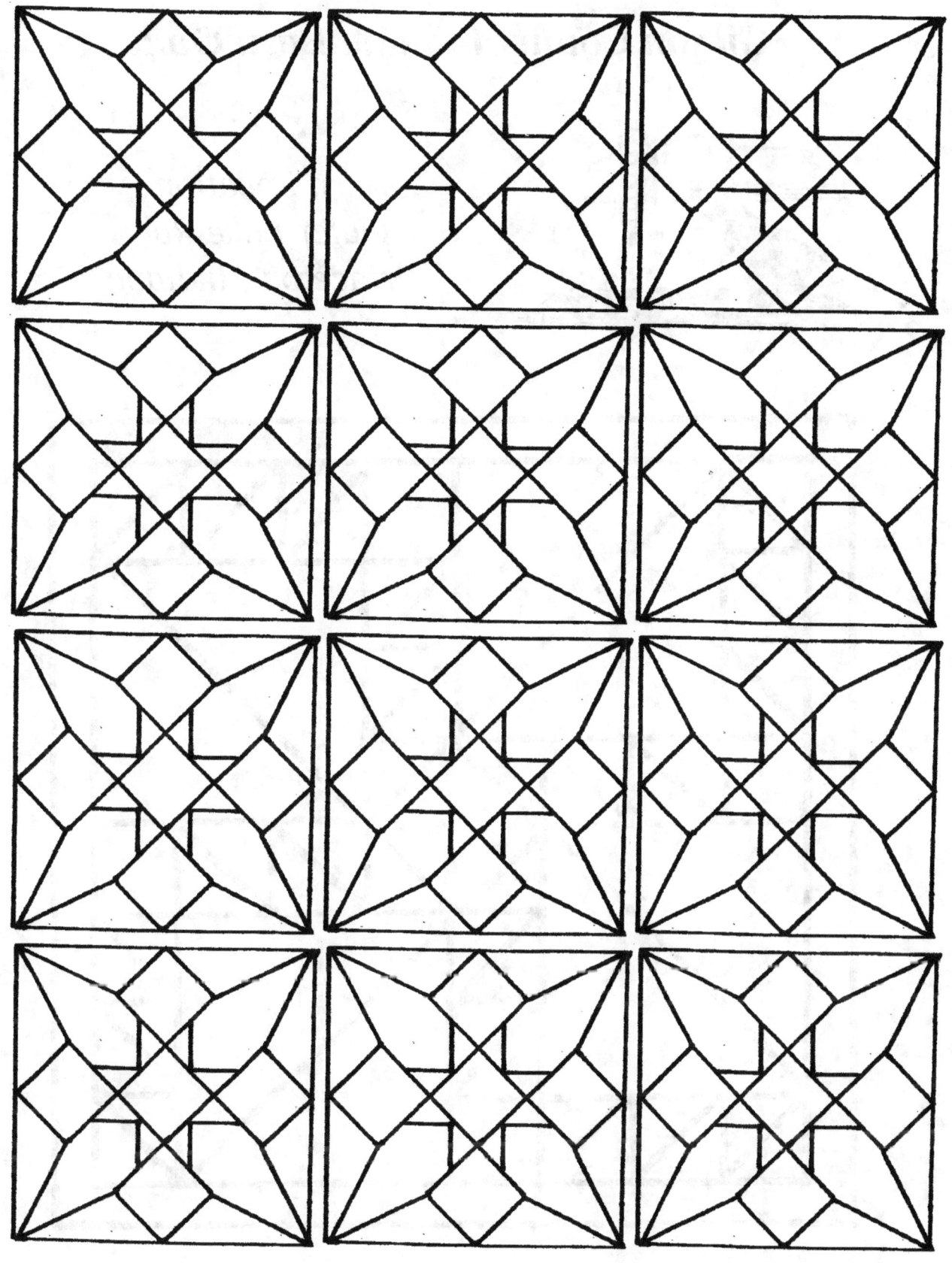

Indian Trails
Gibson County Indiana Barn Quilt

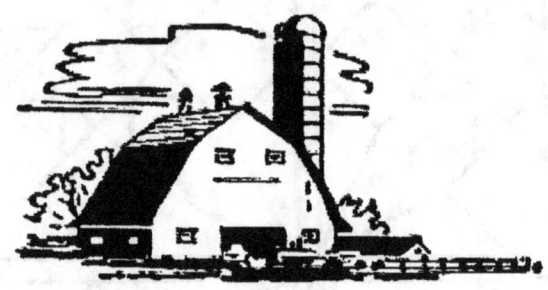

Barn Location
Outer Lake Rd
Princeton , Indiana

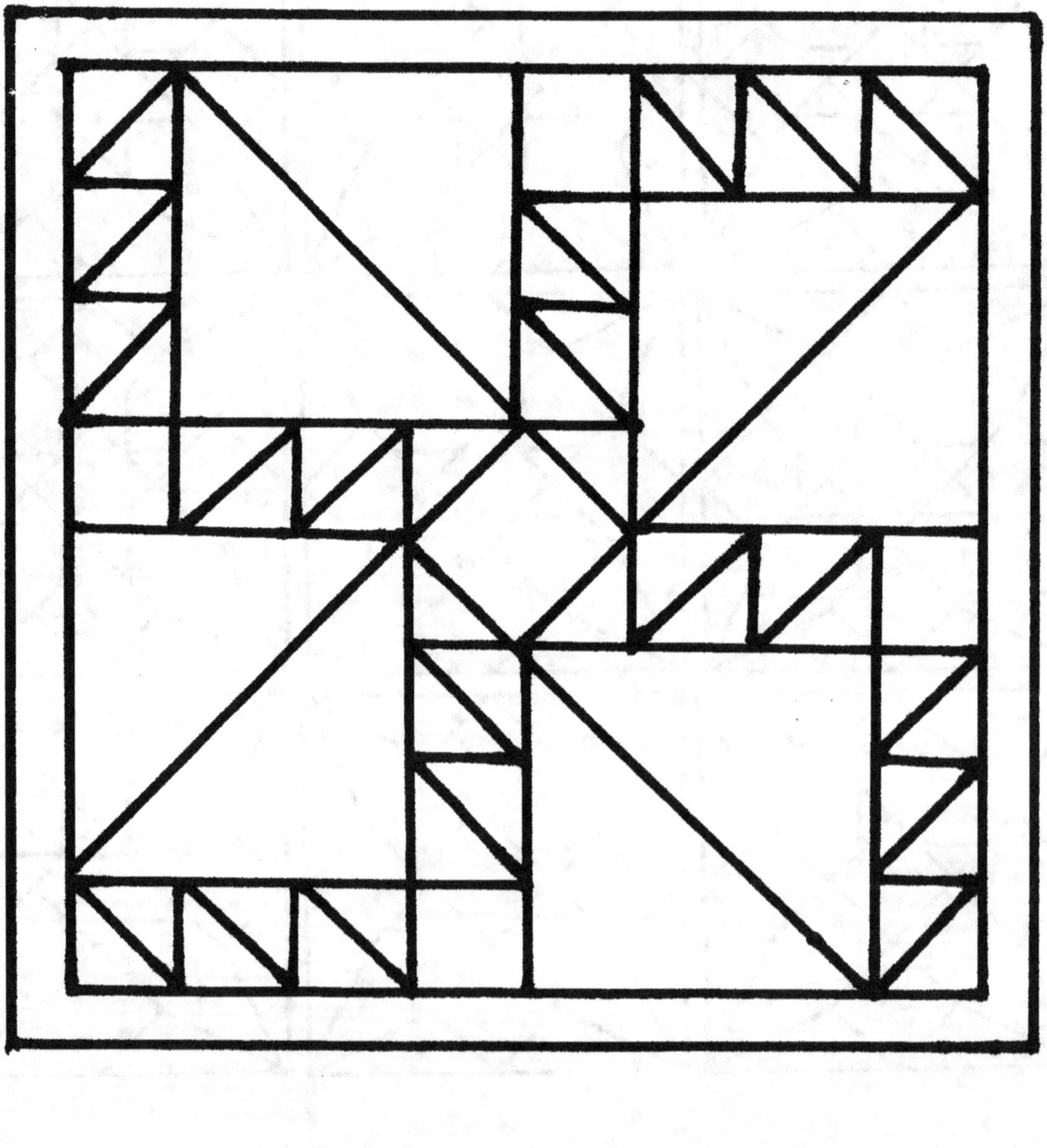

Gibson County Barn Quilt Indian Trails

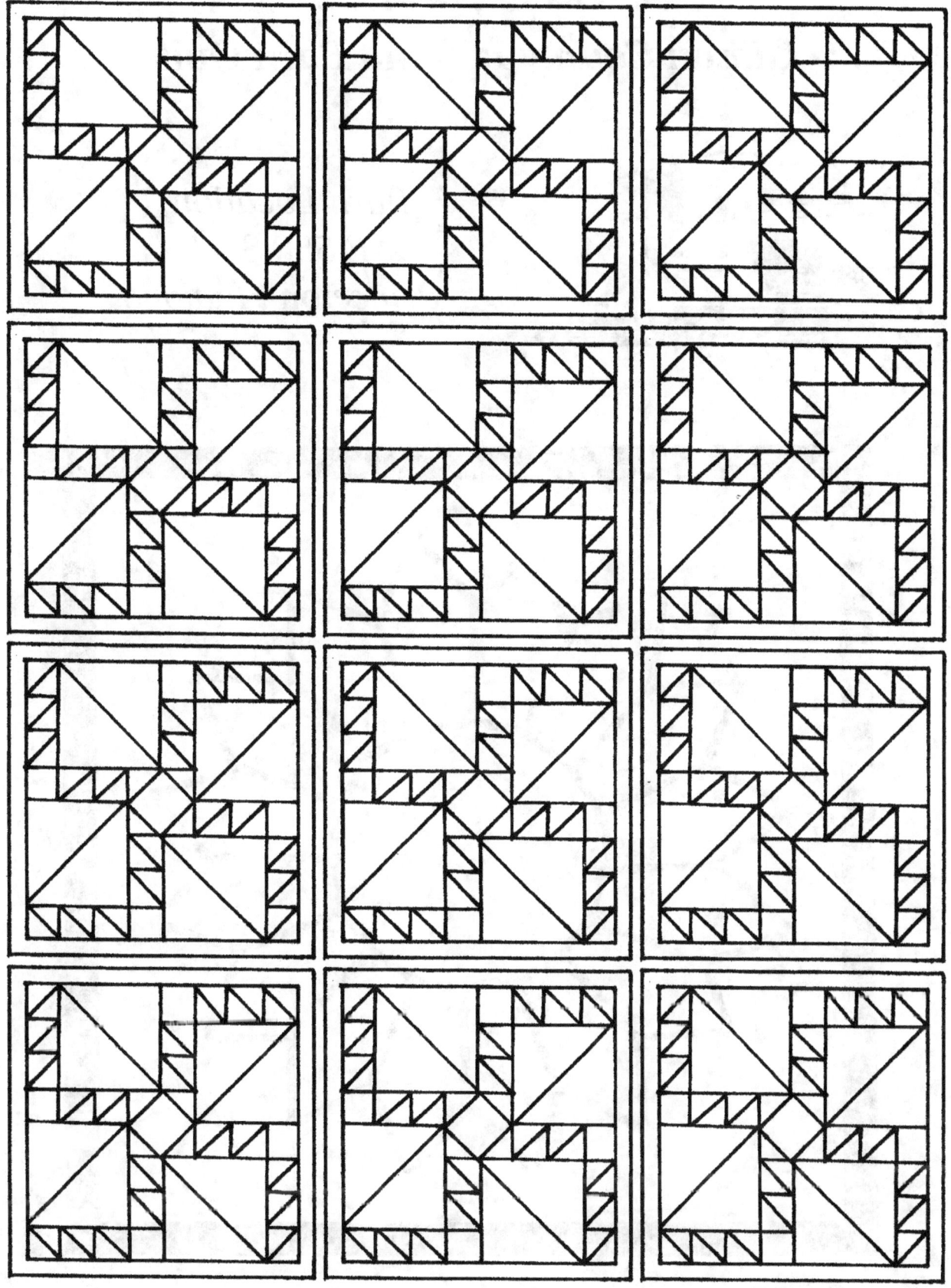

Sunflower

Gibson County Indiana Barn Quilt

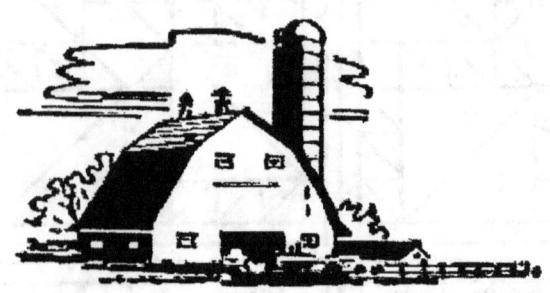

*Barn Location
E 550 S
Princeton , Indiana*

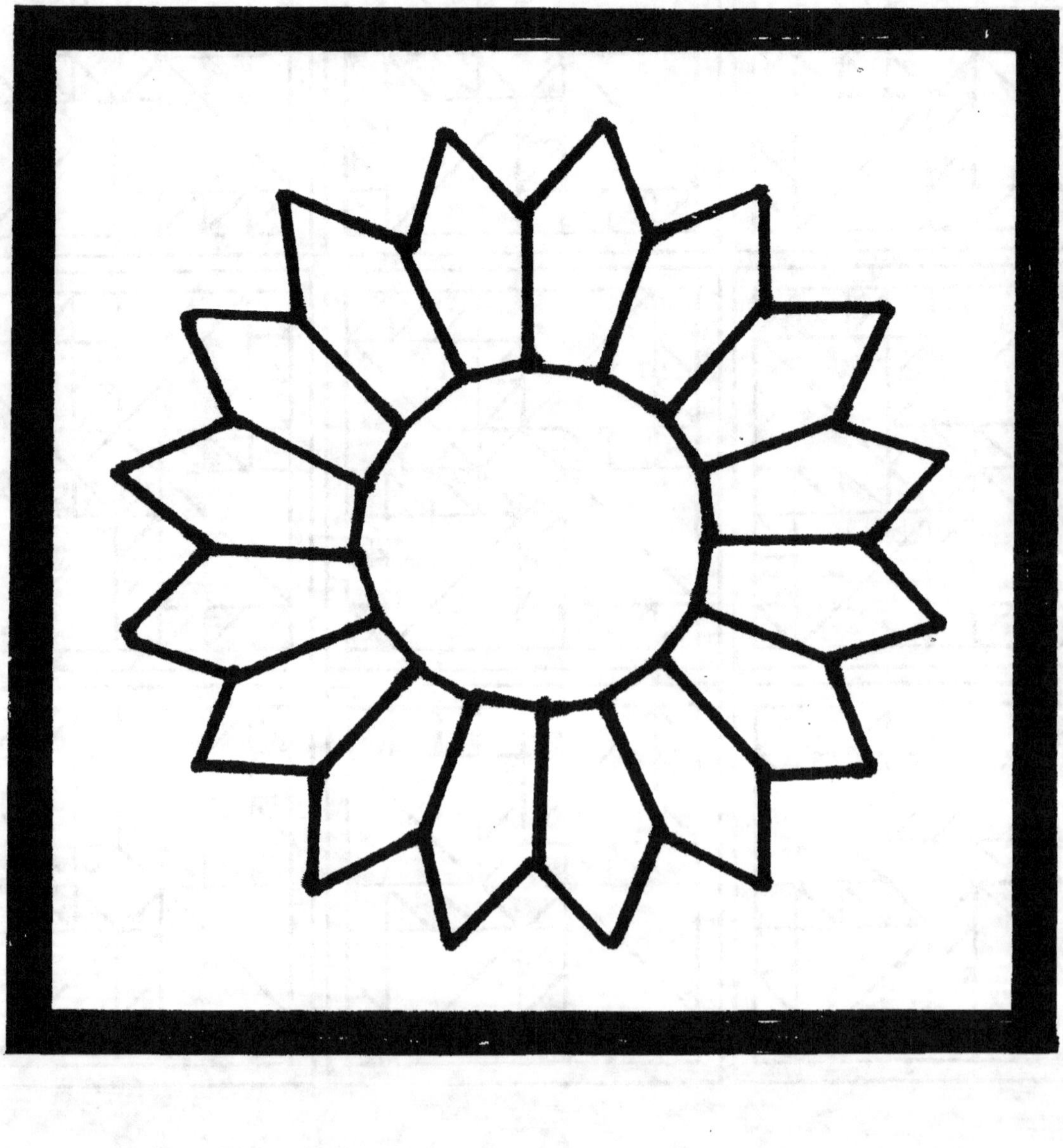

Gibson County Barn Quilt Sunflower

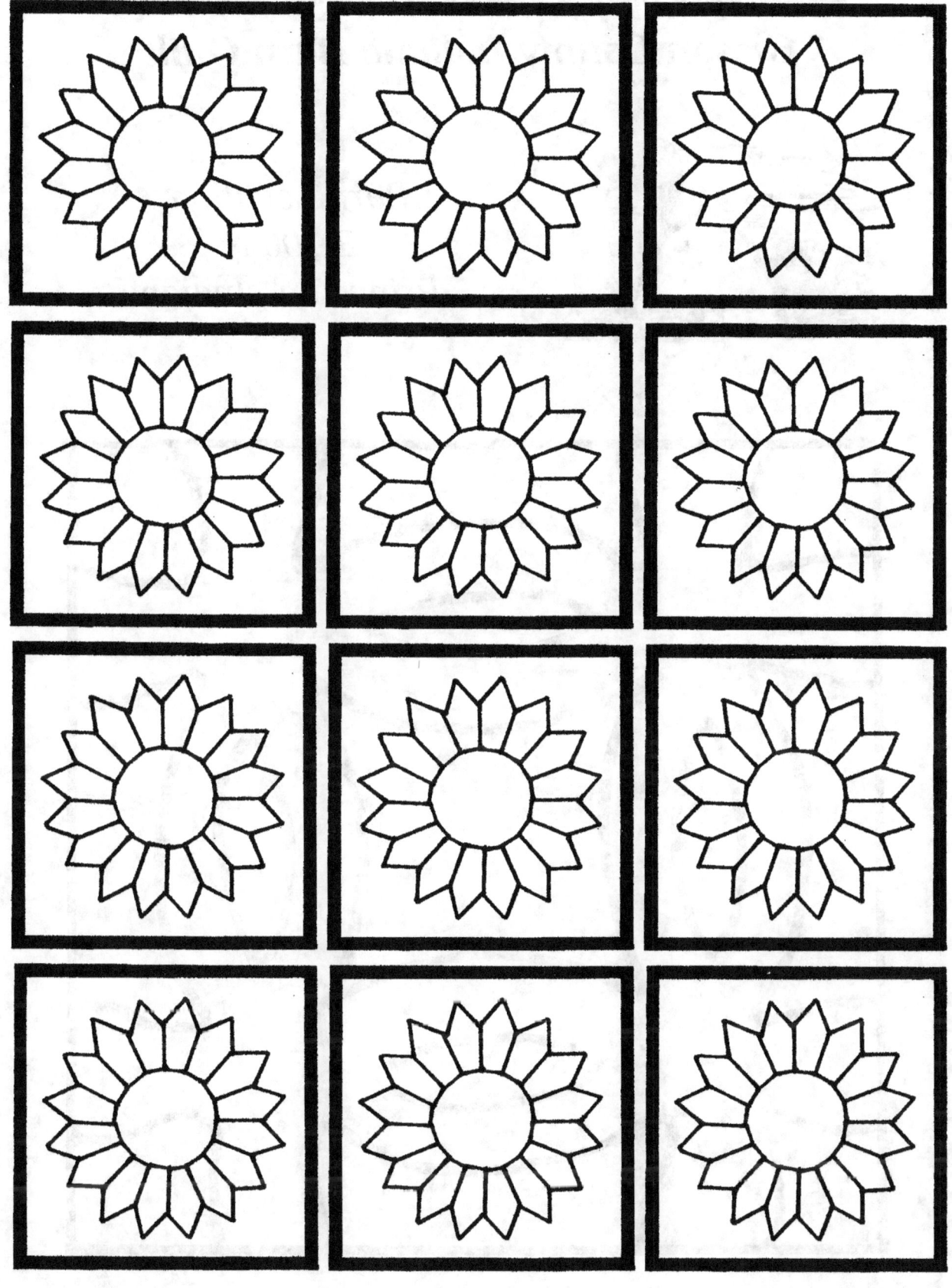

Double Wedding Ring

Gibson County Indiana Barn Quilt

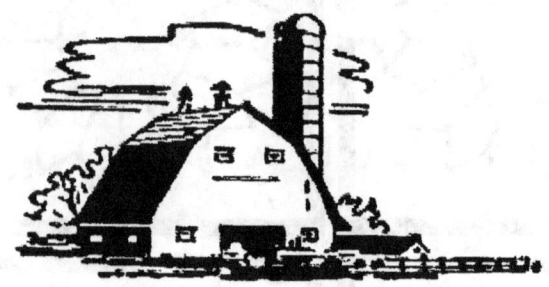

Barn Location
E 100 N
Princeton , Indiana

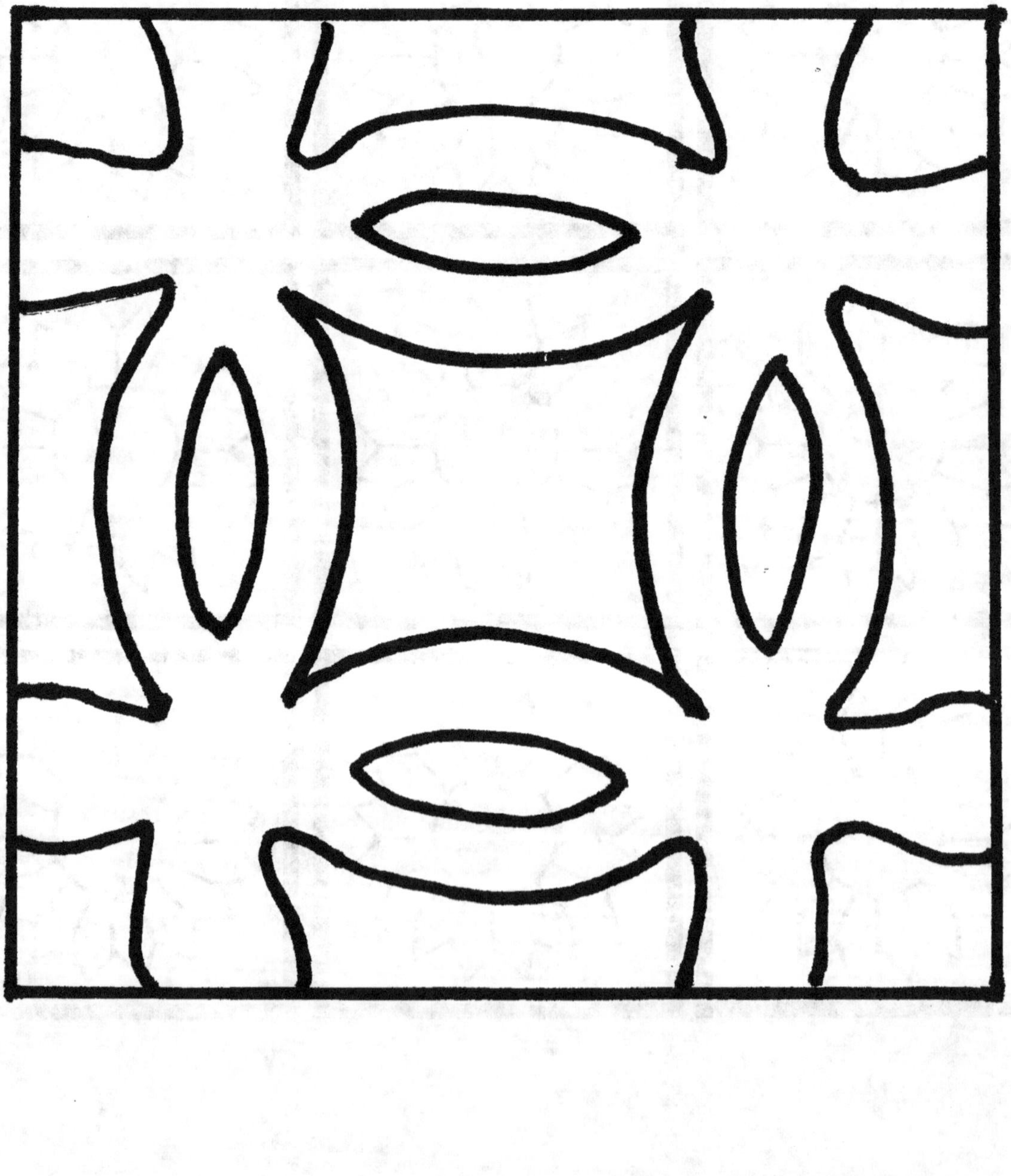

Gibson County Barn Quilt Double Wedding Ring

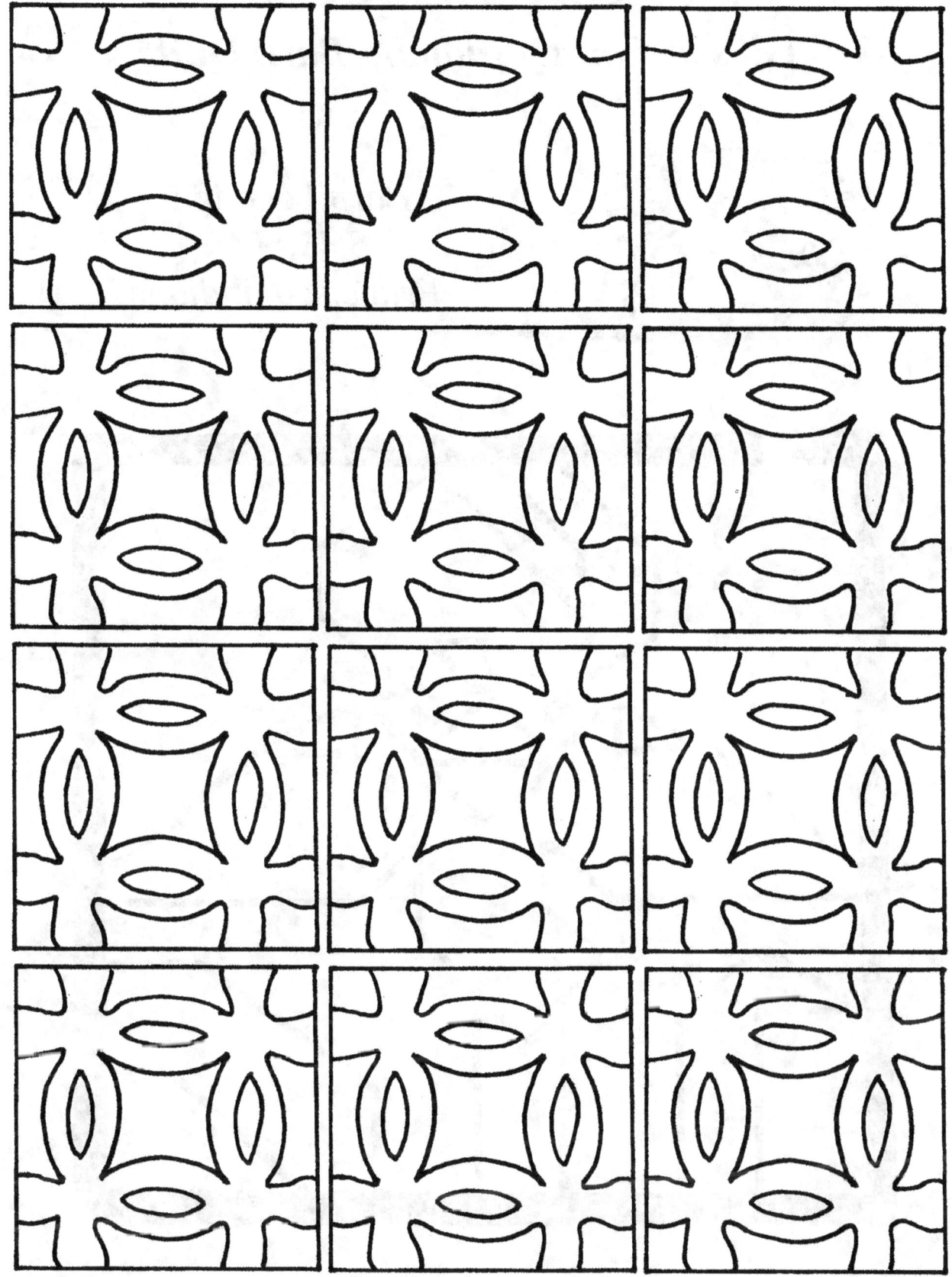

Tennessee
Gibson County Indiana Barn Quilt

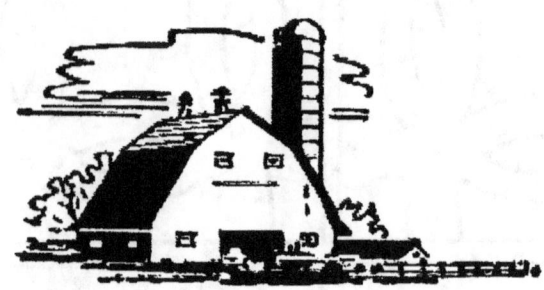

Barn Location
S 450 E
Francisco, Indiana

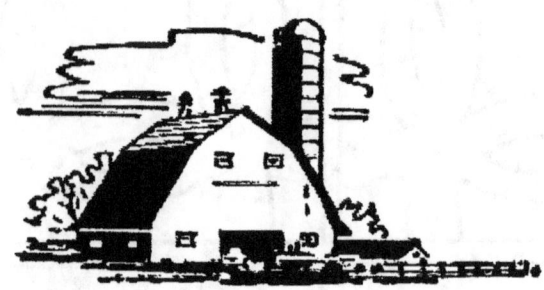

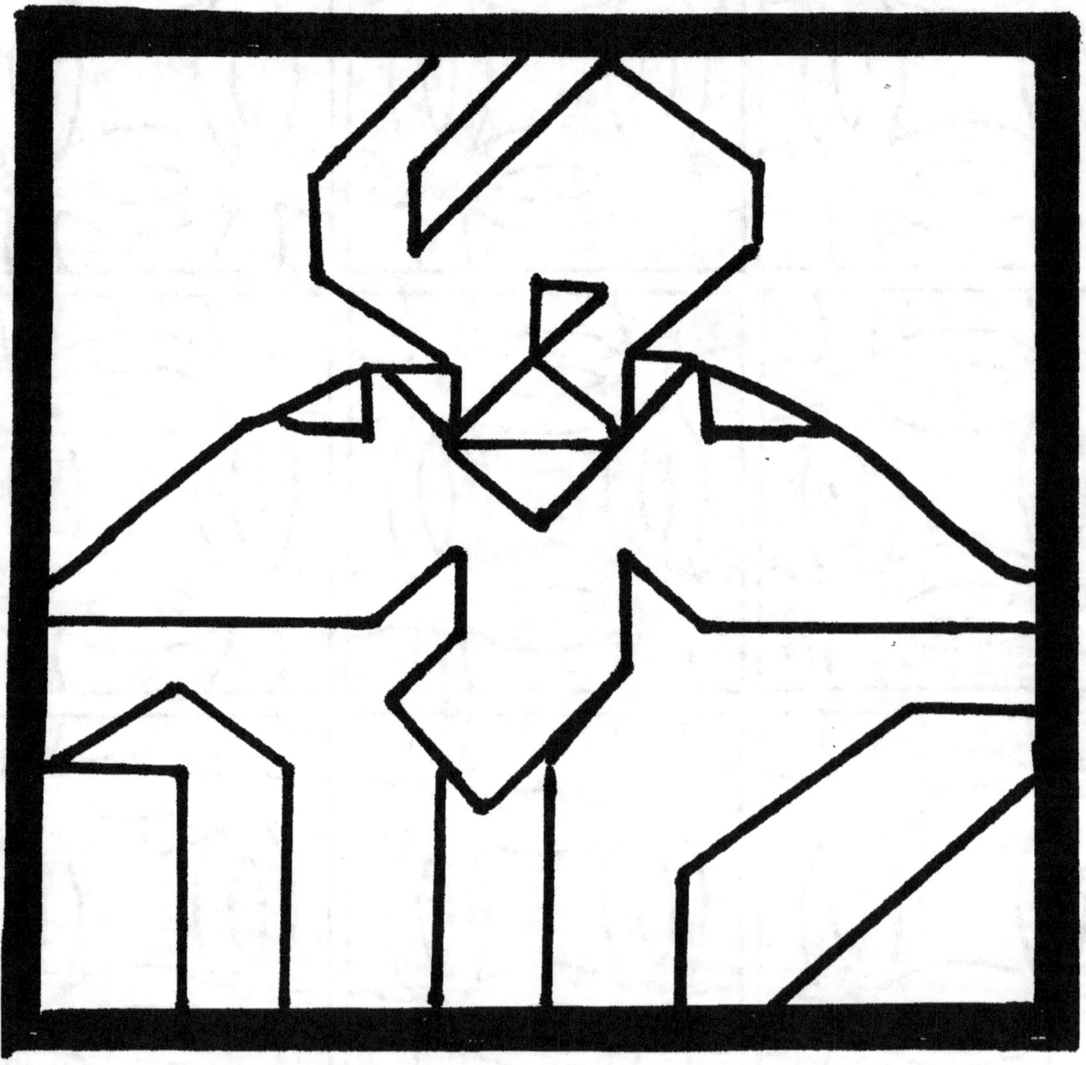

Gibson County Barn Quilt Tennessee

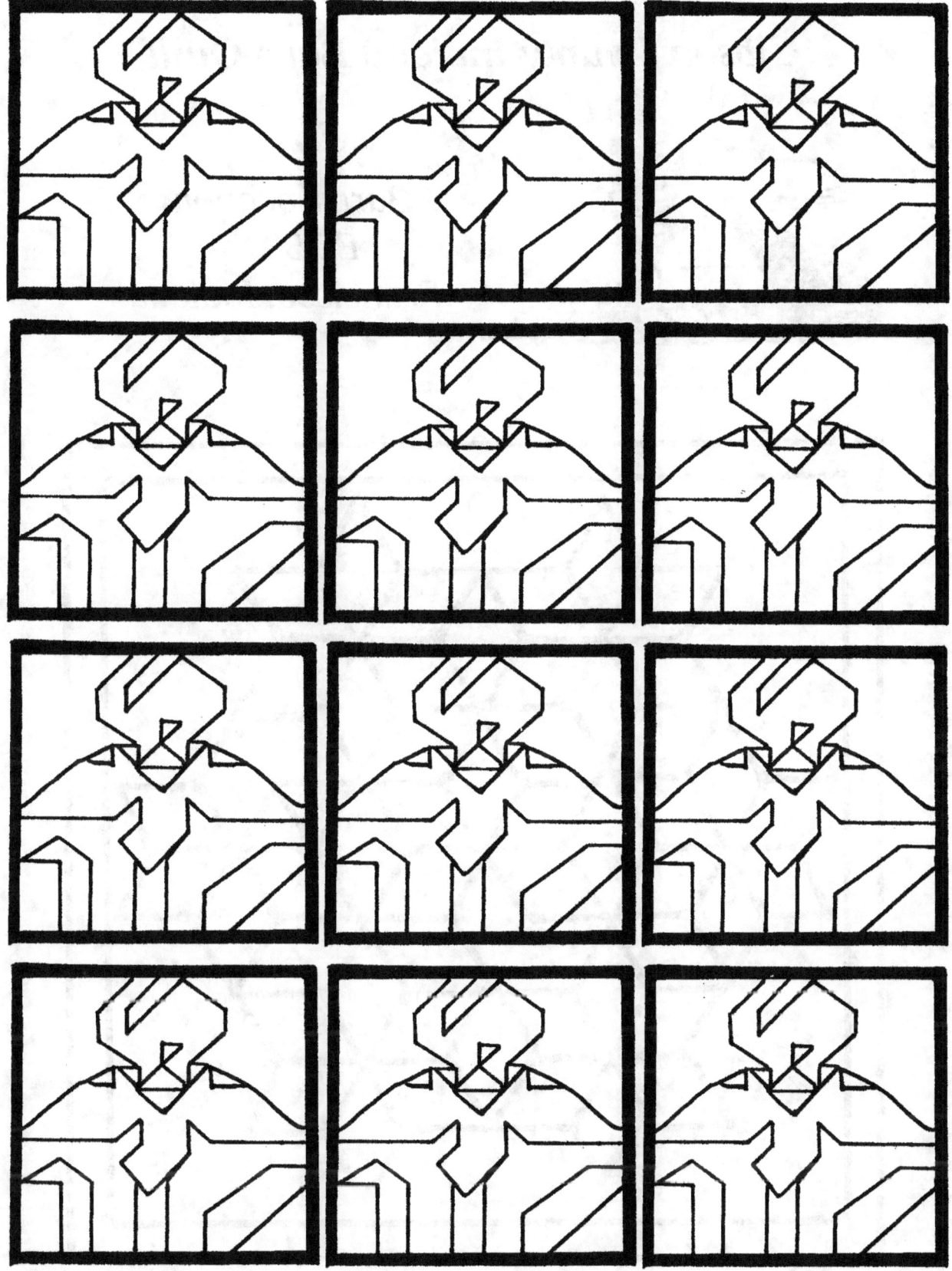

Seven Sisters
Gibson County Indiana Barn Quilt

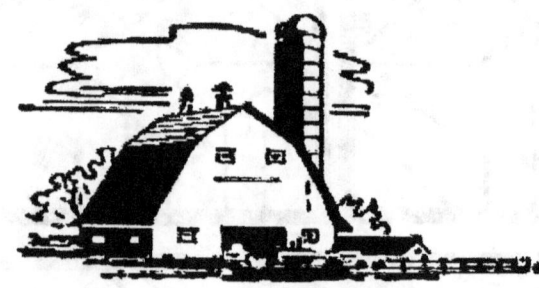

Barn Location
E 350 S
Francisco, Indiana

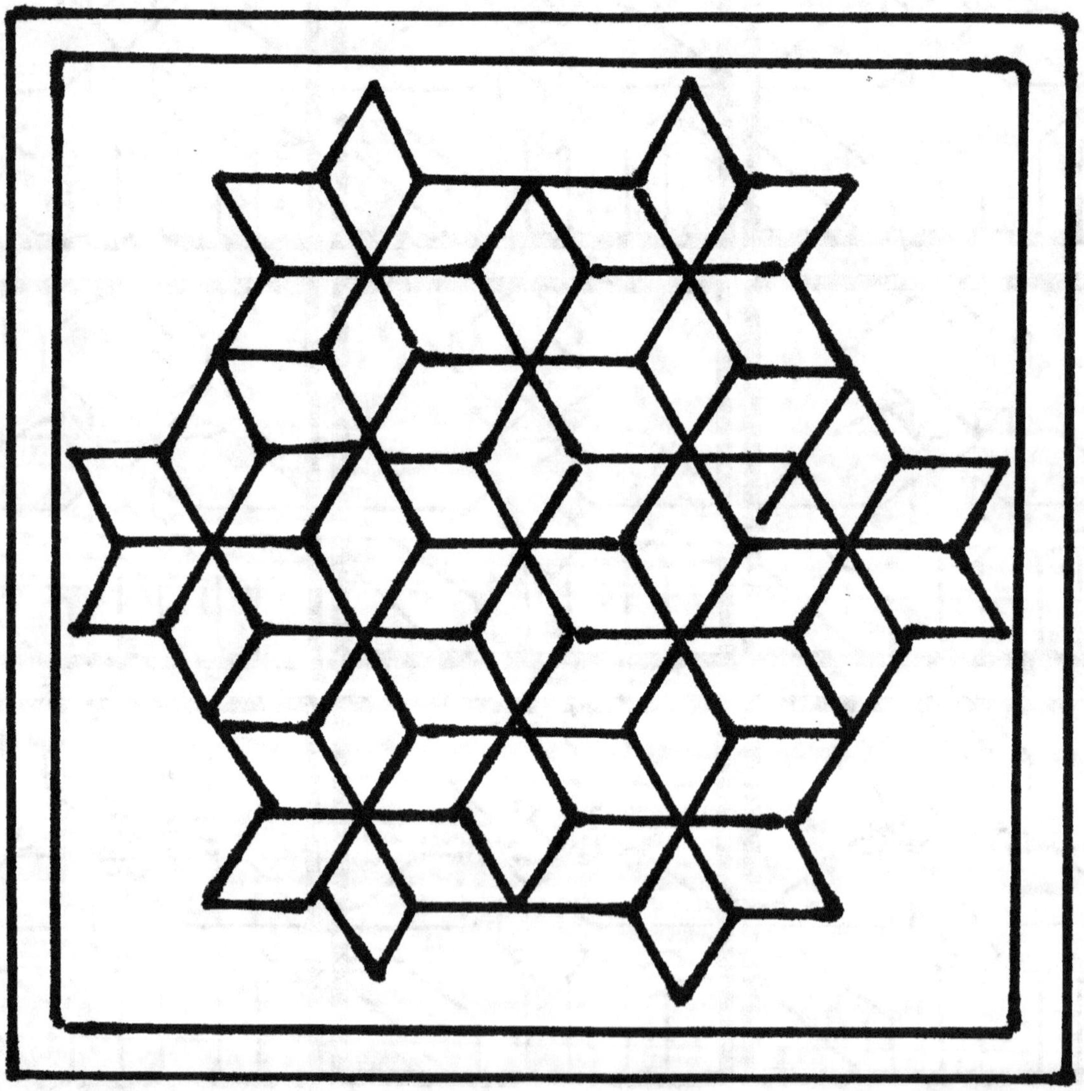

Gibson County Barn Quilt Seven Sisters

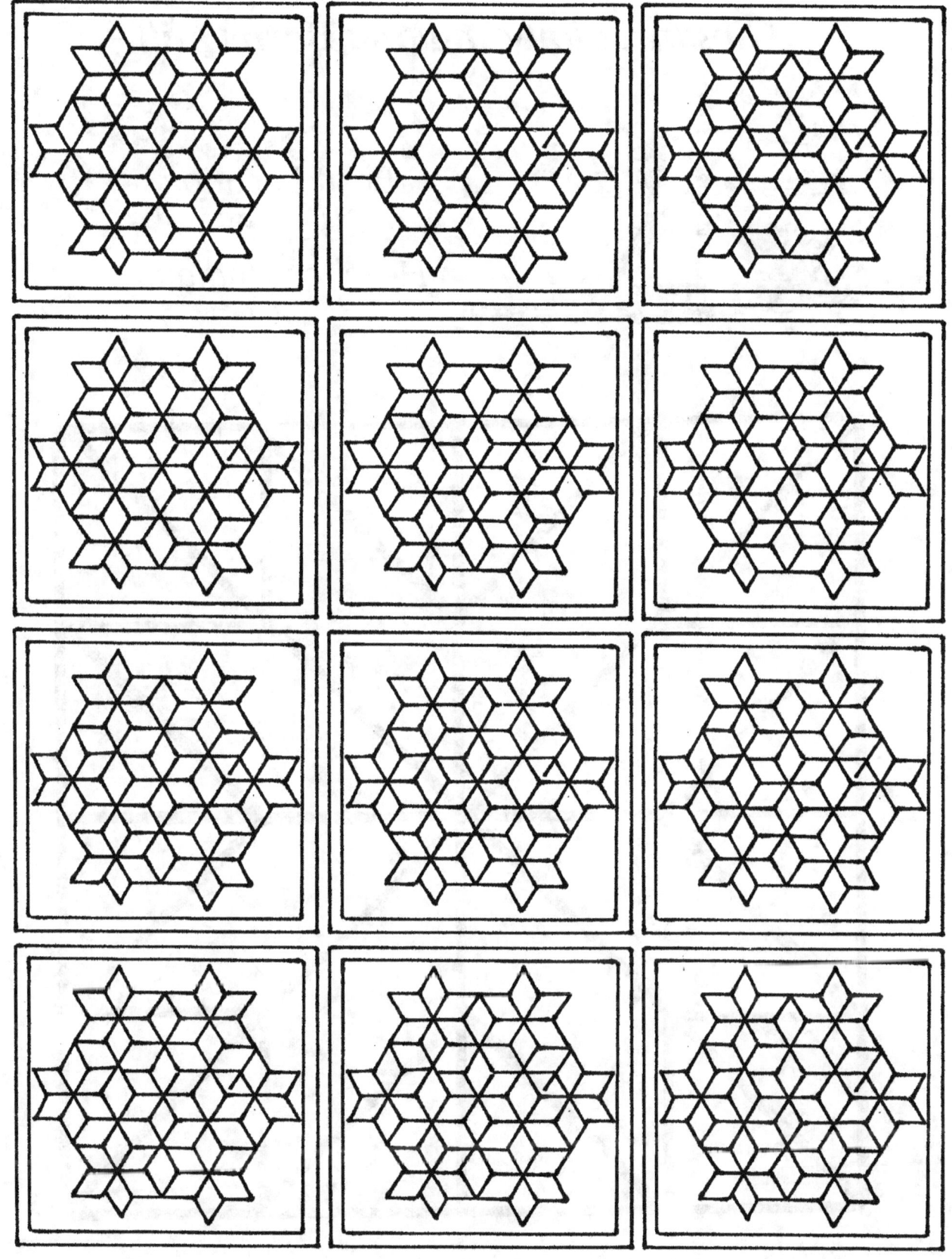

Star Burst

Gibson County Indiana Barn Quilt

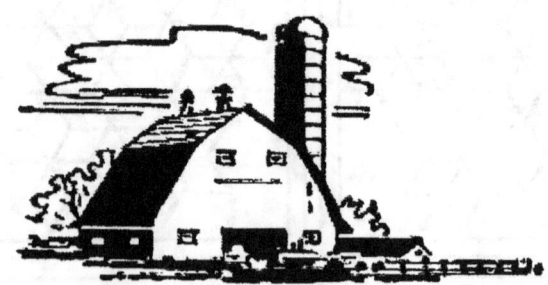

Barn Location
E SR 56
Hazelton, Indiana

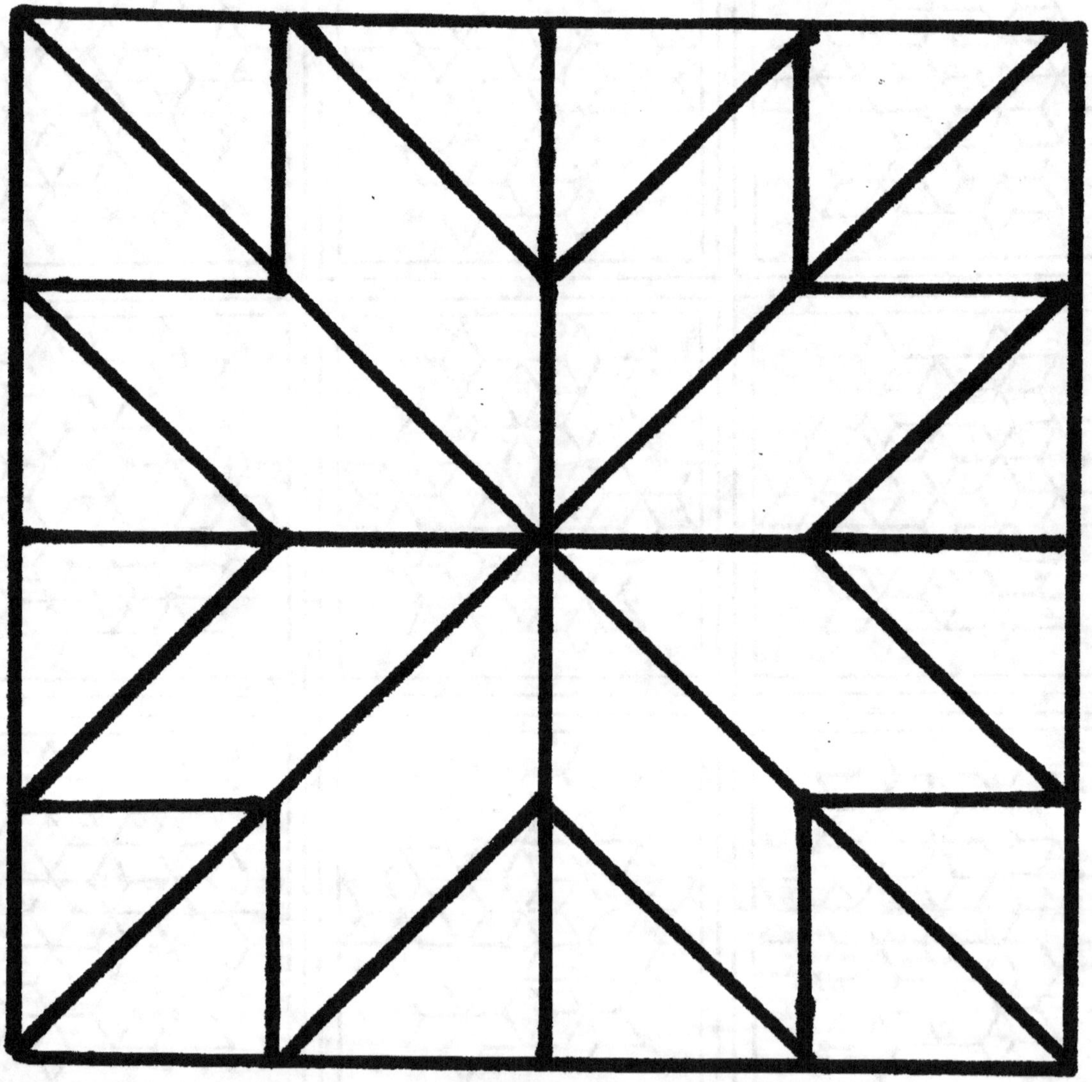

Gibson County Barn Quilt Star Burst

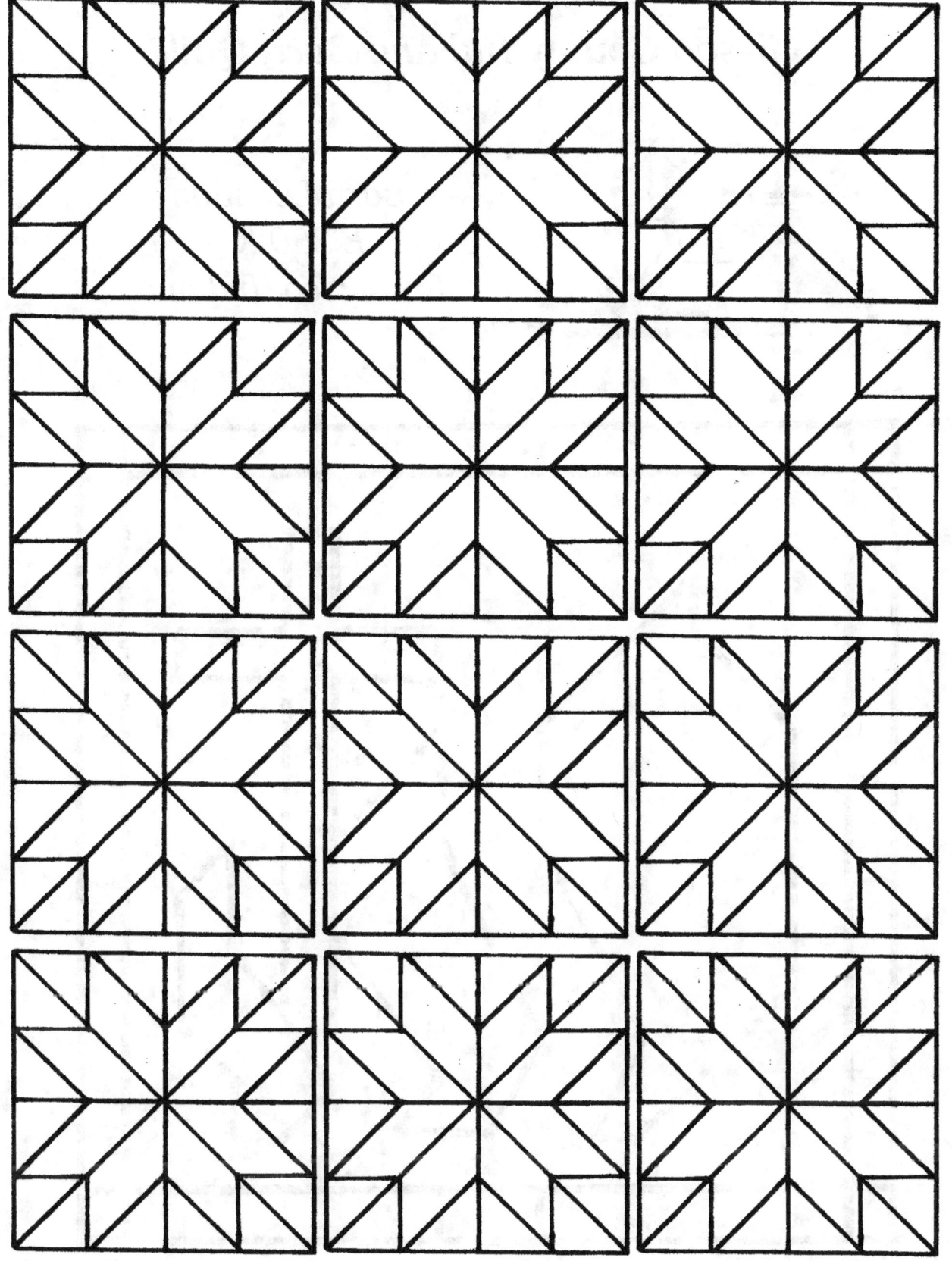

Church of God Flames
Gibson County Indiana Barn Quilt

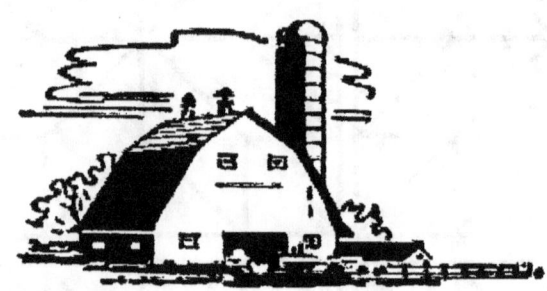

Barn Location
E 350 N
Francisco, Indiana

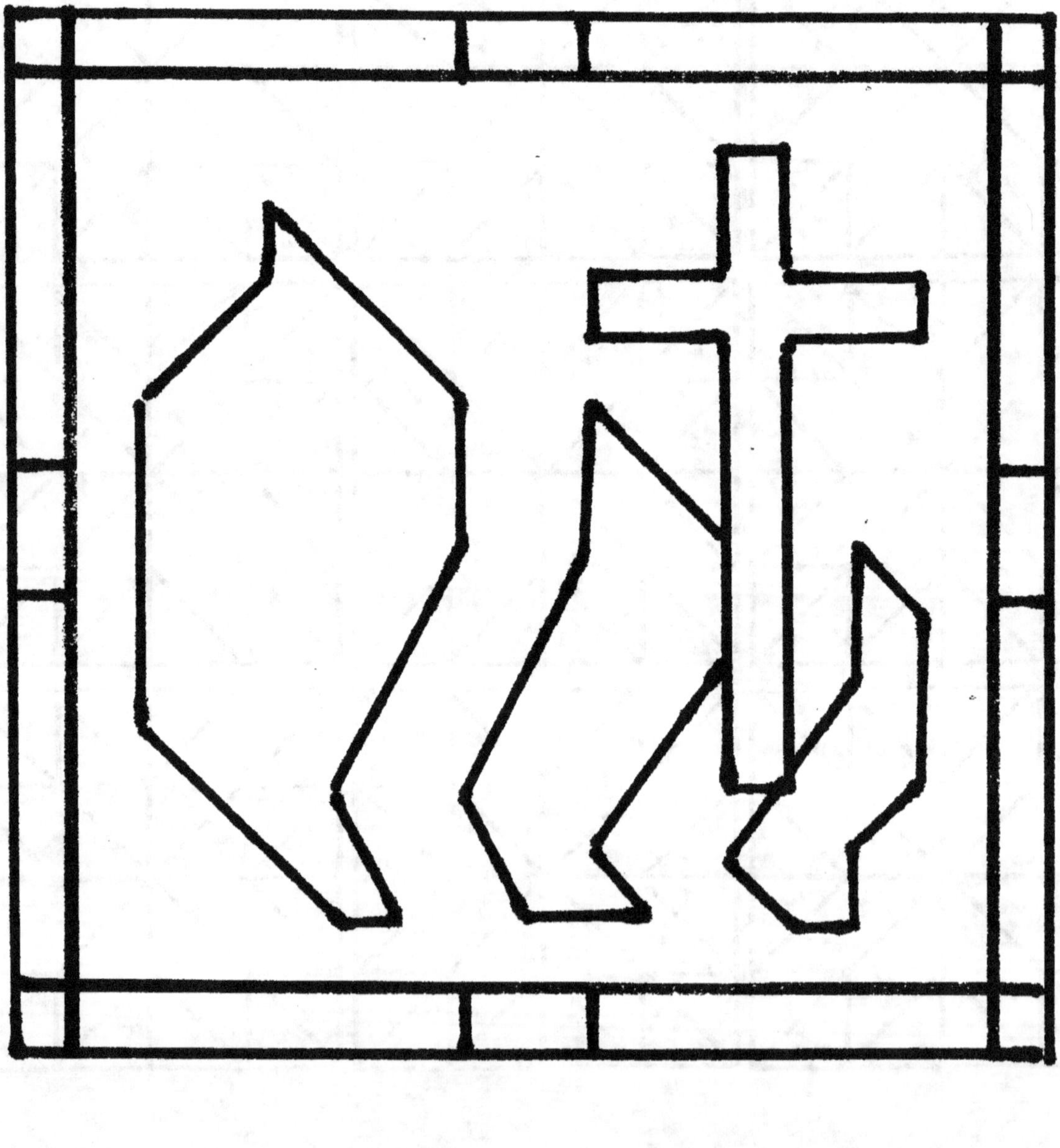

Gibson County Barn Quilt Church of God Flames

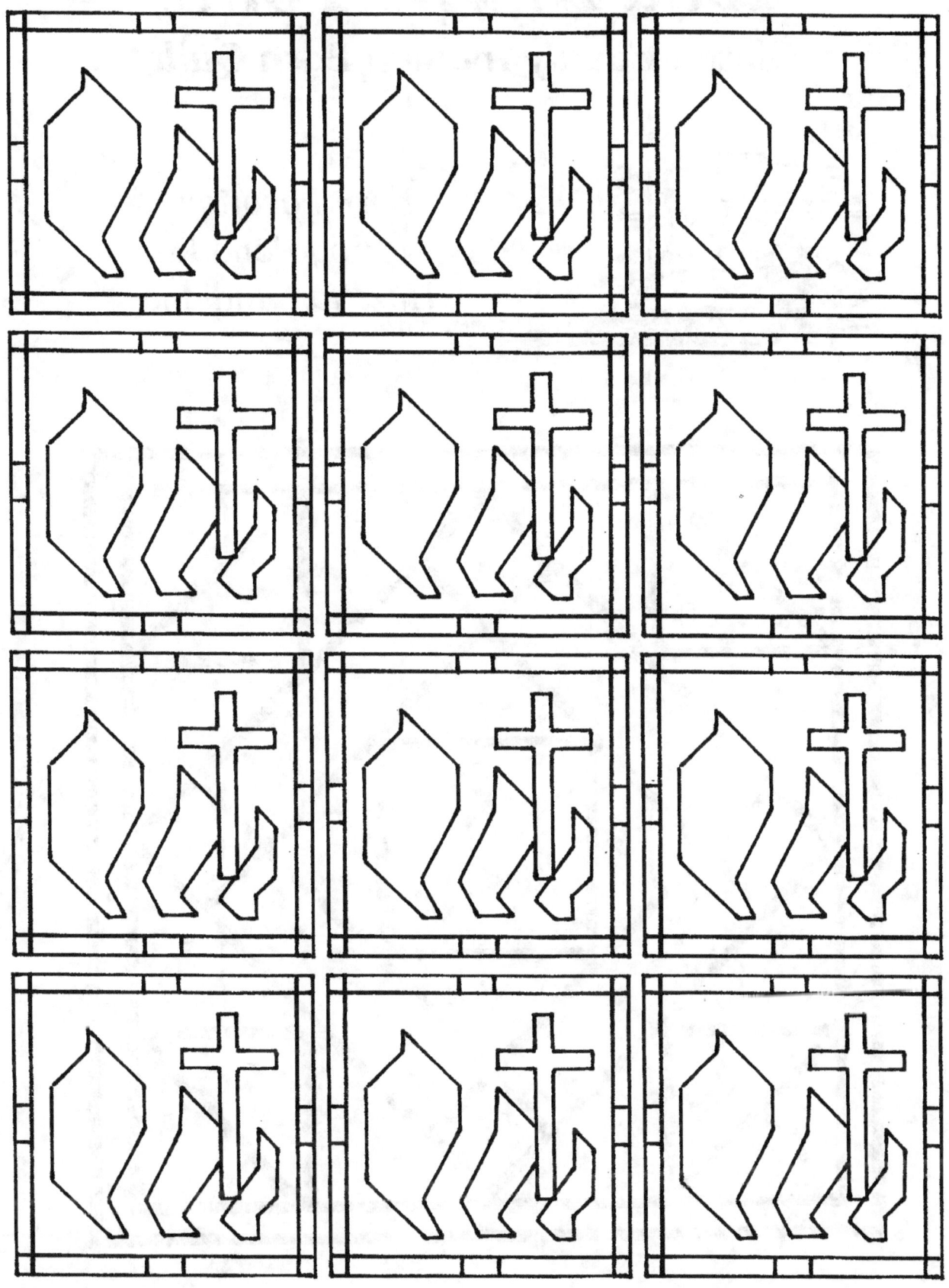

Toad In The Pond
Gibson County Indiana Barn Quilt

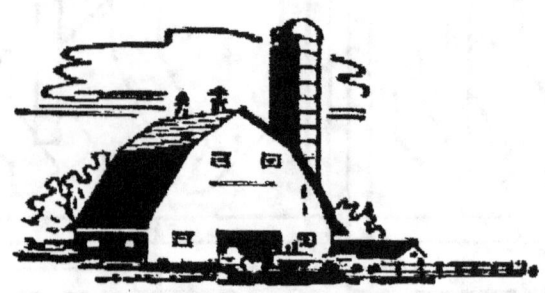

Barn Location
N Frog Pond Rd
Hazelton, Indiana

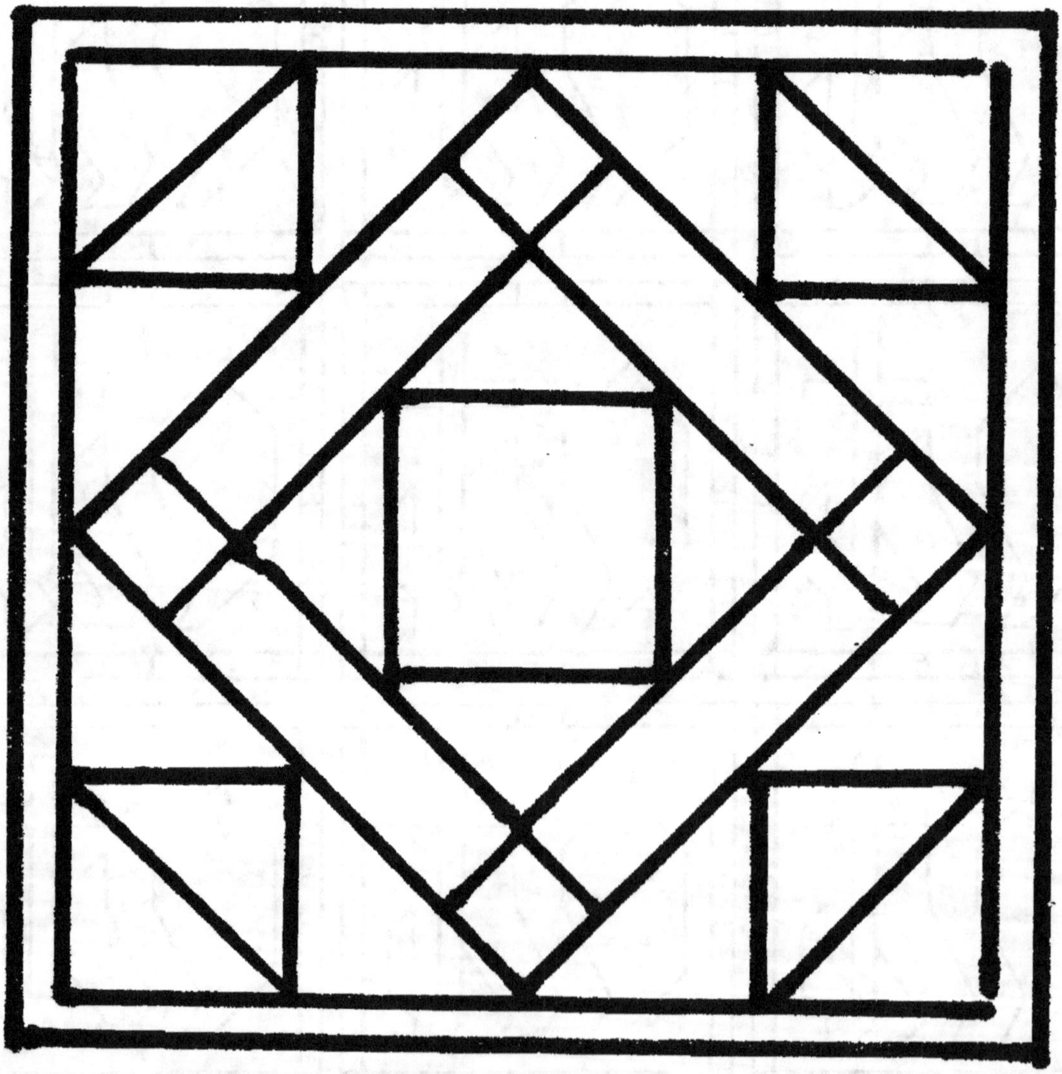

Gibson County Barn Quilt Toad in the Pond

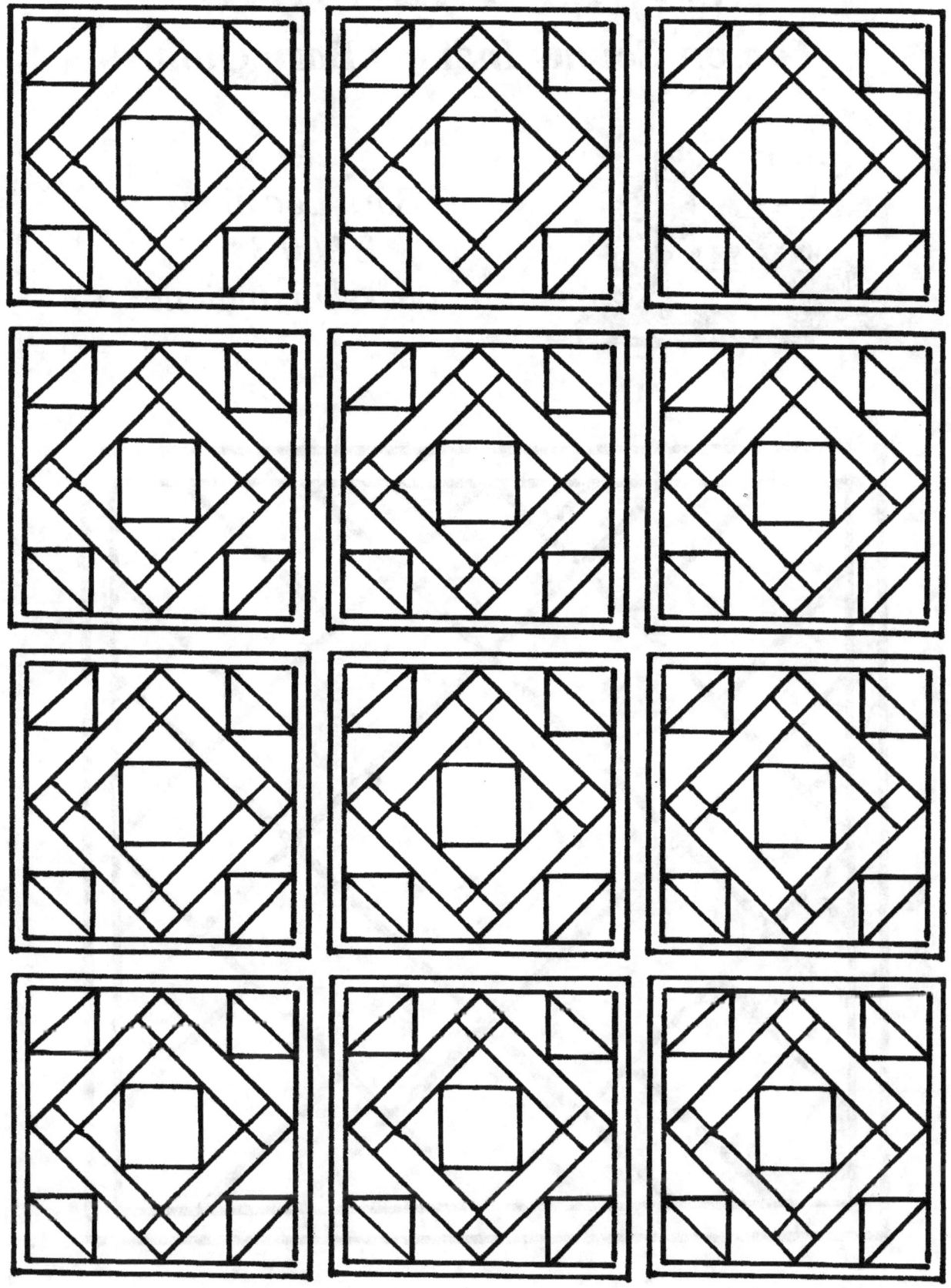

Stripes and Nine

Gibson County Indiana Barn Quilt

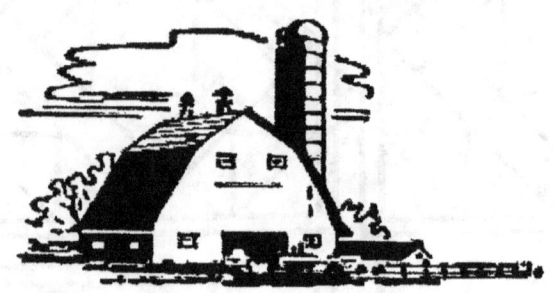

Barn Location
E 900 S
Buckskin, Indiana

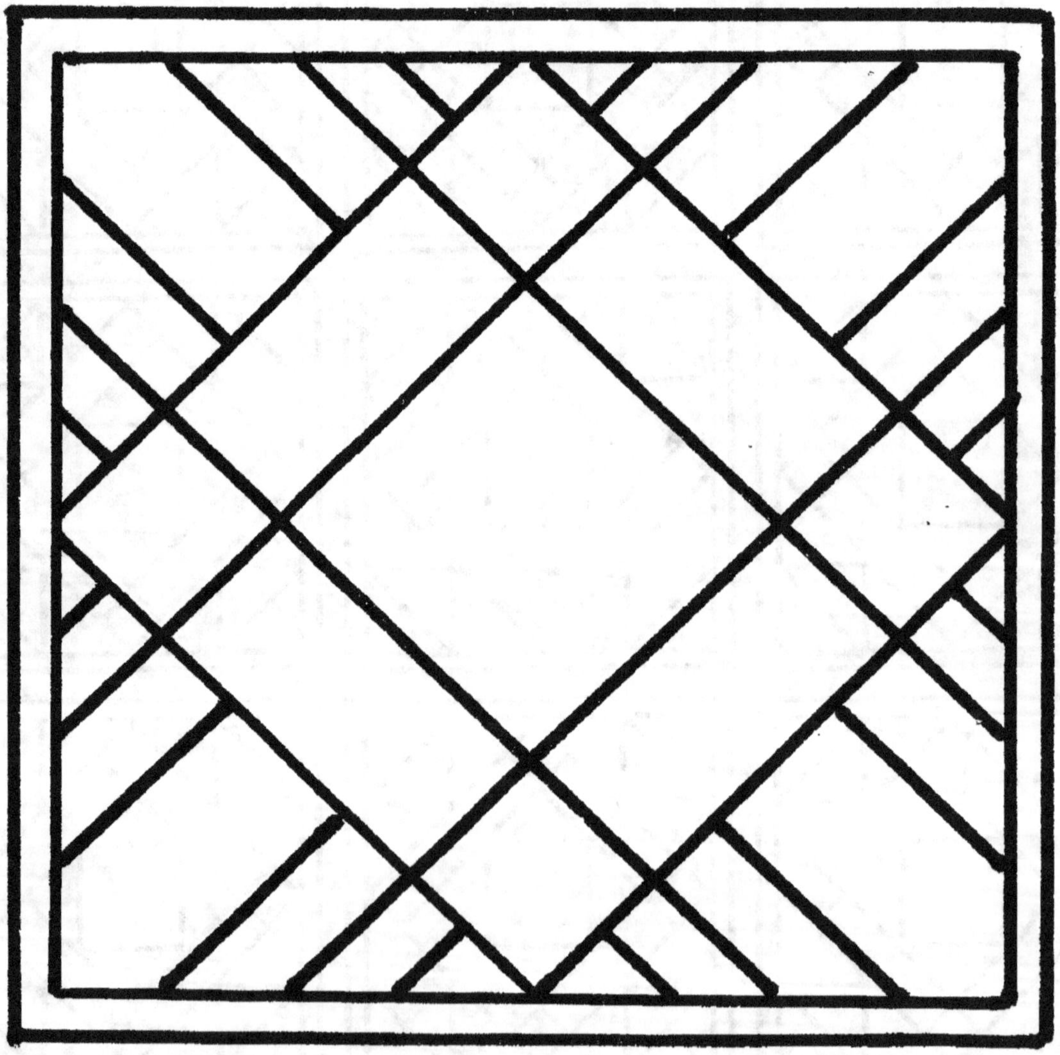

Gibson County Barn Quilt Stripes and Nine

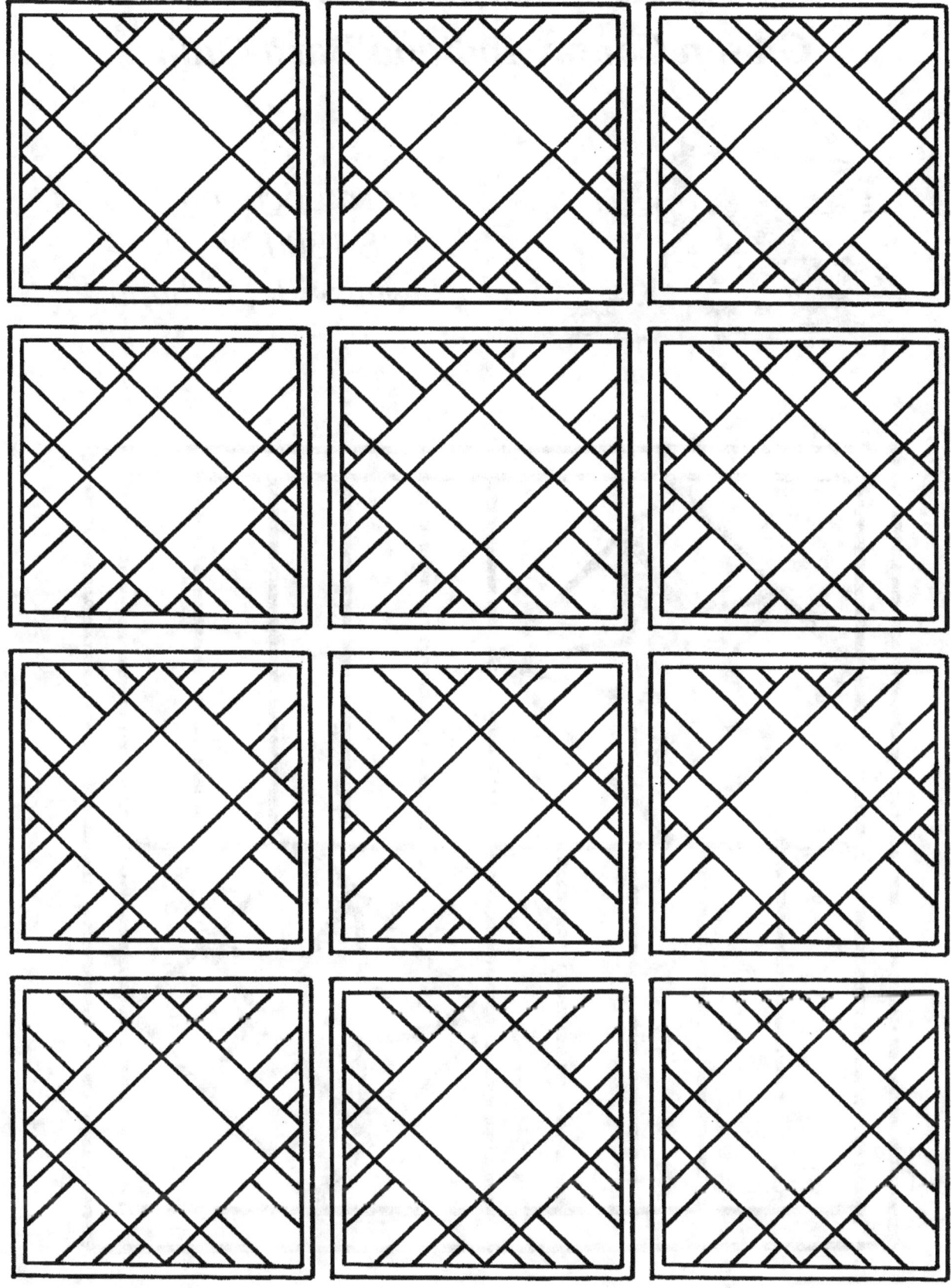

Stars and Bars
Gibson County Indiana Barn Quilt

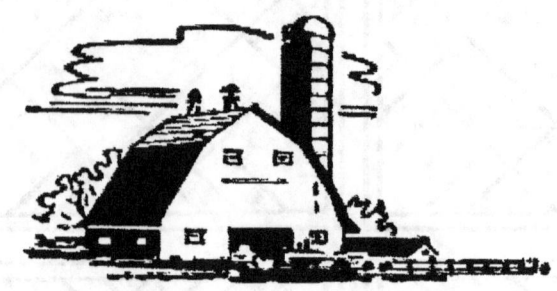

Barn Location
S 1500 W
Owensville, Indiana

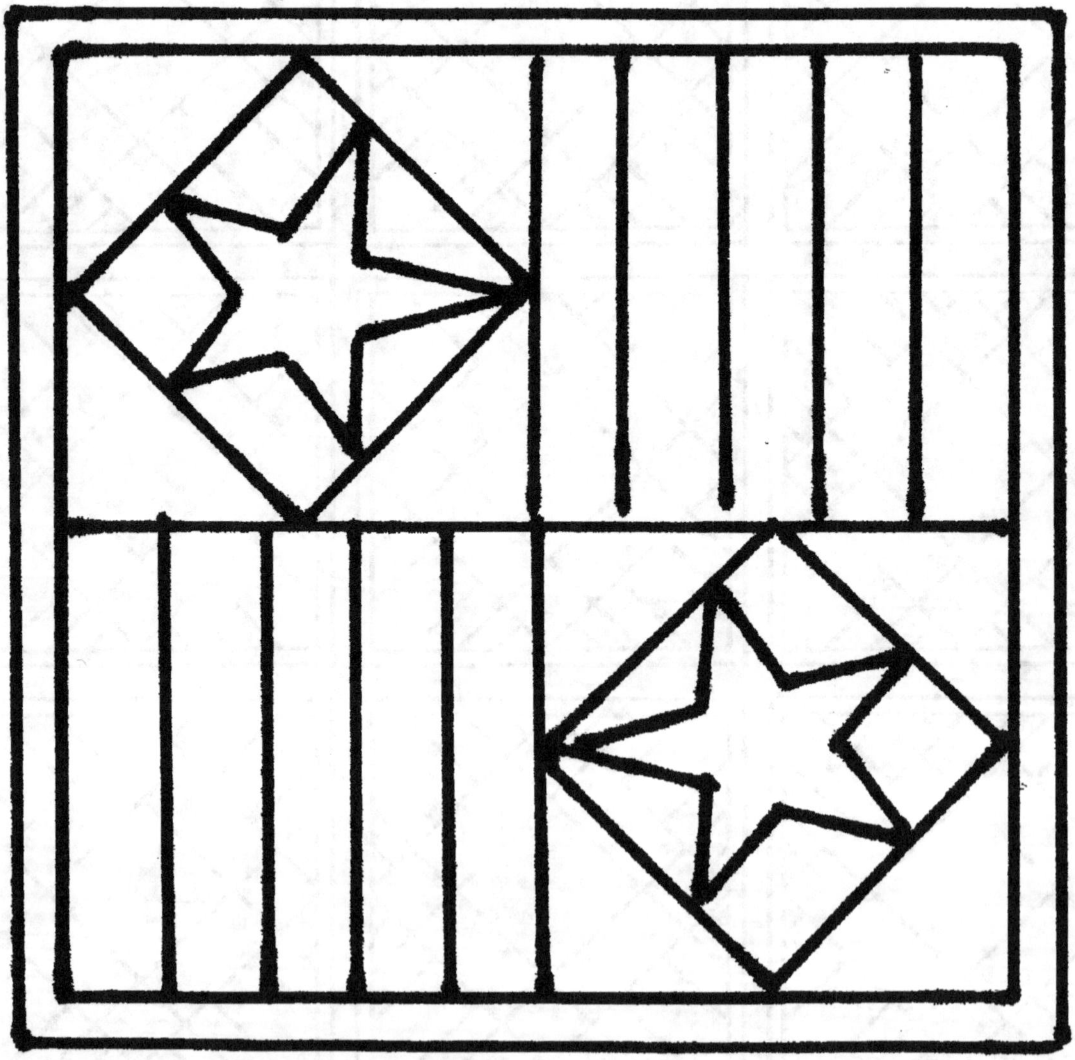

Gibson County Barn Quilt Stars & Bars

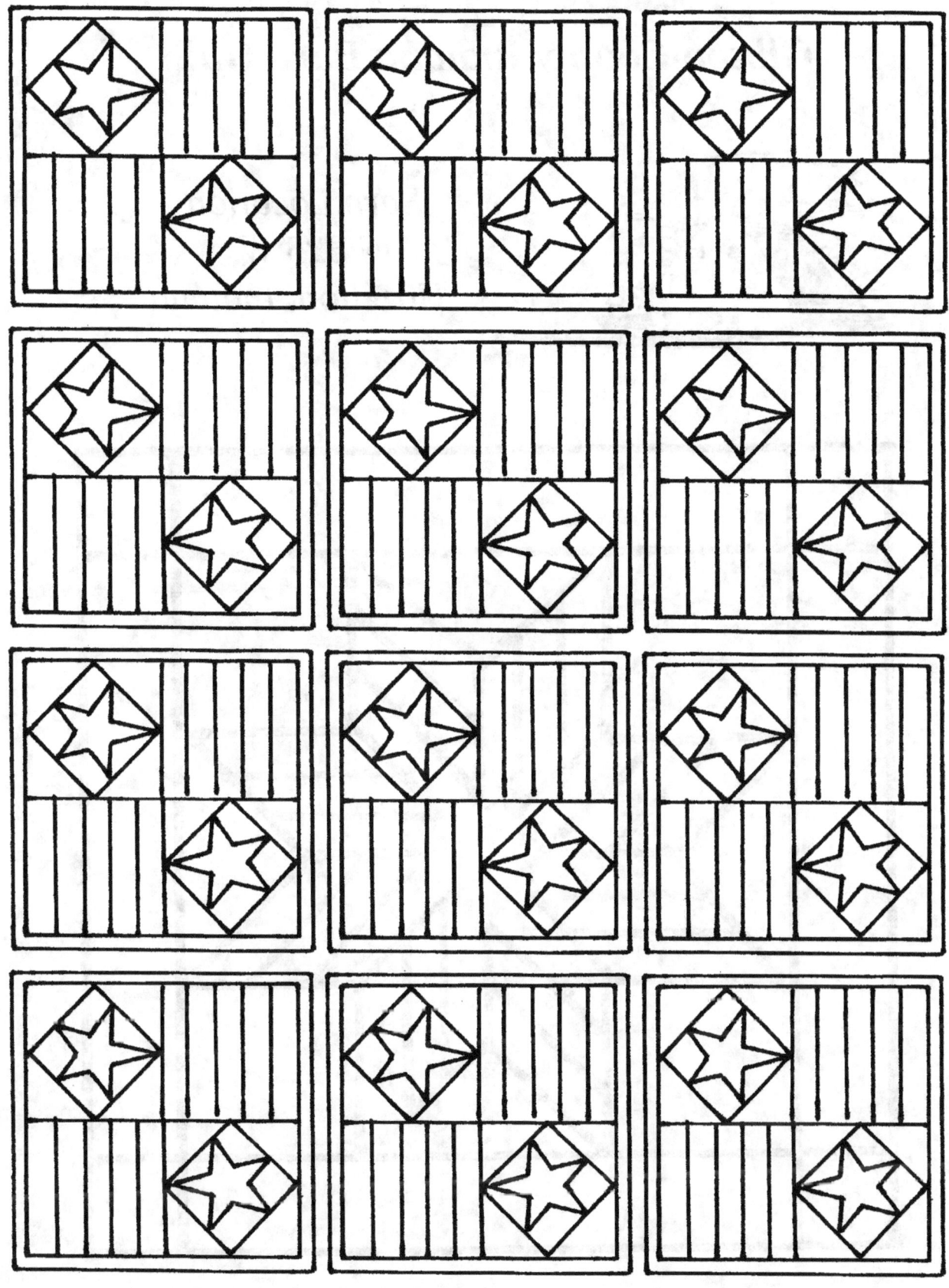

Liberty Star
Gibson County Indiana Barn Quilt

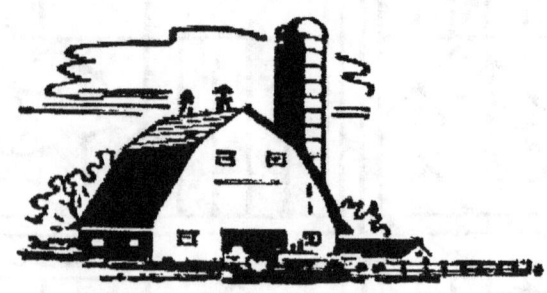

Barn Location
N 825 W
Hazelton, Indiana

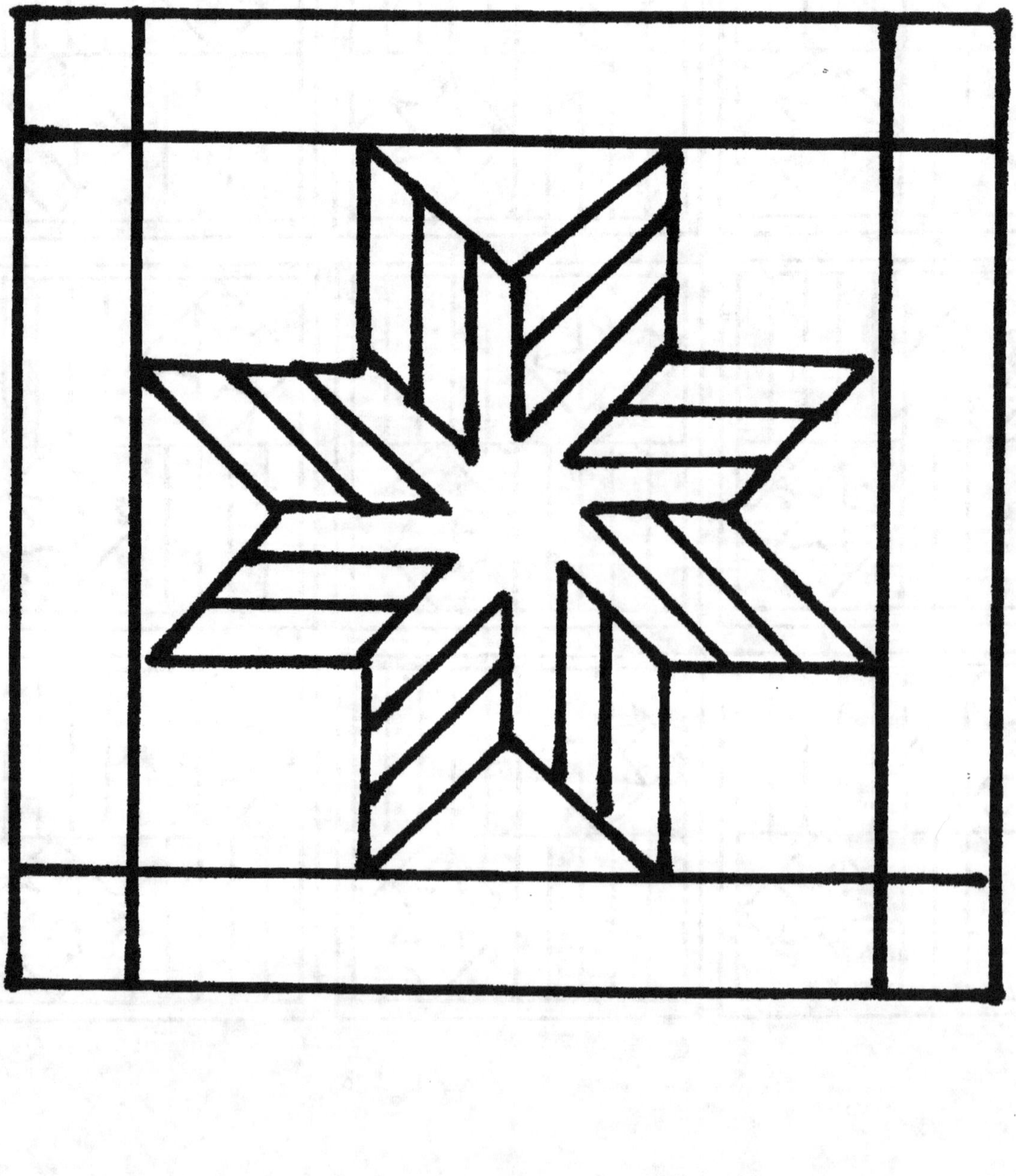

Gibson County Barn Quilt Liberty Star

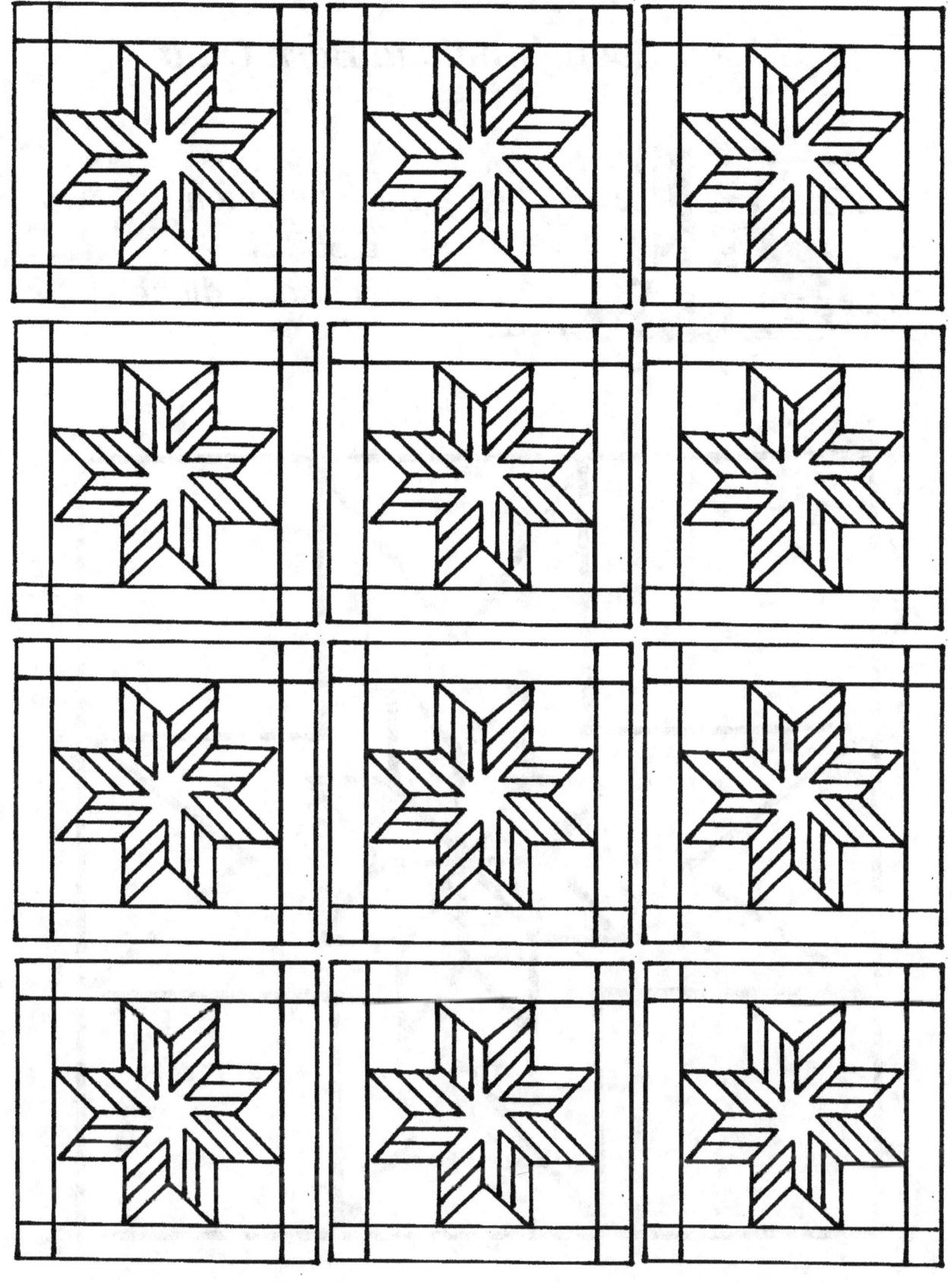

Compass Star
Gibson County Indiana Barn Quilt

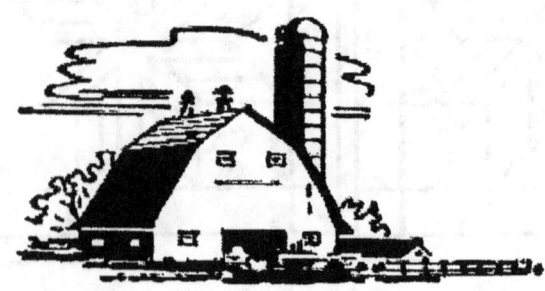

Barn Location
E 350 N
Francisco, Indiana

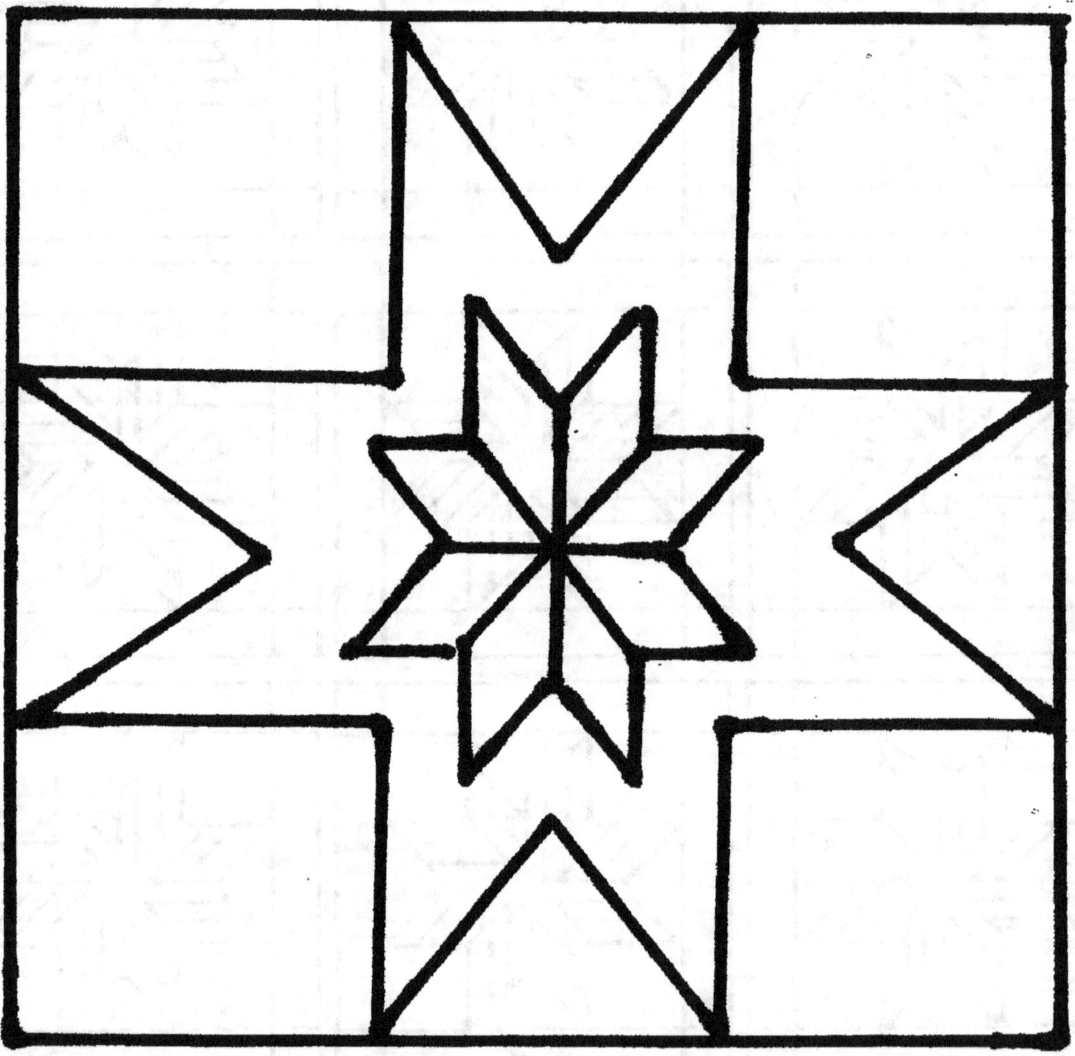

Gibson County Barn Quilt Compass Star

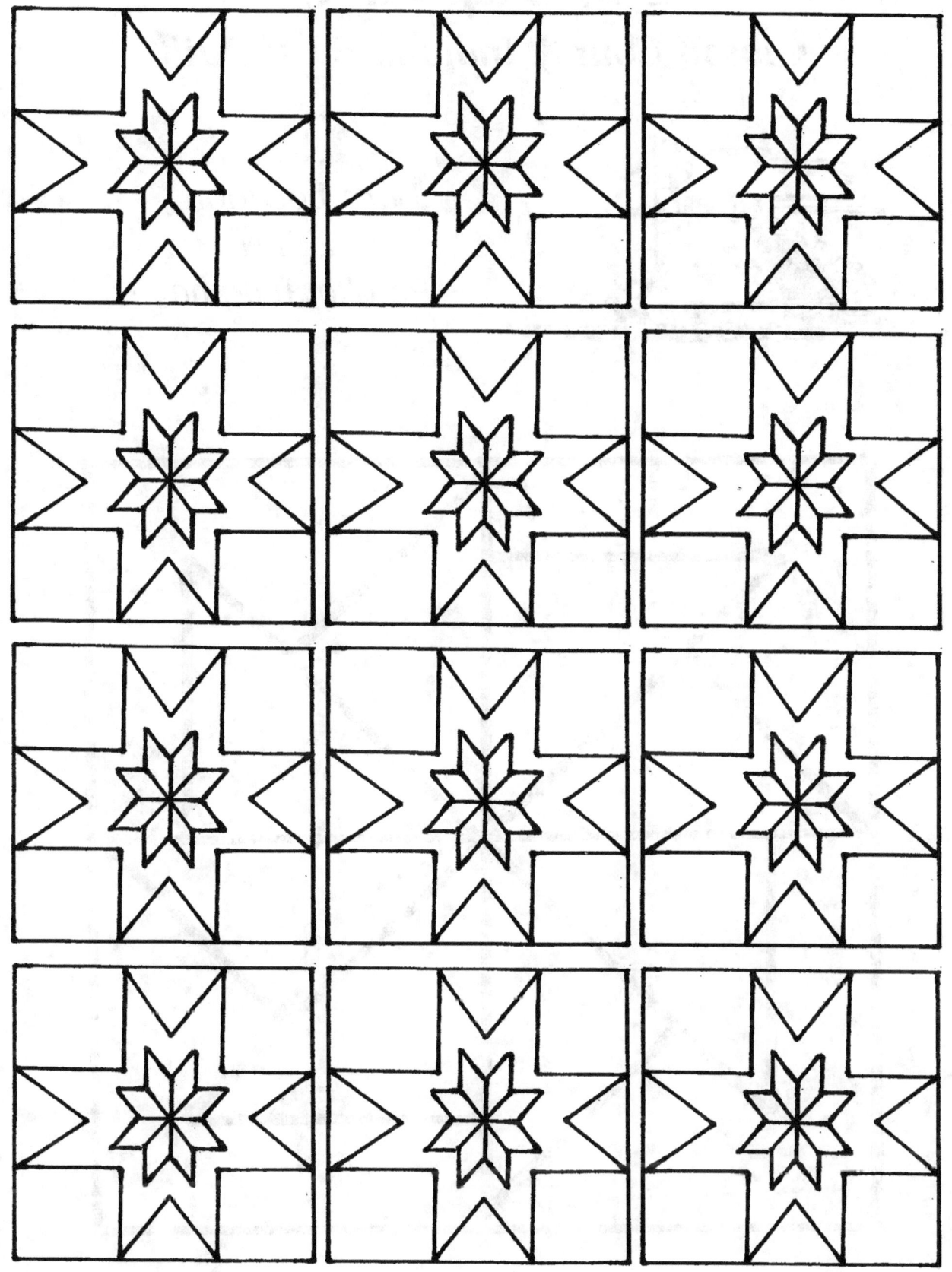

Flying Kite
Gibson County Indiana Barn Quilt

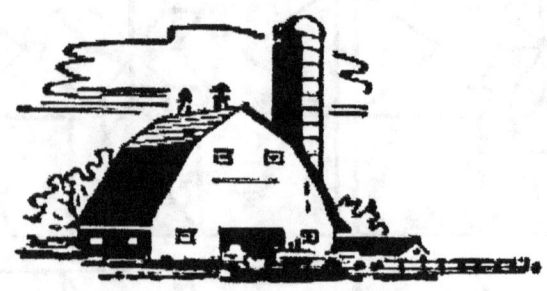

Barn Location
W 225 N
Patoka, Indiana

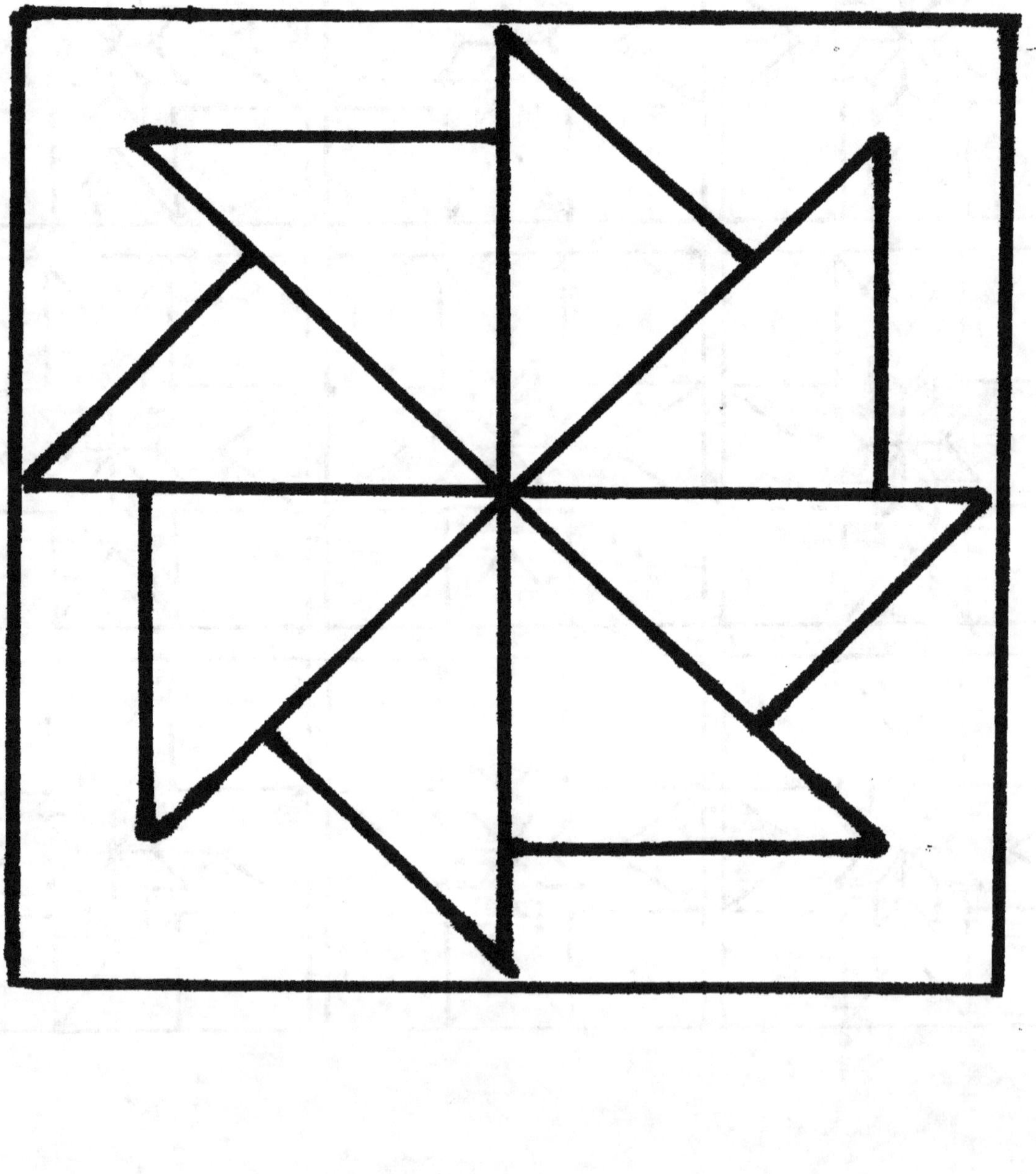

Gibson County Barn Quilt Flying Kite

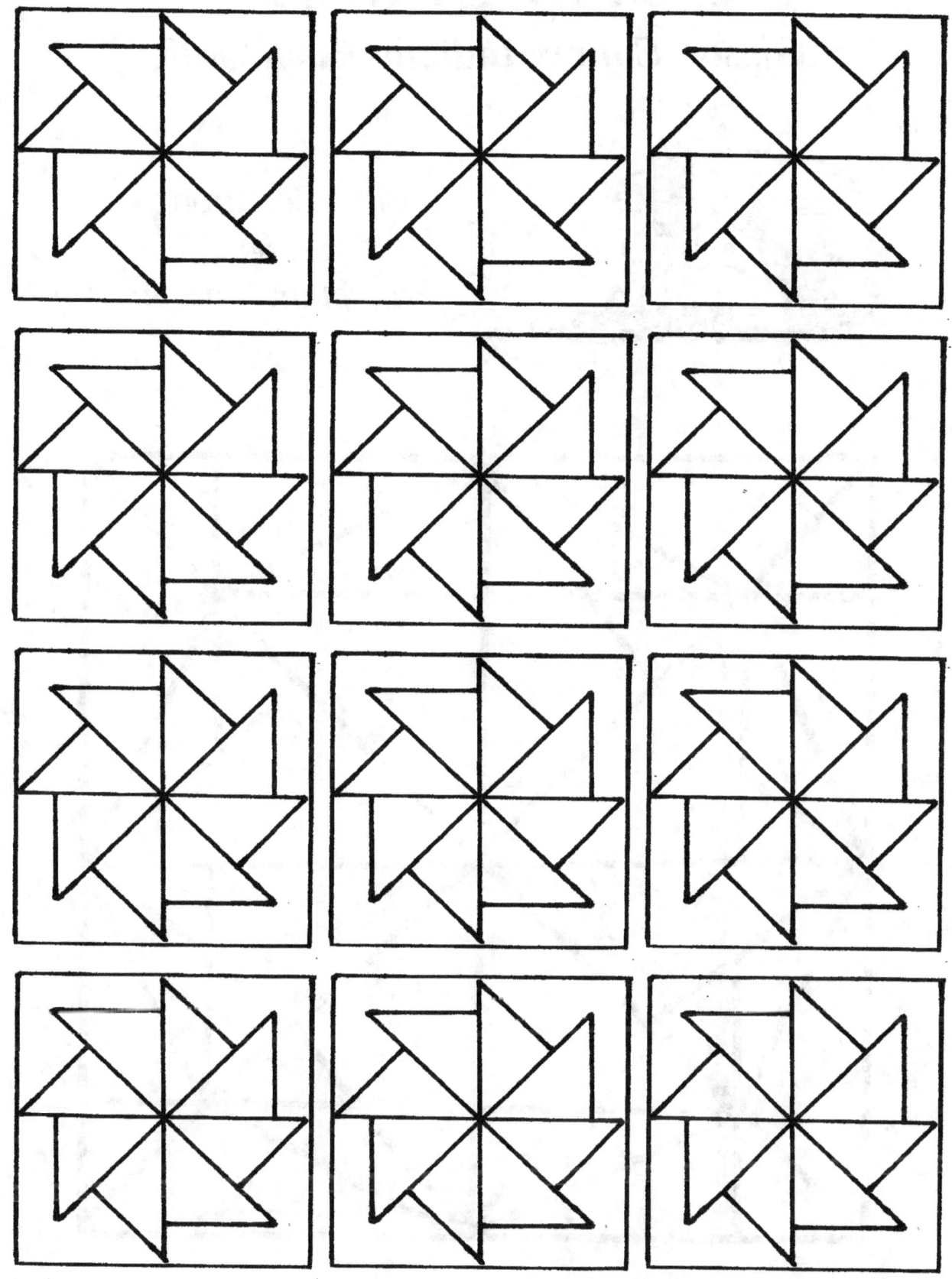

Lucky Star #2

Gibson County Indiana Barn Quilt

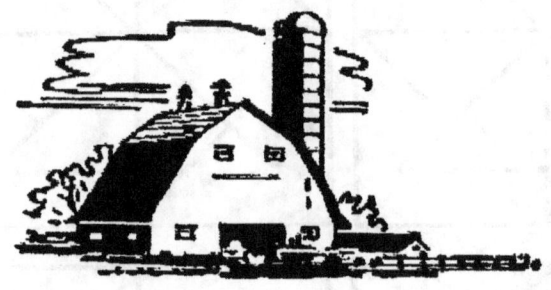

Barn Location
E SR 64
Princeton, Indiana

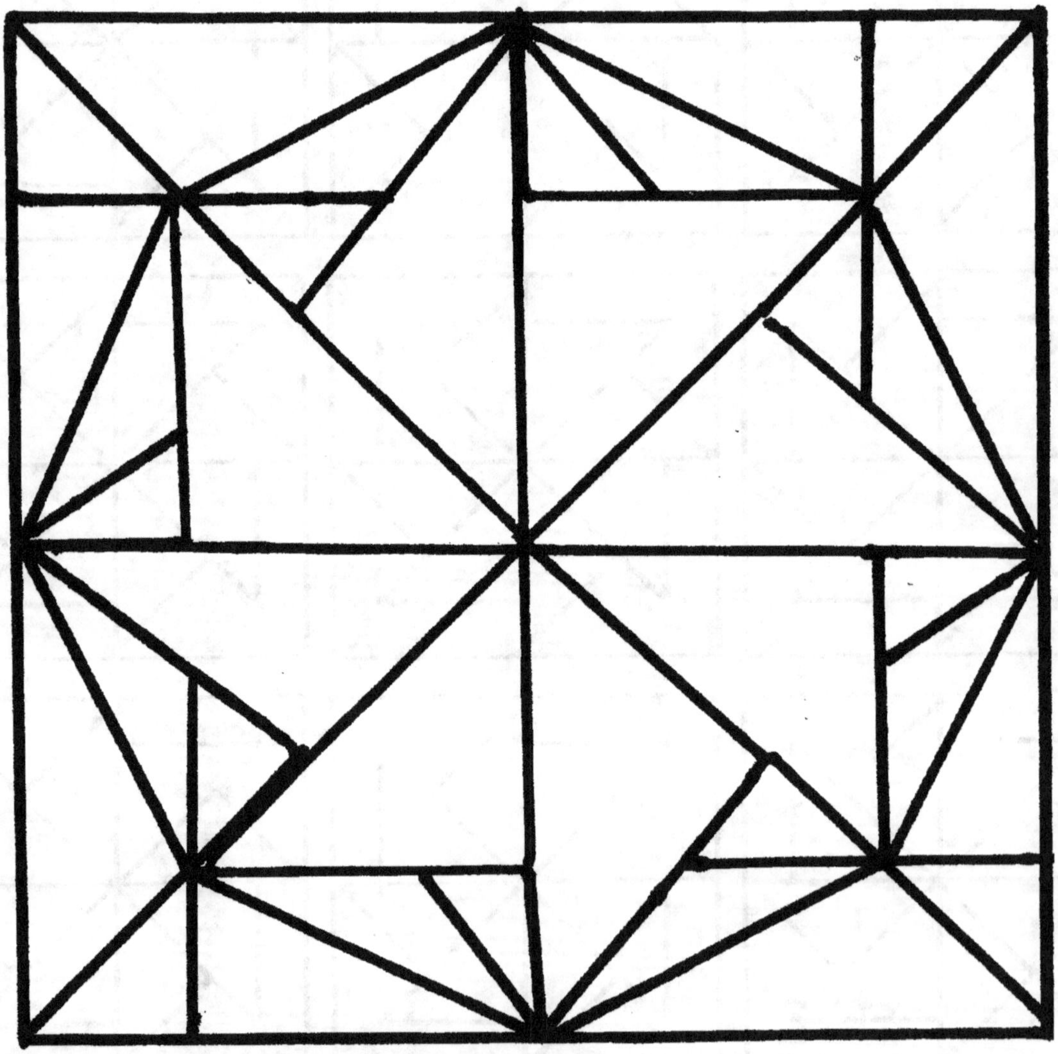

Gibson County Barn Quilt Lucky Star #2

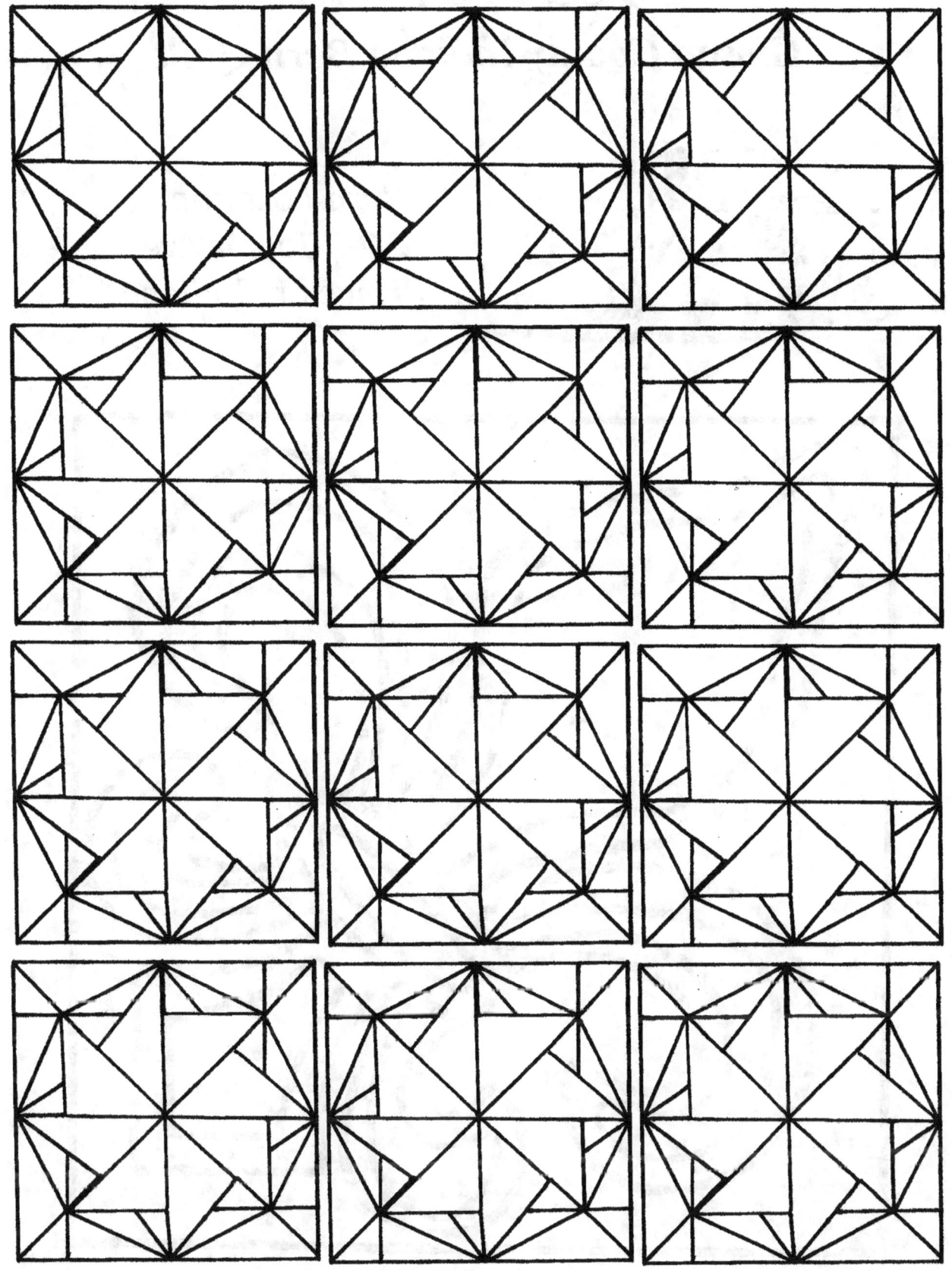

Fleur-de-lis

Gibson County Indiana Barn Quilt

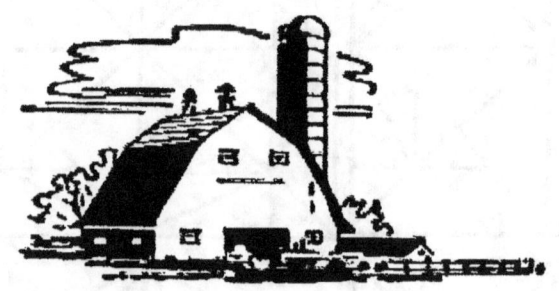

Barn Location
2400 Taylor Ave
Princeton, Indiana

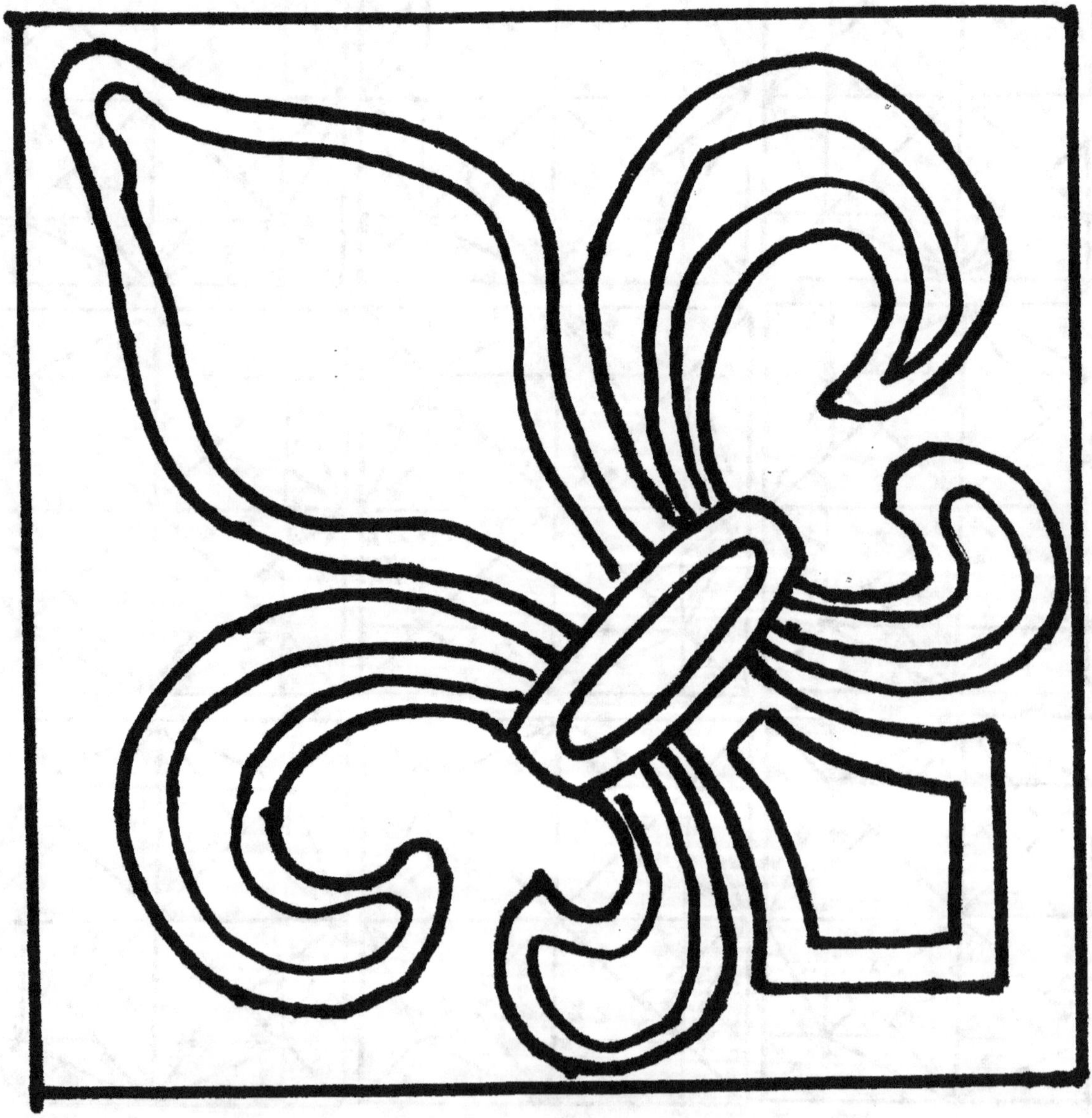

Gibson County Barn Quilt Fleur-de-lis

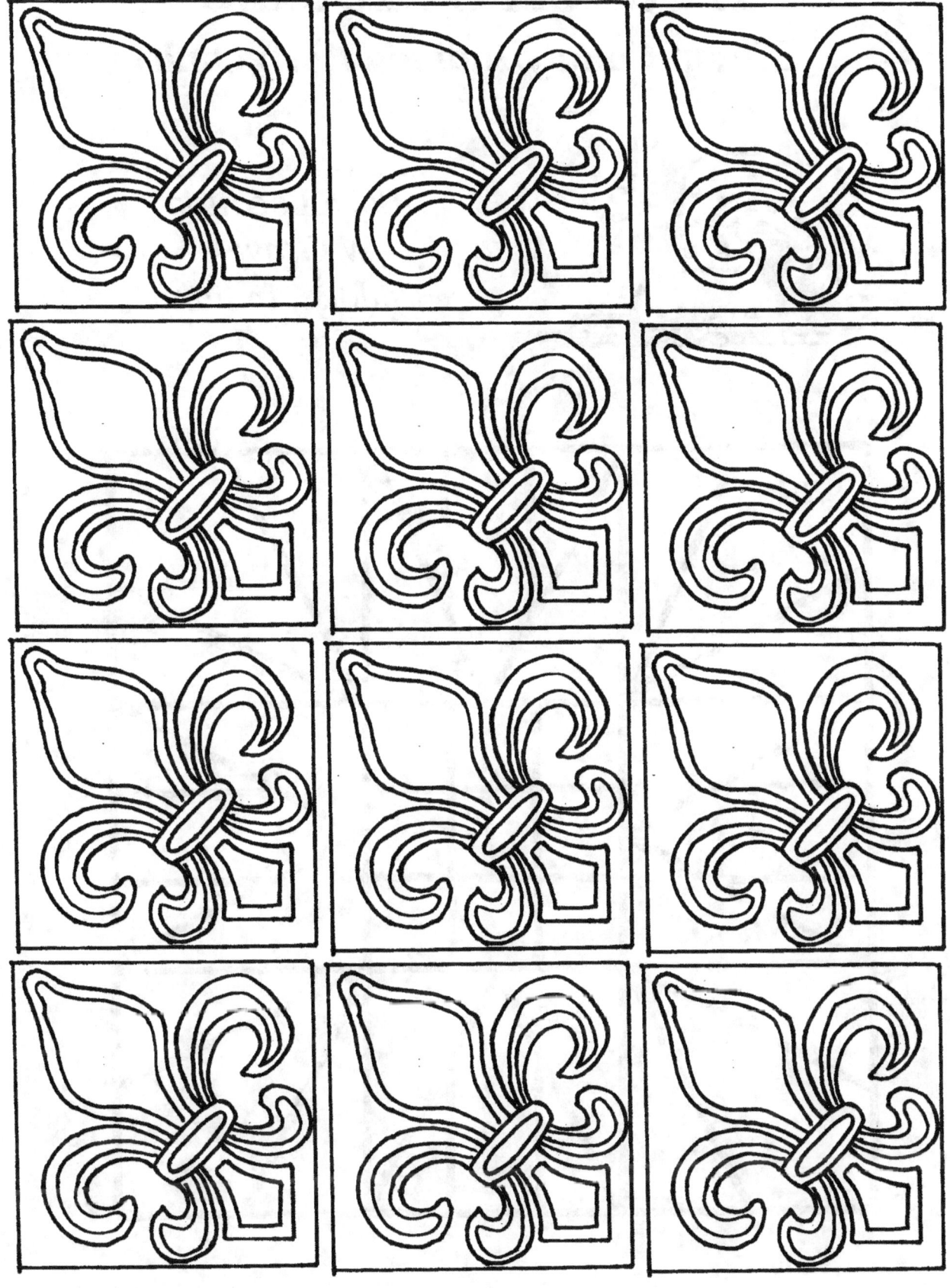

Heaven's Ablaze
Gibson County Indiana Barn Quilt

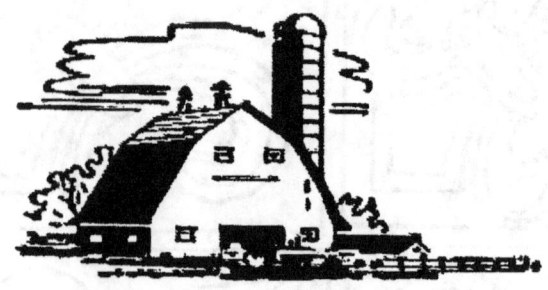

Barn Location
W Grave
Padoka, Indiana

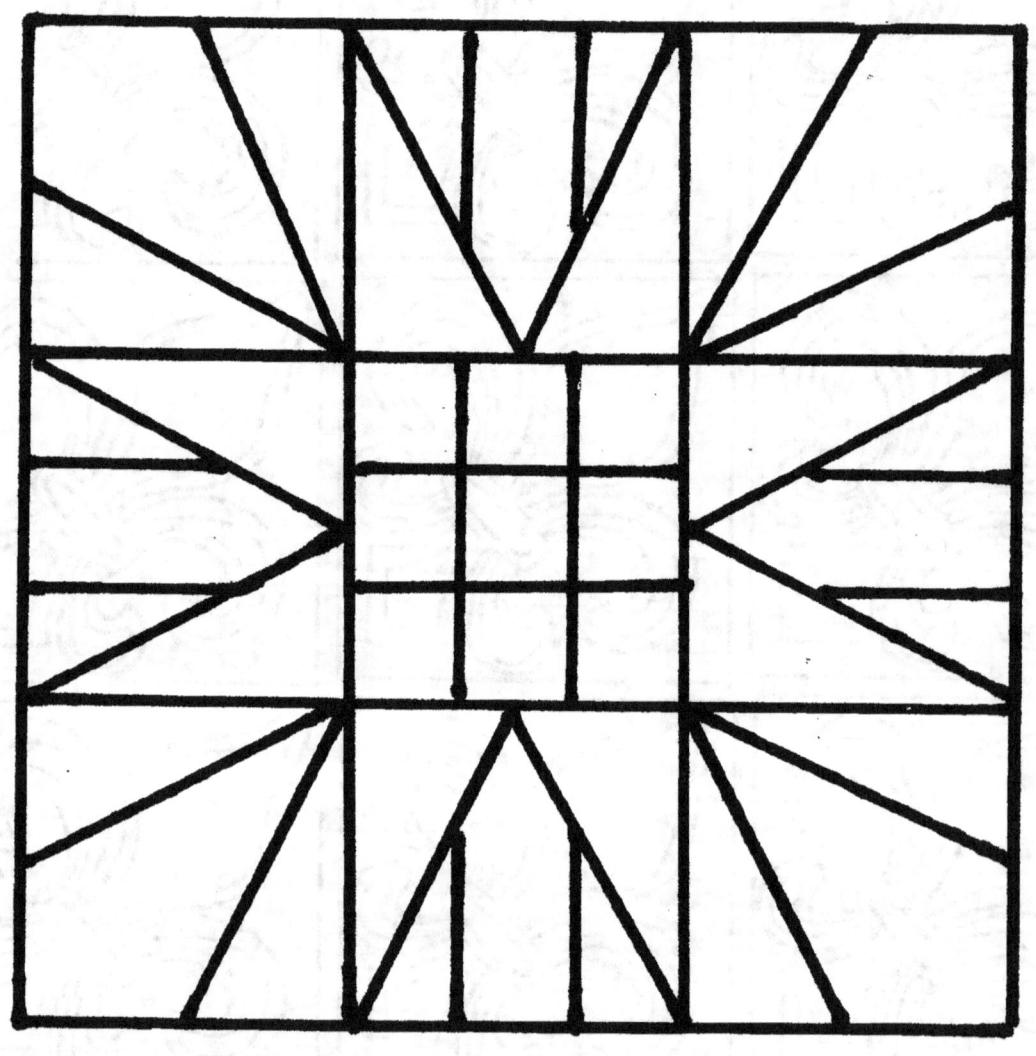

Gibson County Barn Quilt Heaven's Ablaze

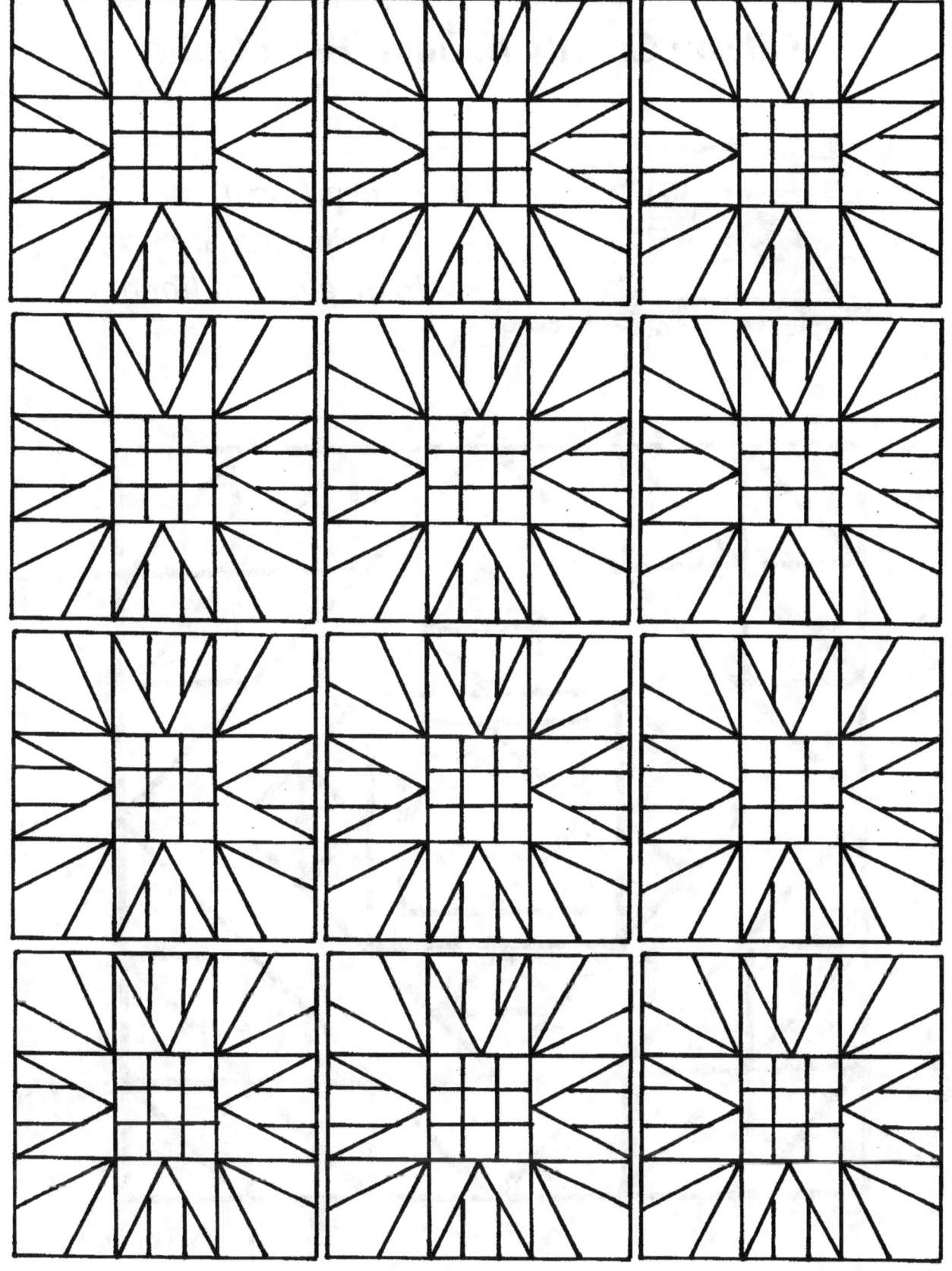

County Fair
Gibson County Indiana Barn Quilt

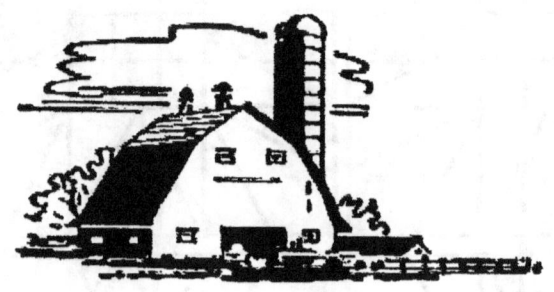

Barn Location
N Embree St
Princeton, Indiana

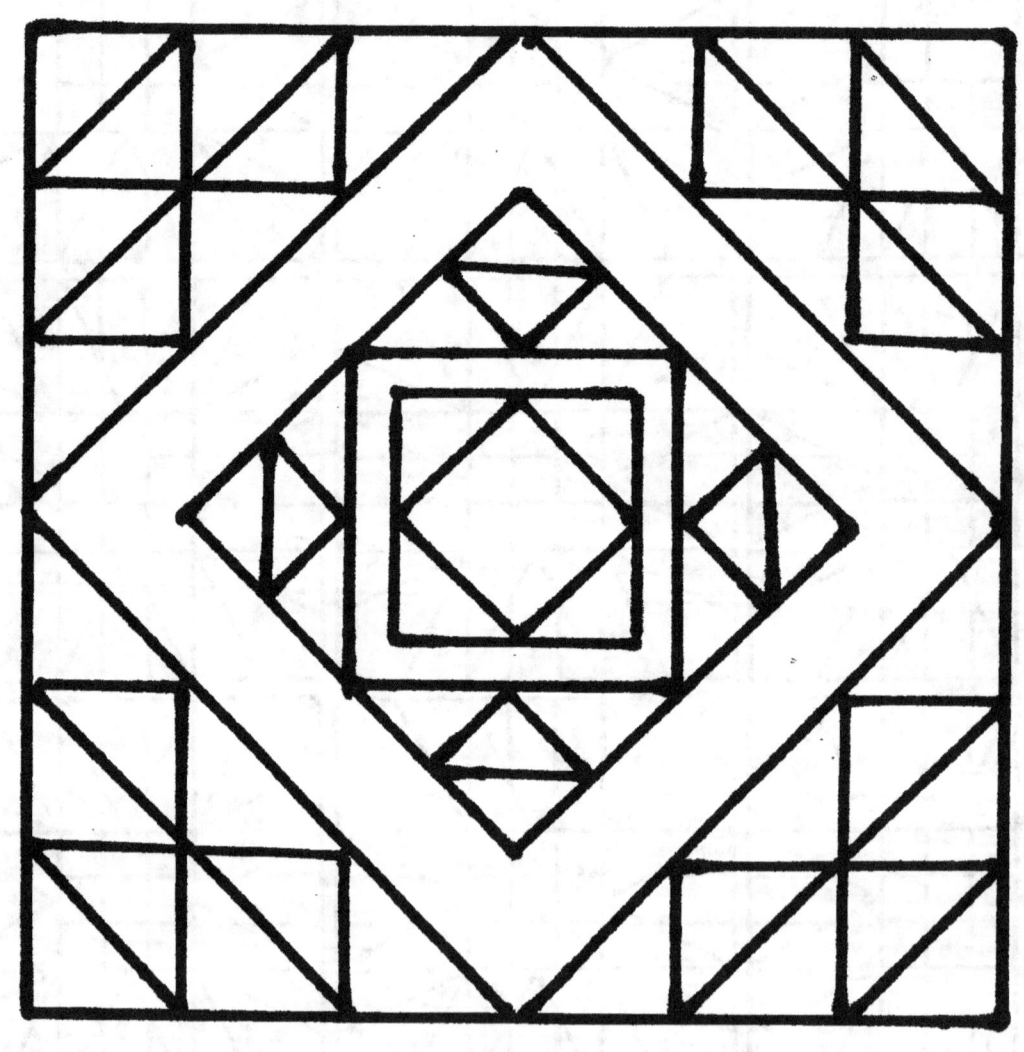

Gibson County Barn Quilt County Fair

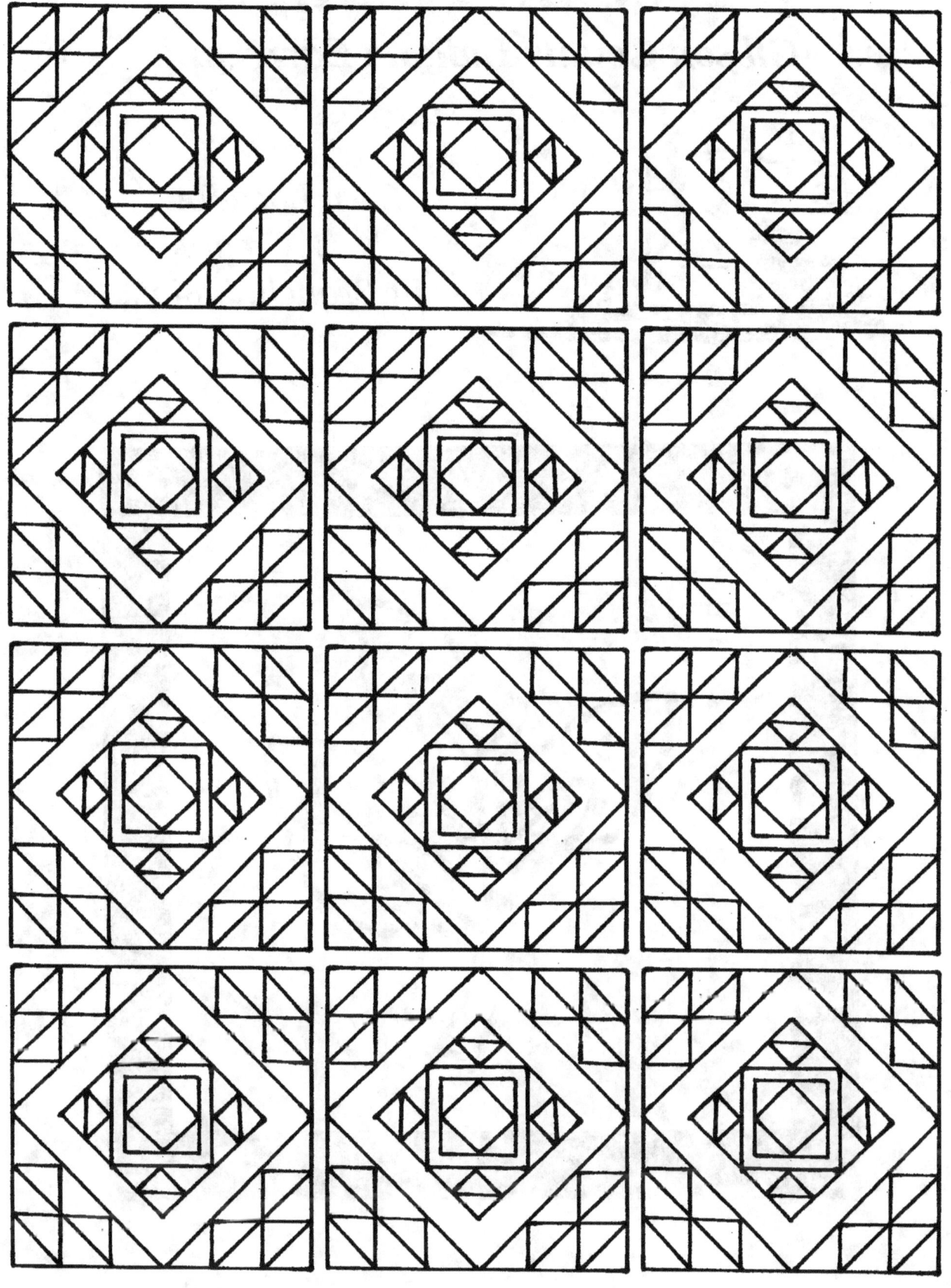

Tree and Tulips
Gibson County Indiana Barn Quilt

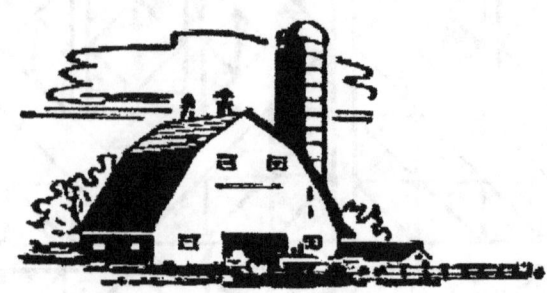

Barn Location
N McCreary
Ft Branch, Indiana

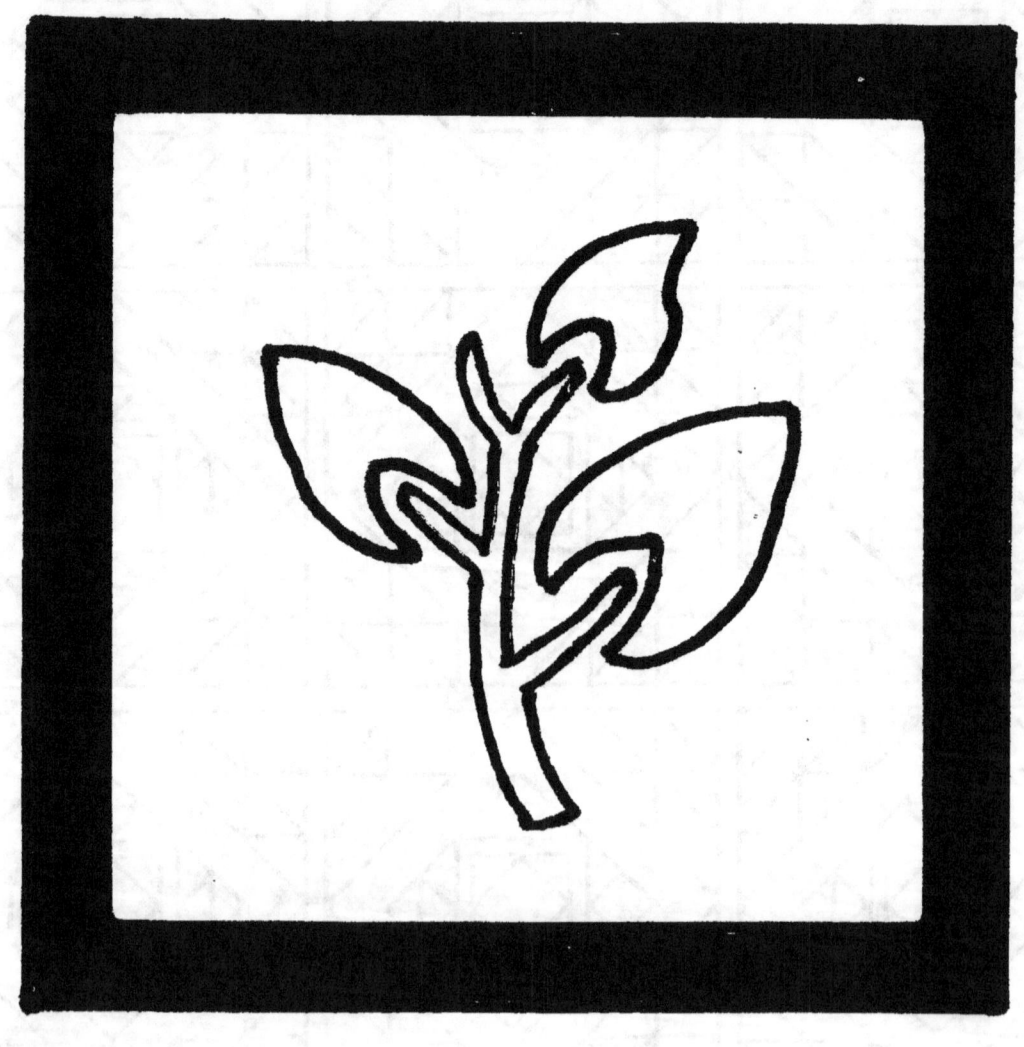

Gibson County Barn Quilt Tree and Tulips

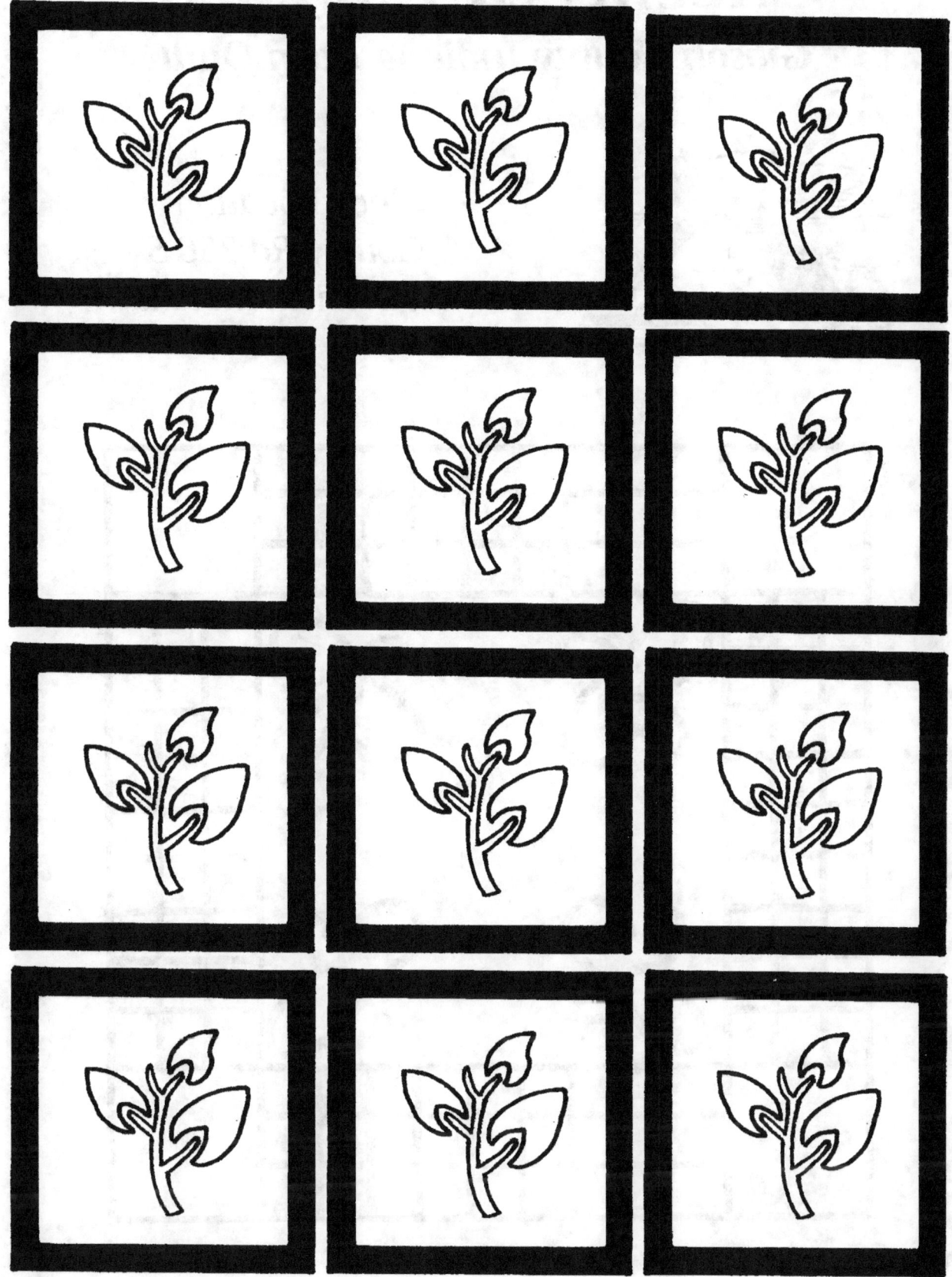

Checkered Popcorn
Gibson County Indiana Barn Quilt

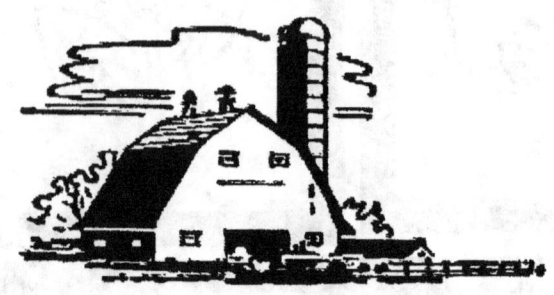

Barn Location
County Rd 750 S
Ft Branch, Indiana

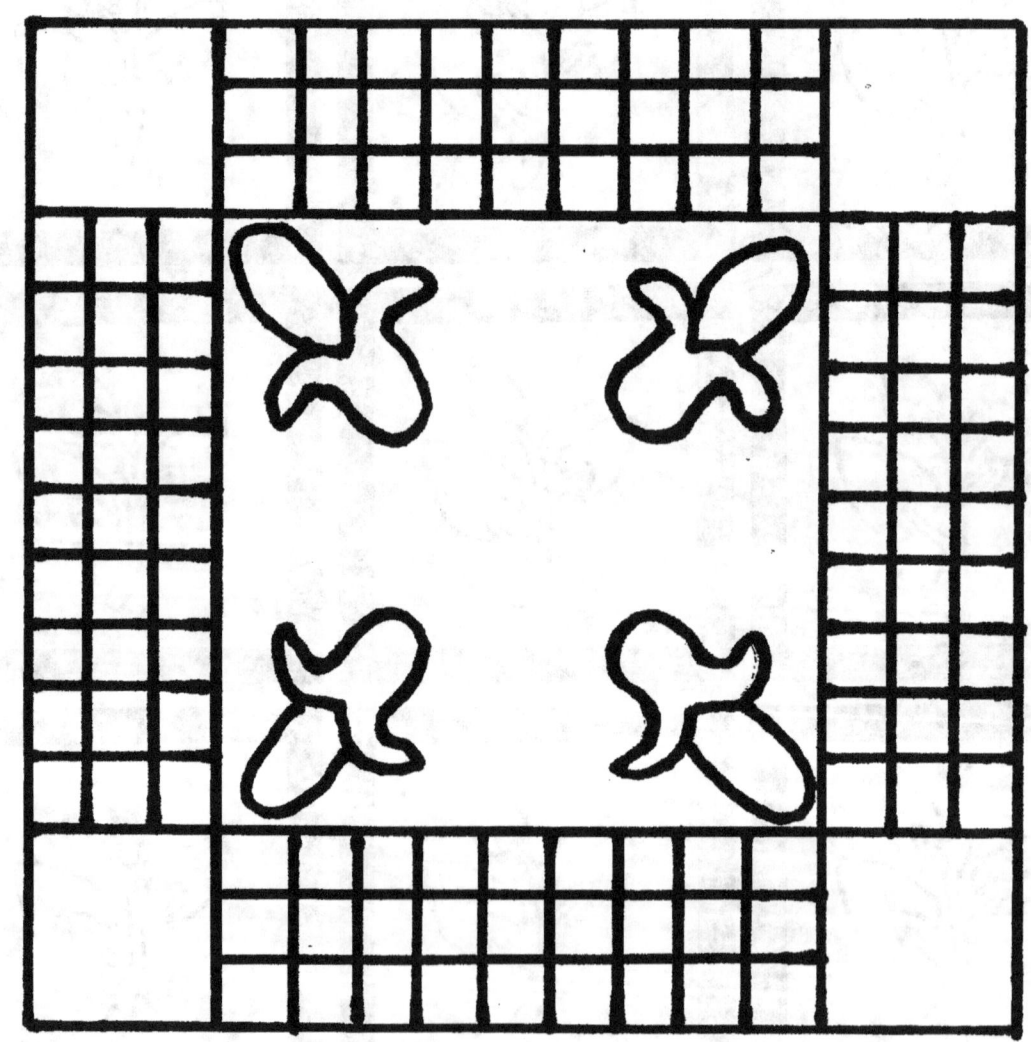

Gibson County Barn Checkered Popcorn

Patriot
Gibson County Indiana Barn Quilt

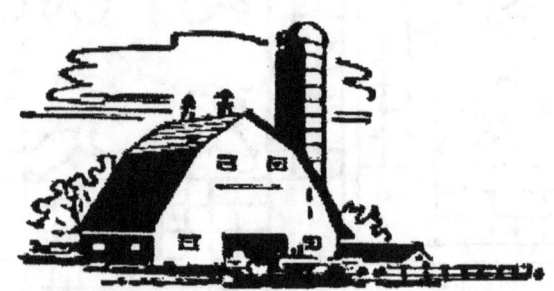

Barn Location
W Brummitt St
Owensville , Indiana

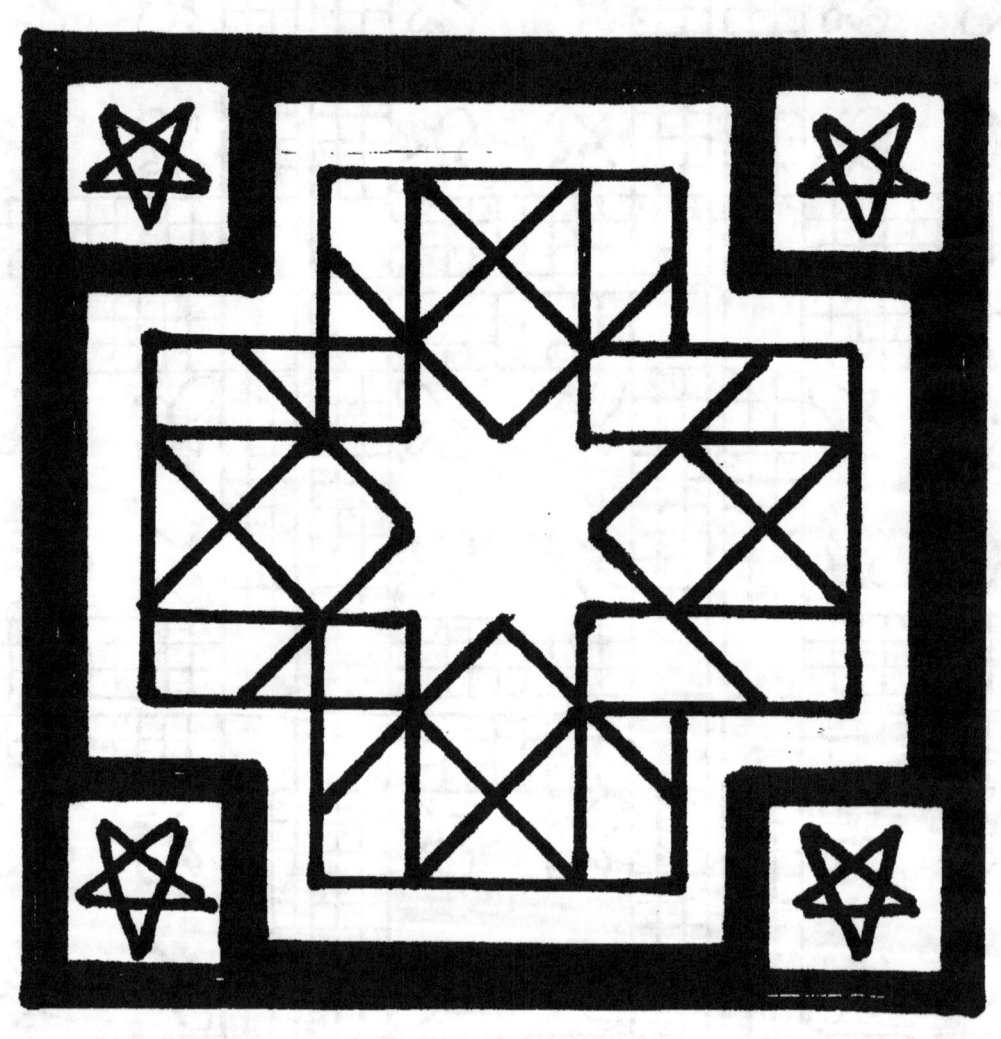

Gibson County Barn Quilt Patriot

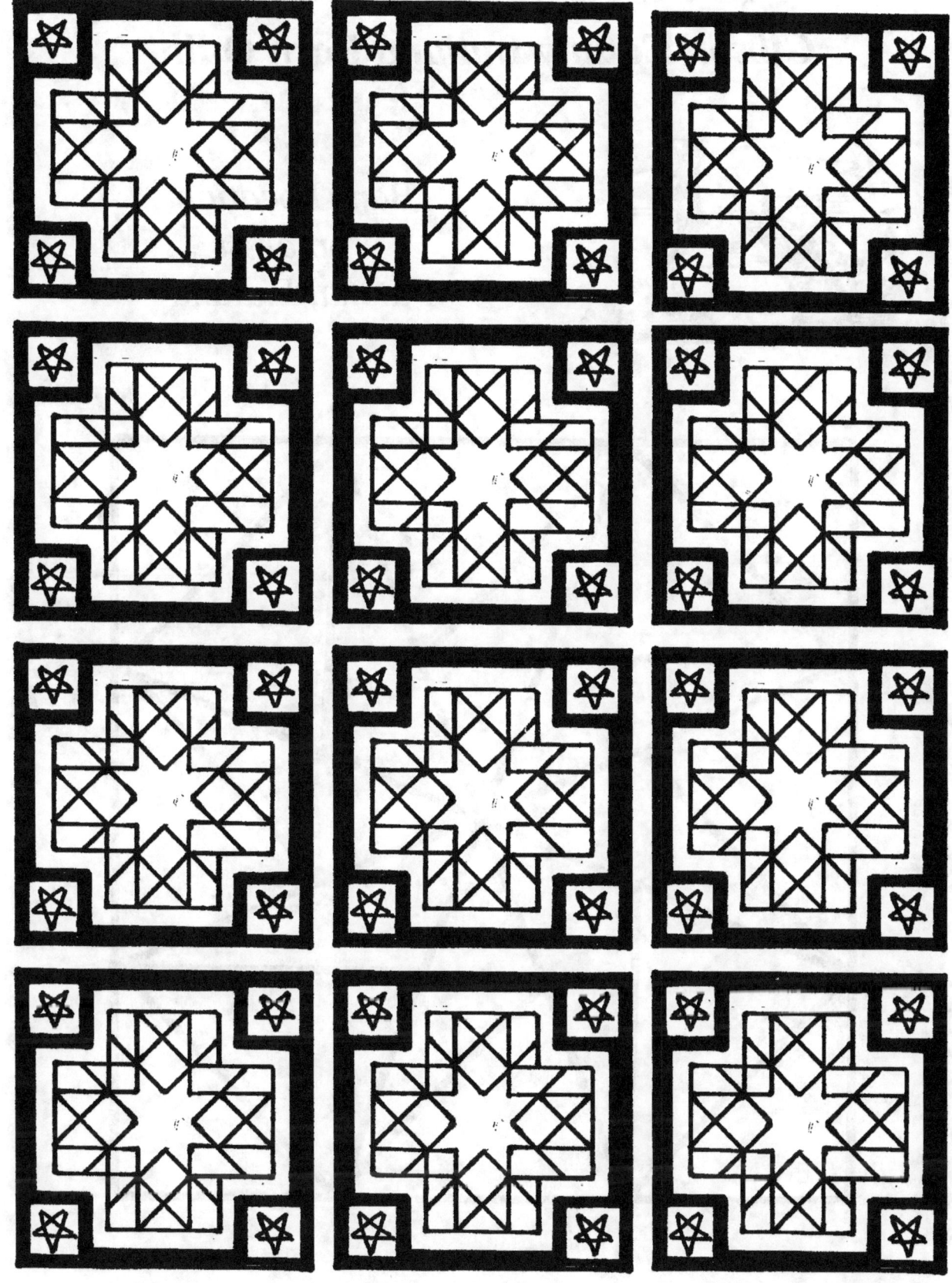

Bob's Pinwheel
Gibson County Indiana Barn Quilt

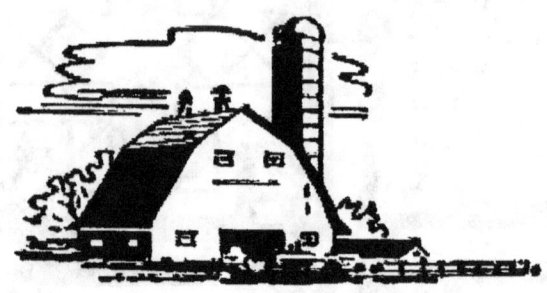

Barn Location
Poplar St
Patoka, Indiana

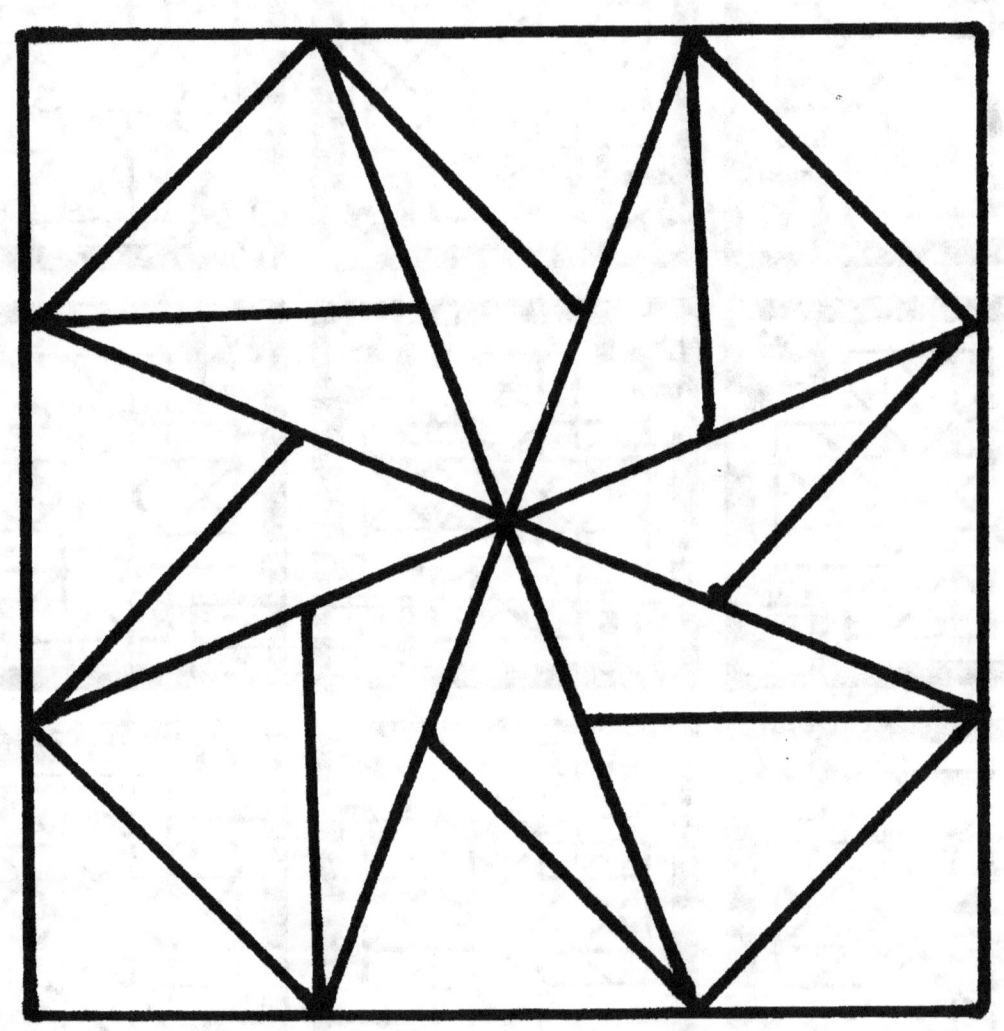

Gibson County Barn Bob's Pinwheel

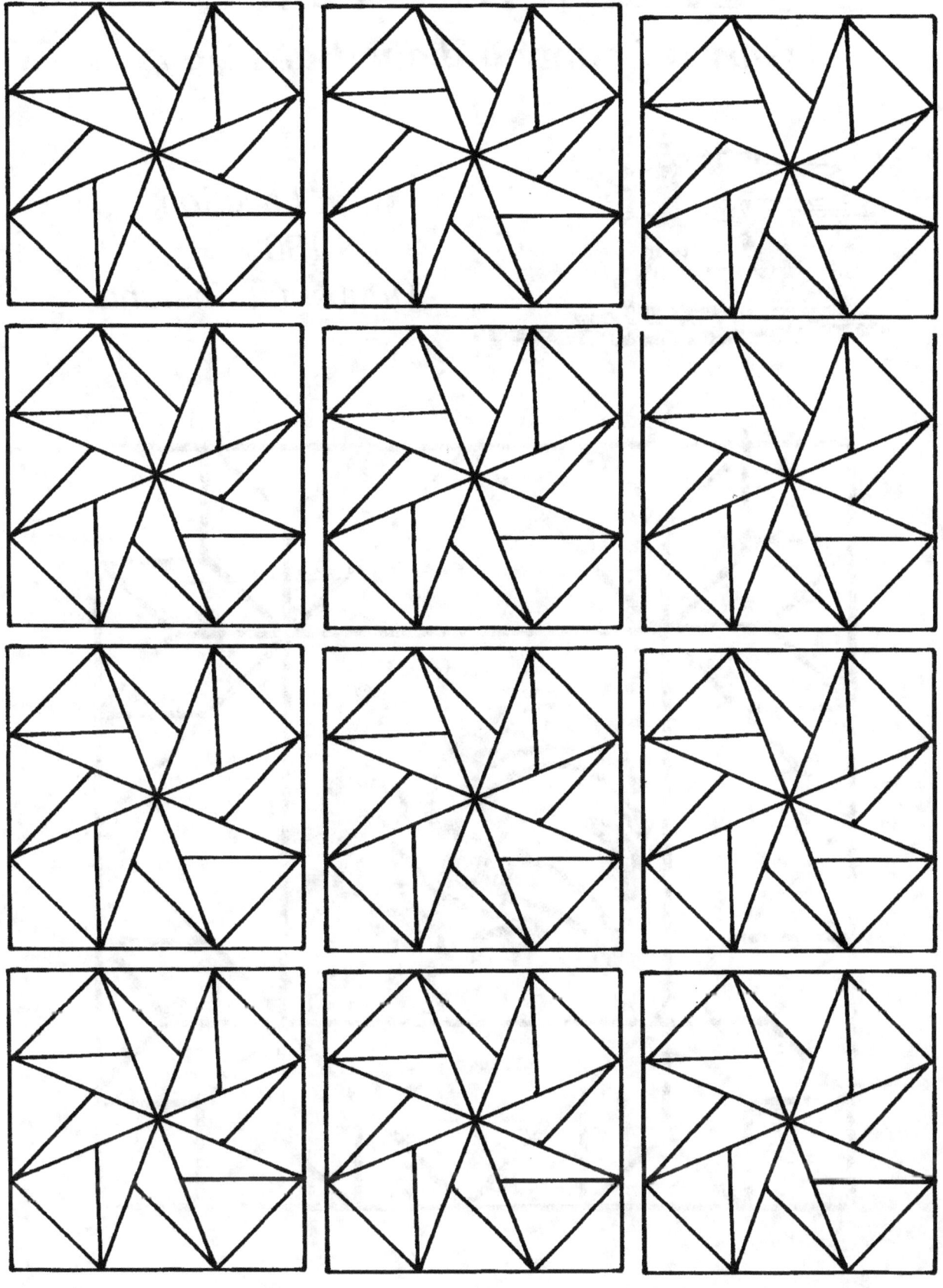

Chicken Scratch
Gibson County Indiana Barn Quilt

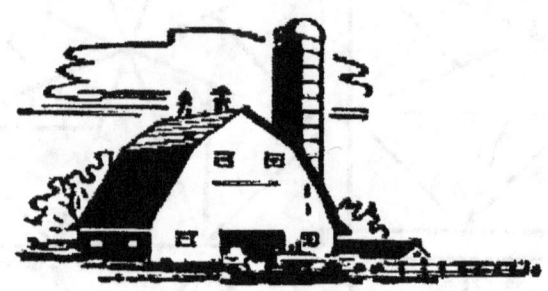

Barn Location
S 150 E
Haubstadt, Indiana

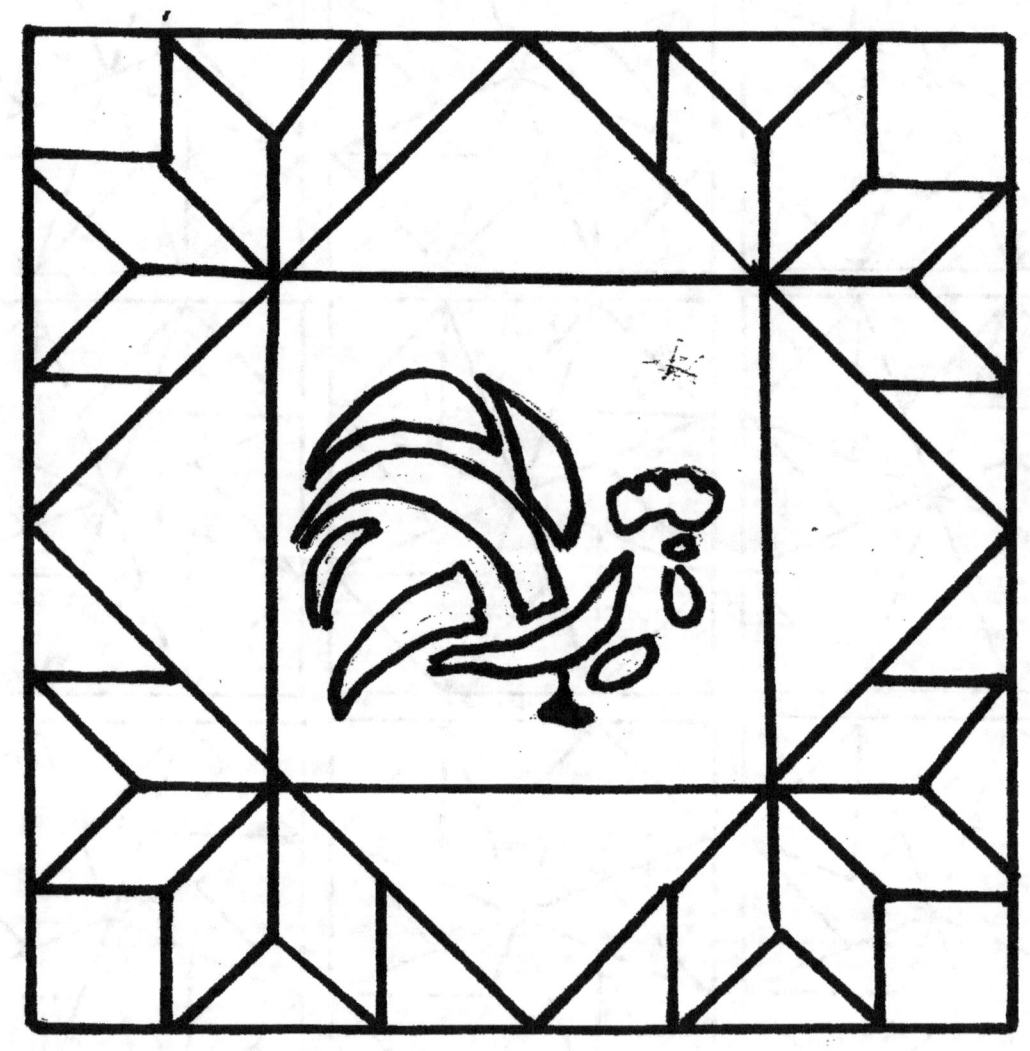

Gibson County Barn Chicken Scratch

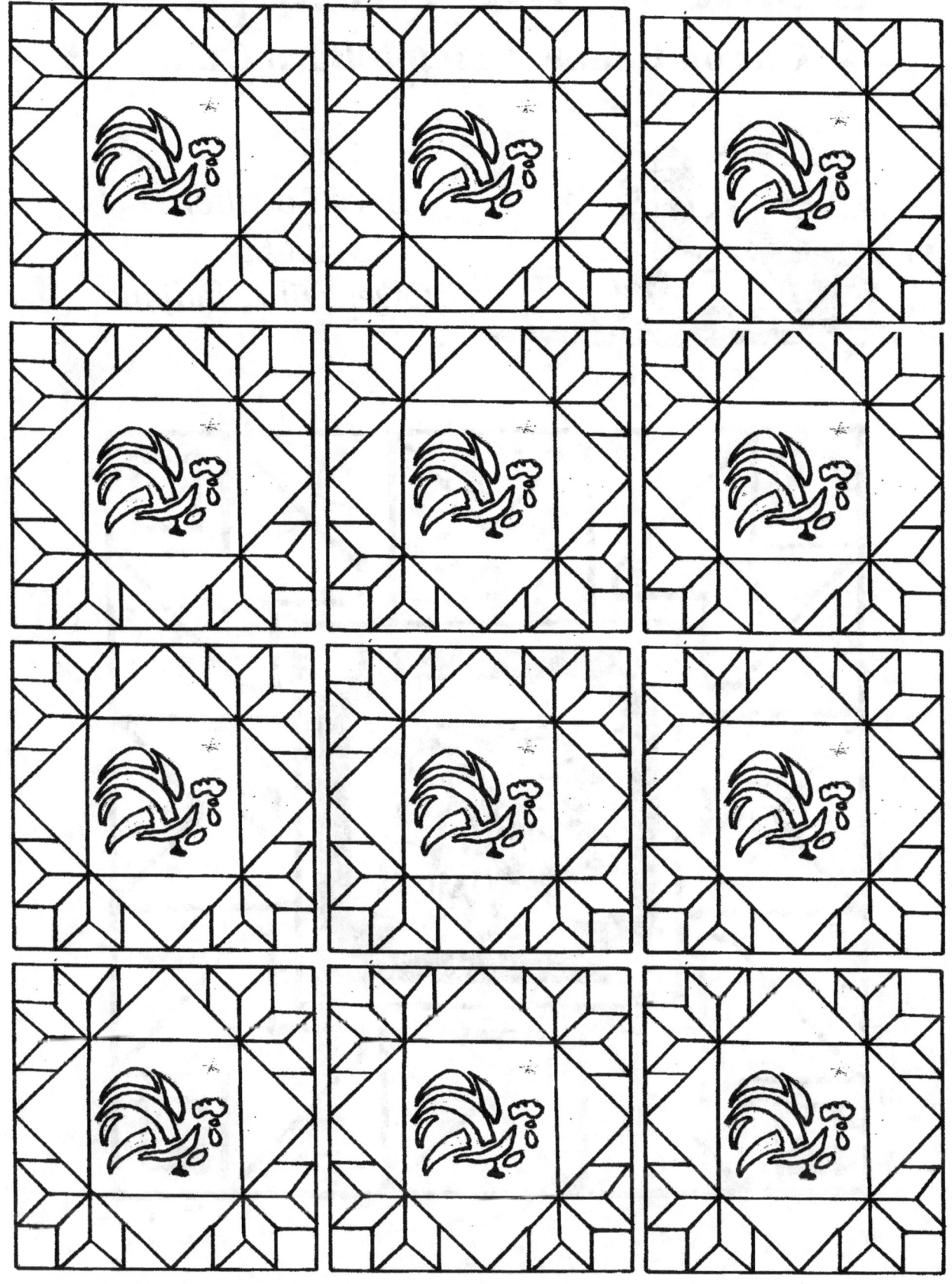

Home of the Kickapoos

Gibson County Indiana Barn Quilt

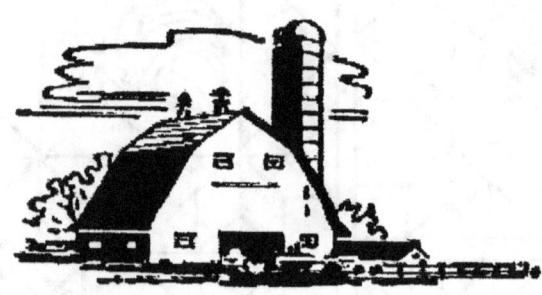

Barn Location
S SR 65
Owensville, Indiana

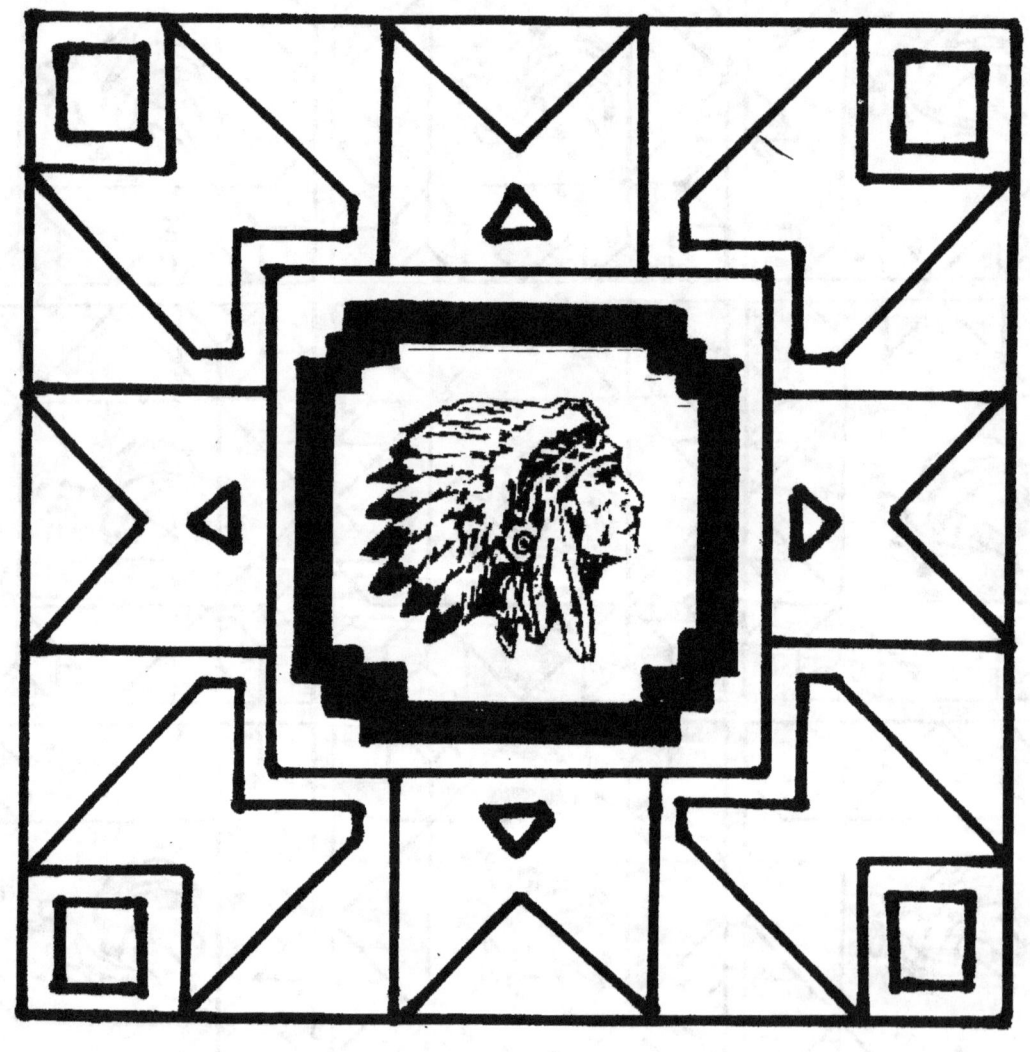

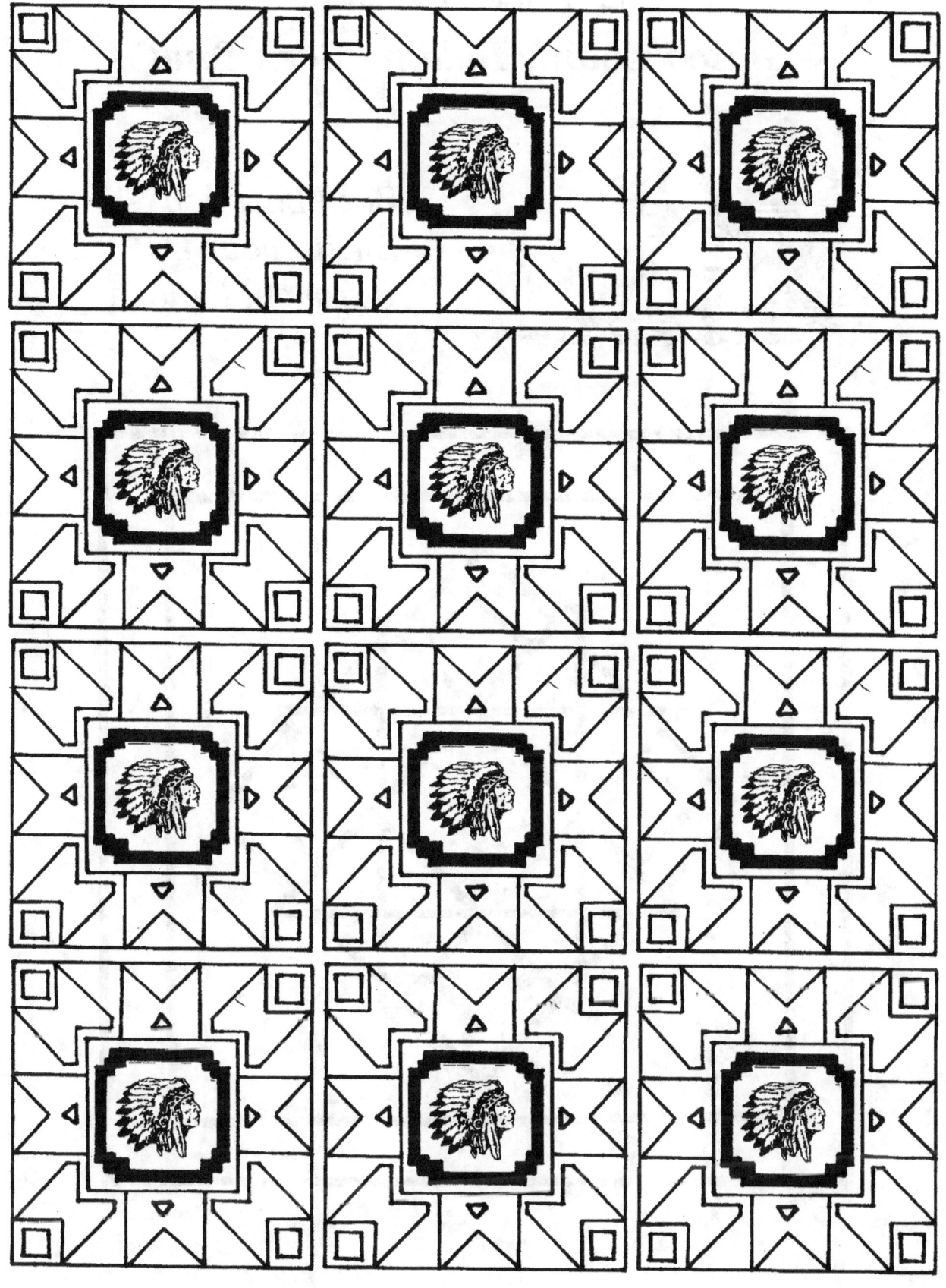

Ohio Star

Gibson County Indiana Barn Quilt

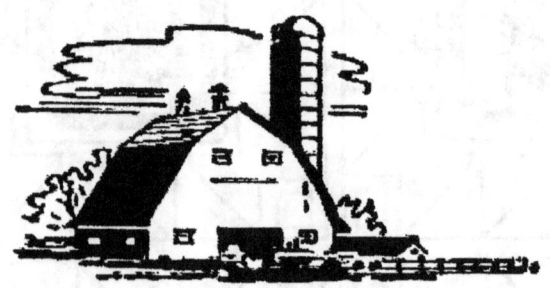

Barn Location
E Hasenour Dr
Ft Branch, Indiana

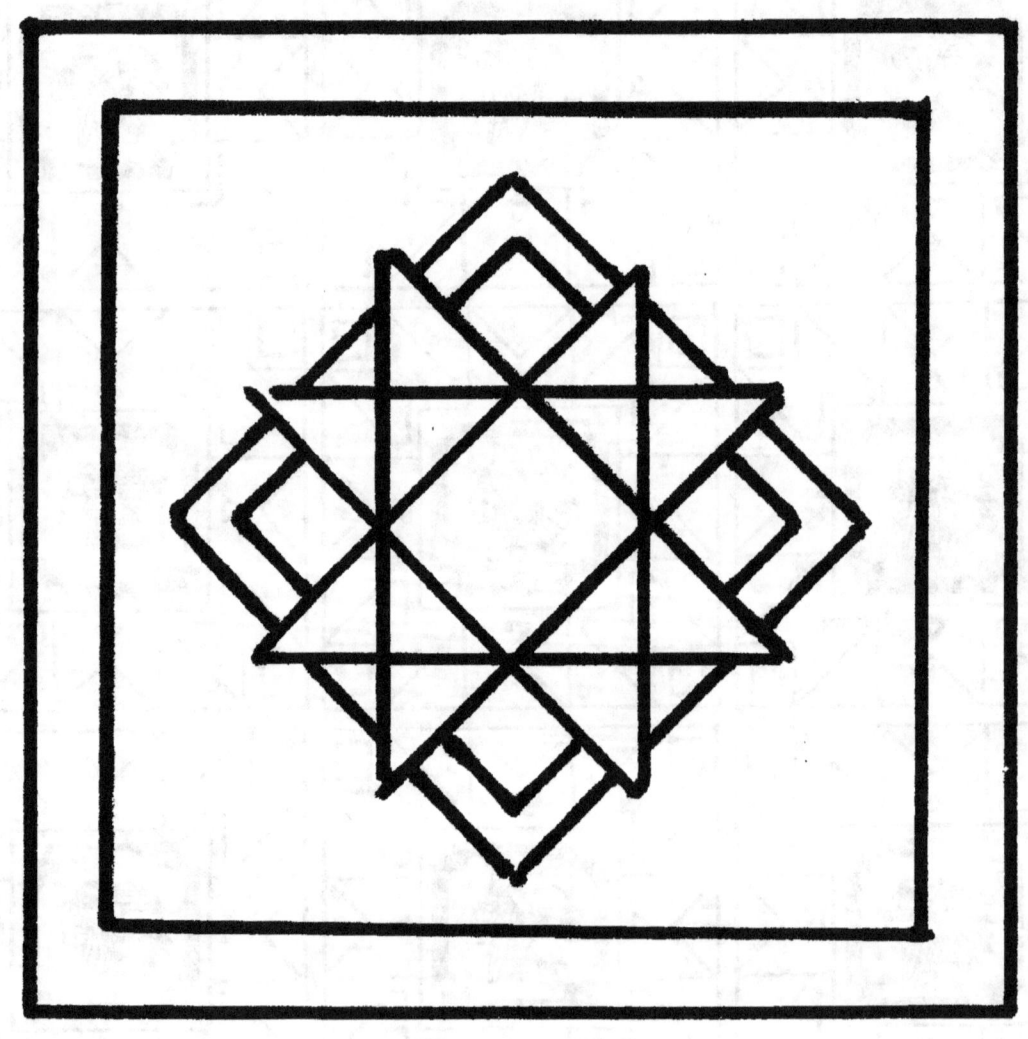

Gibson County Barn Quilt Ohio Star

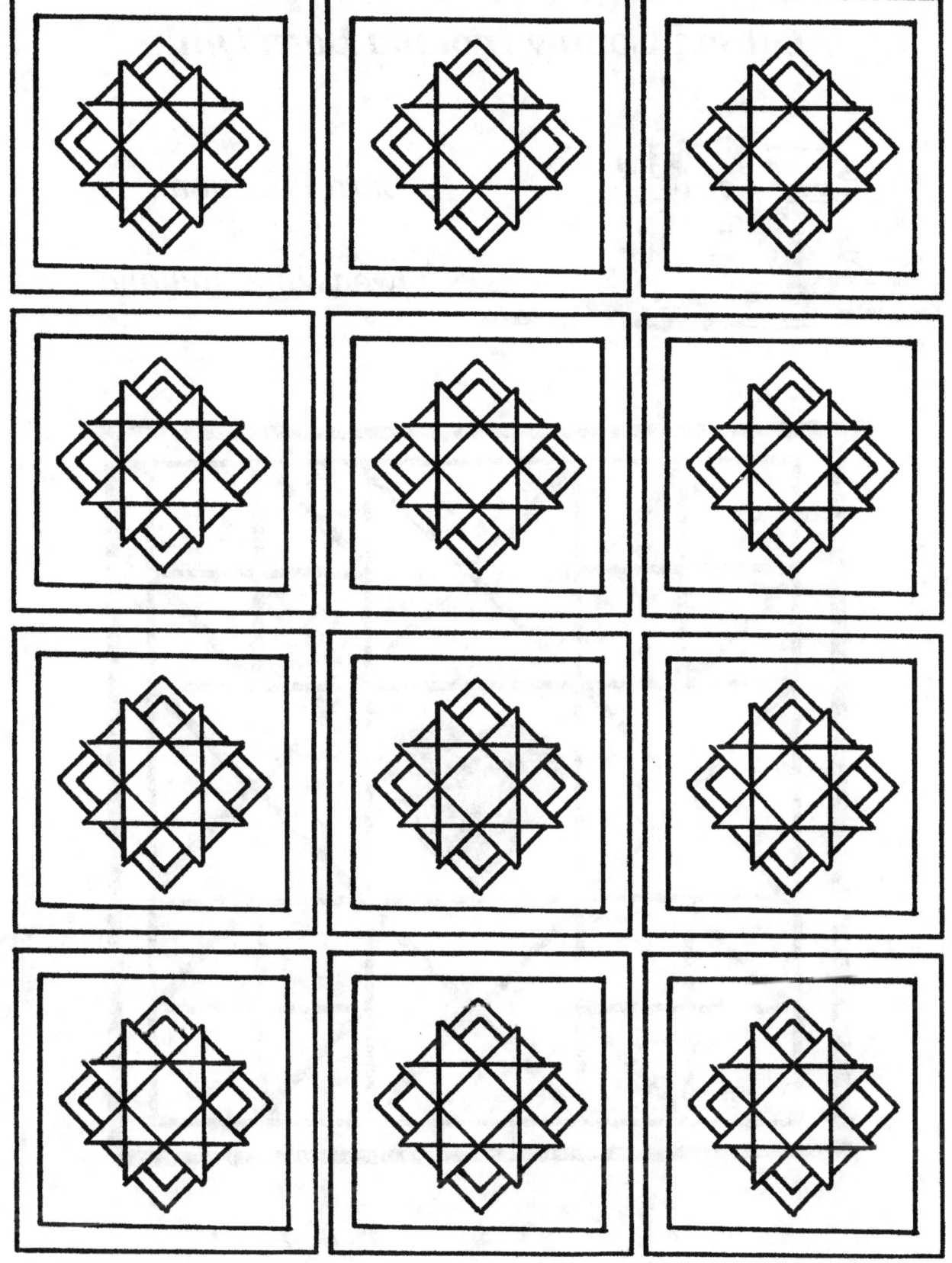

Farmer's Wife
Gibson County Indiana Barn Quilt

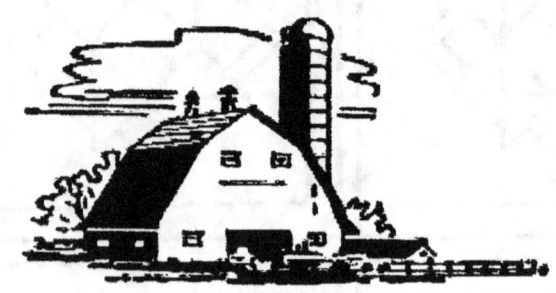

Barn Location
W 950 S
Owensville, Indiana

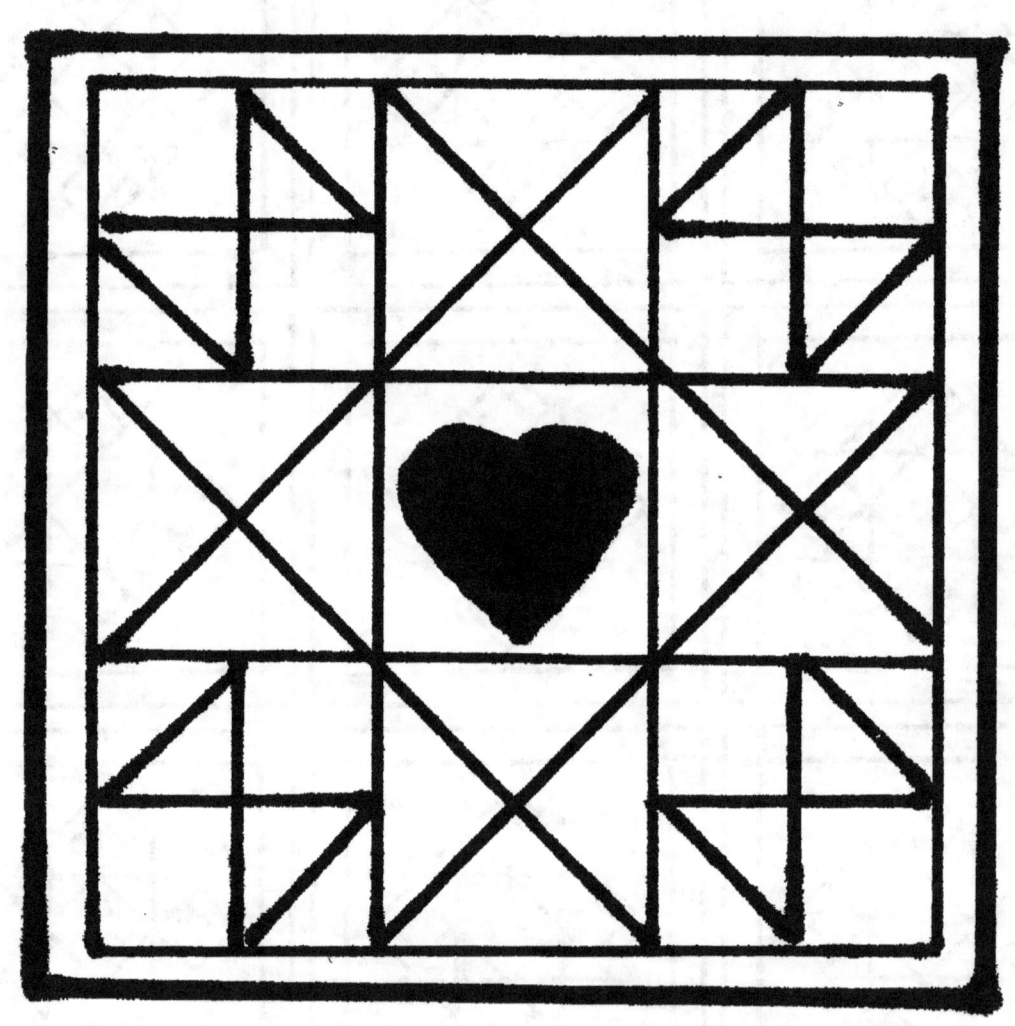

Gibson County Barn Farmer's Wife

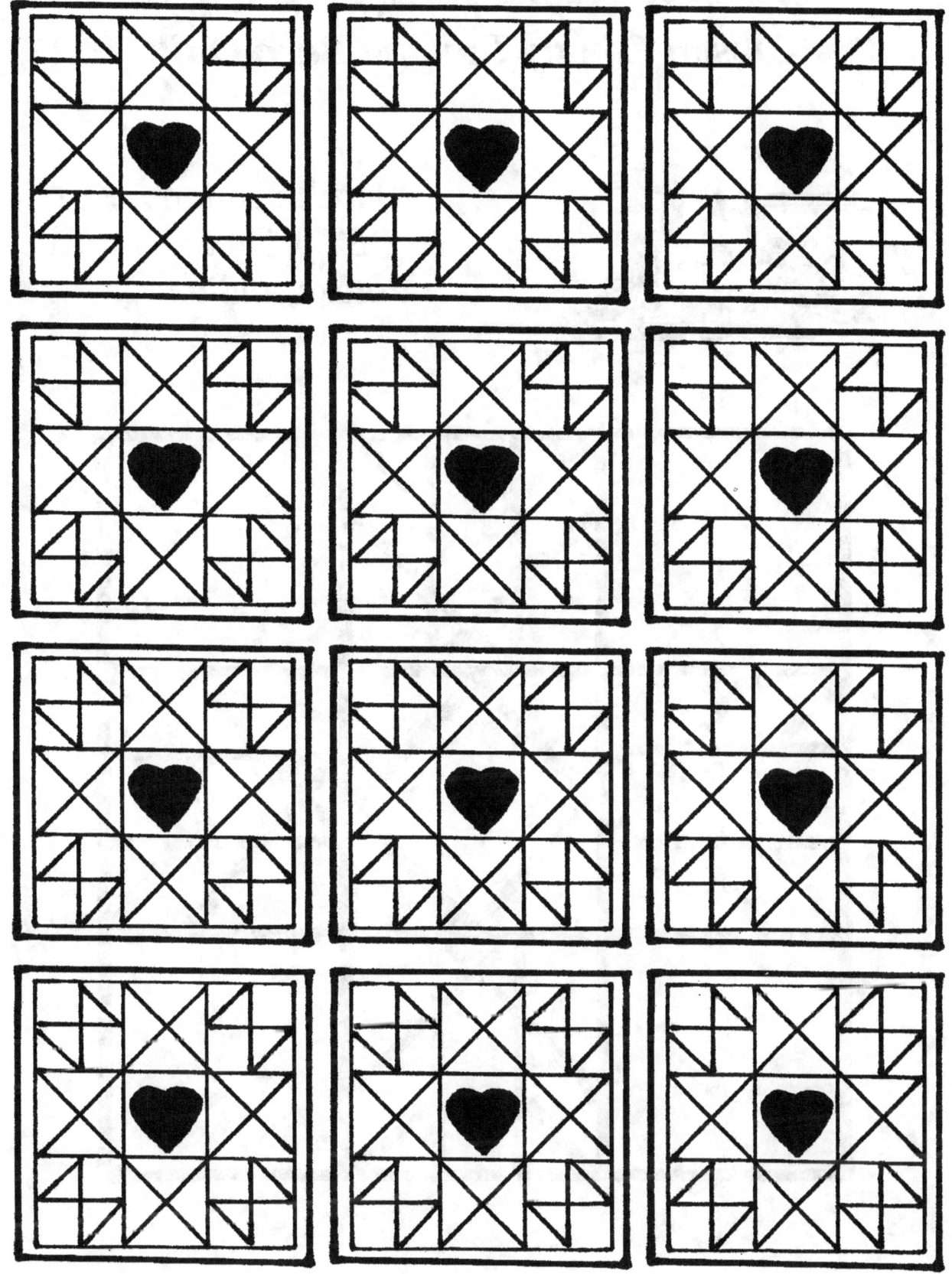

Contemporary Cross
Gibson County Indiana Barn Quilt

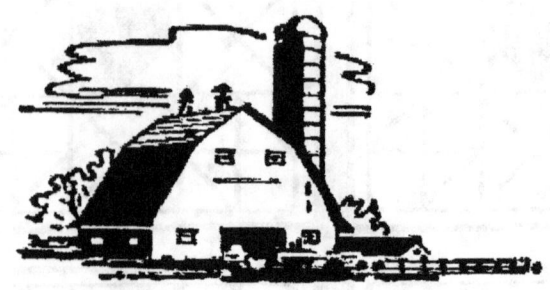

Barn Location
E Spring St
Patoka, Indiana

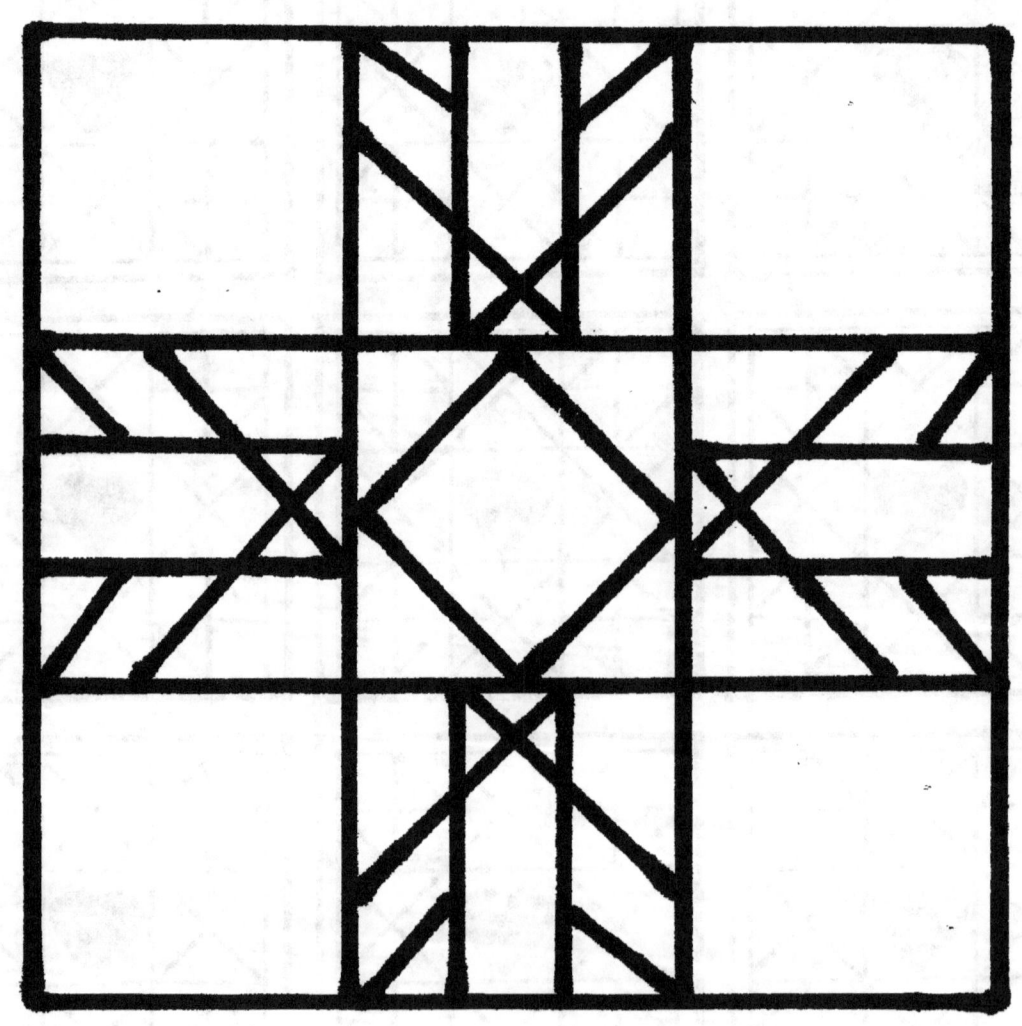

Gibson County Barn Contemporary Cross

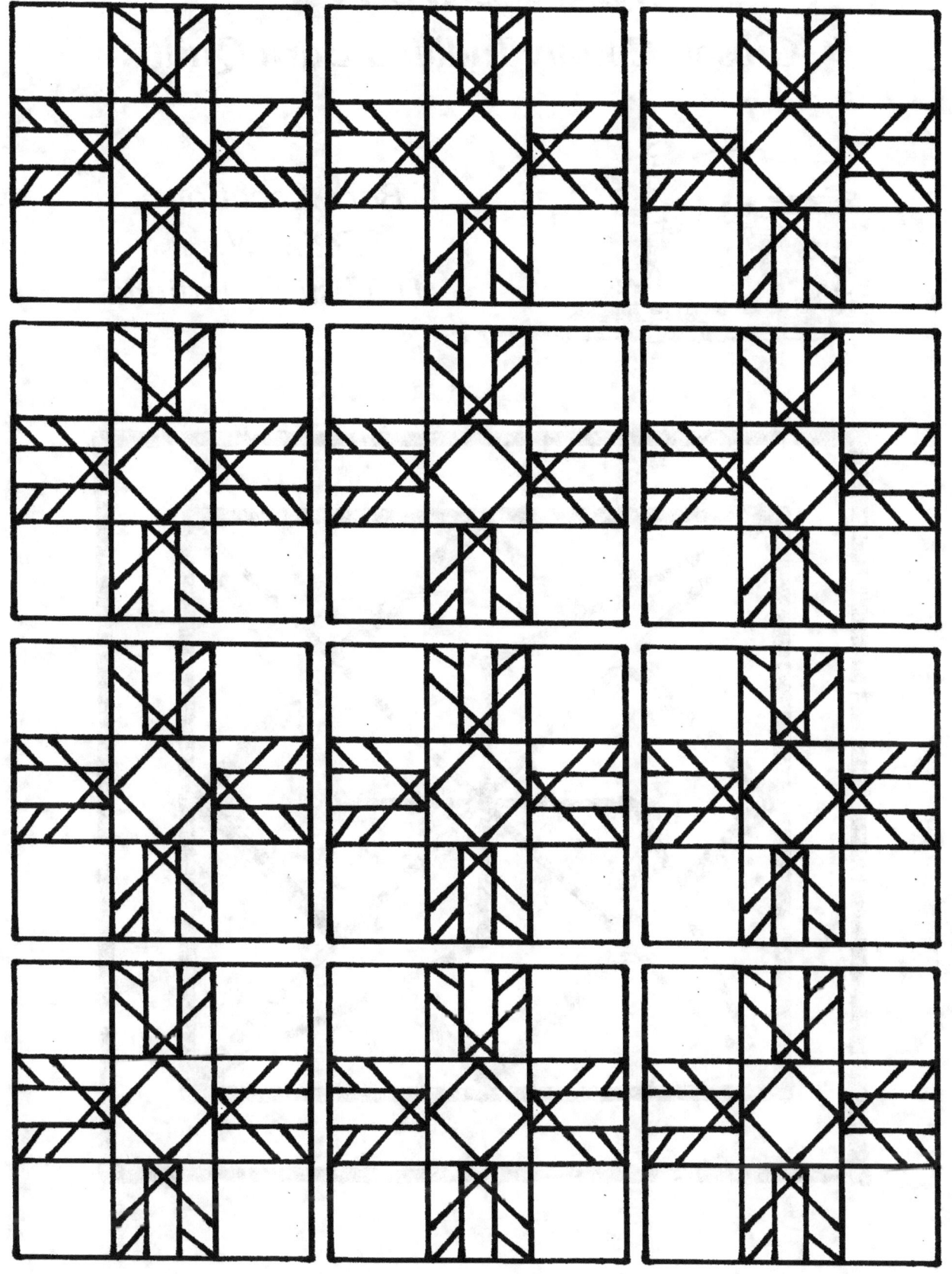

Star Bound

Gibson County Indiana Barn Quilt

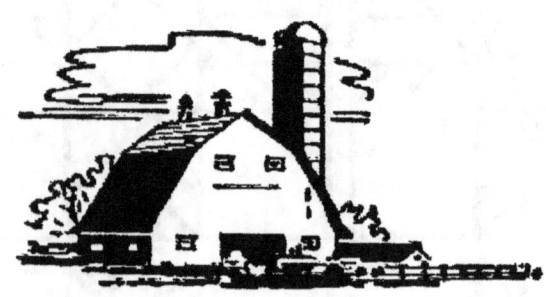

*Barn Location
S 200 W
Haubstadt, Indiana*

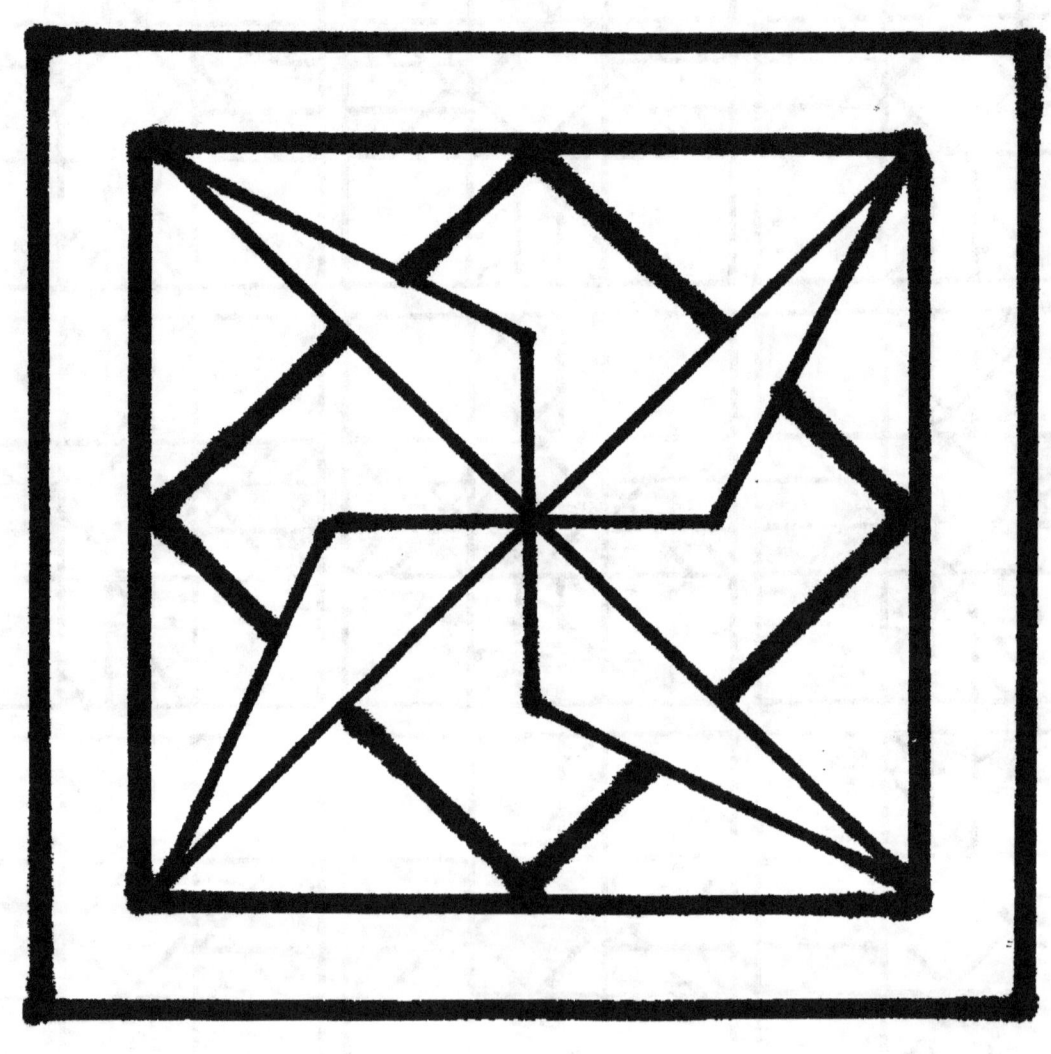

Gibson County Barn Star Bound

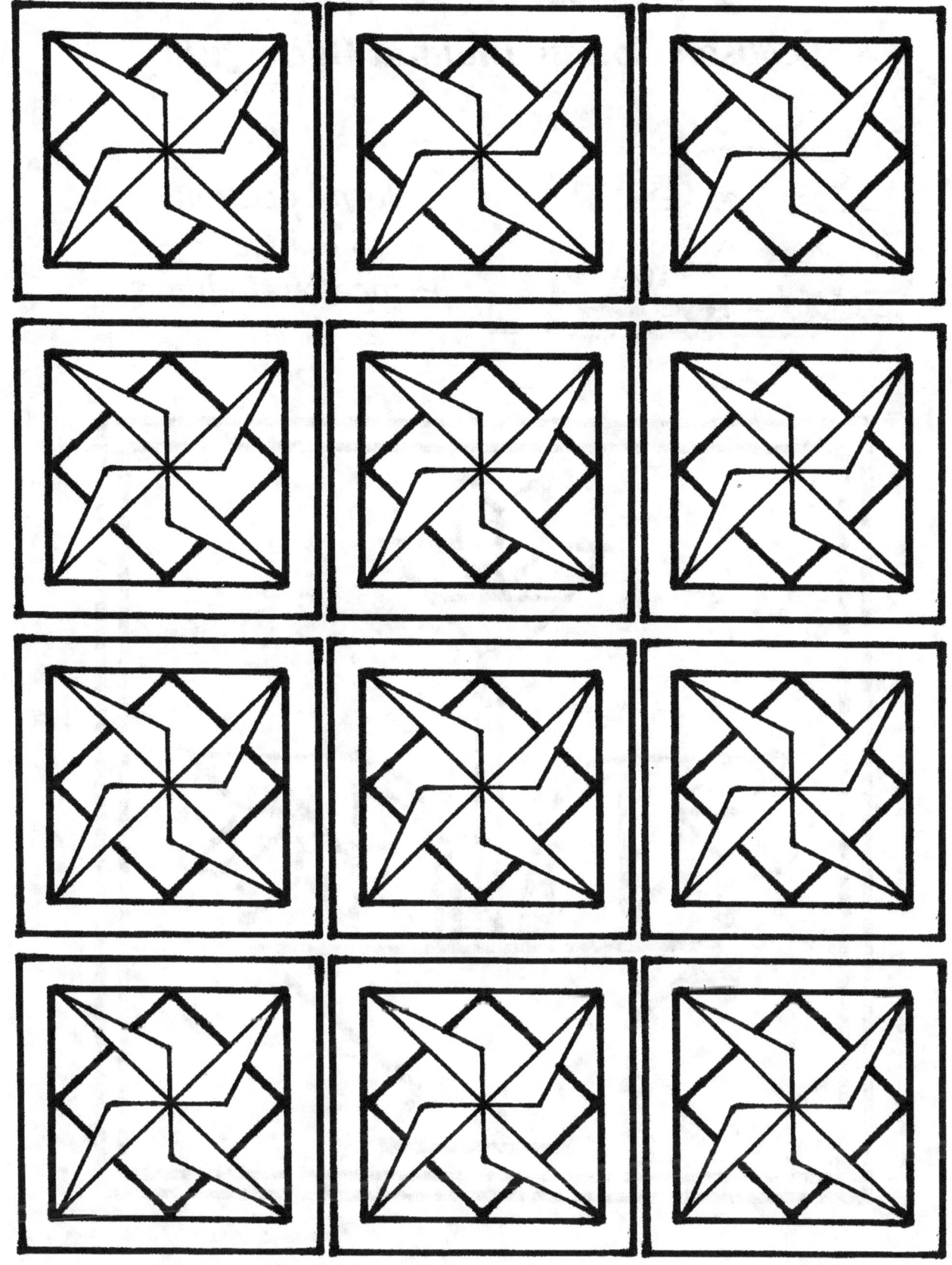

Potted Flowers
Gibson County Indiana Barn Quilt

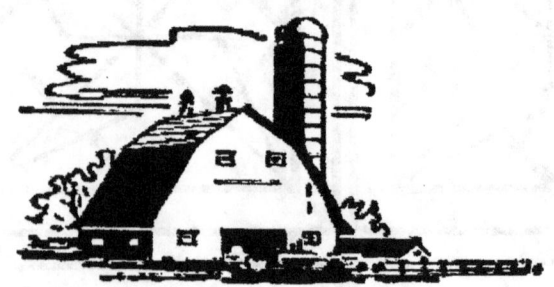

Barn Location
S Prince
Princeton, Indiana

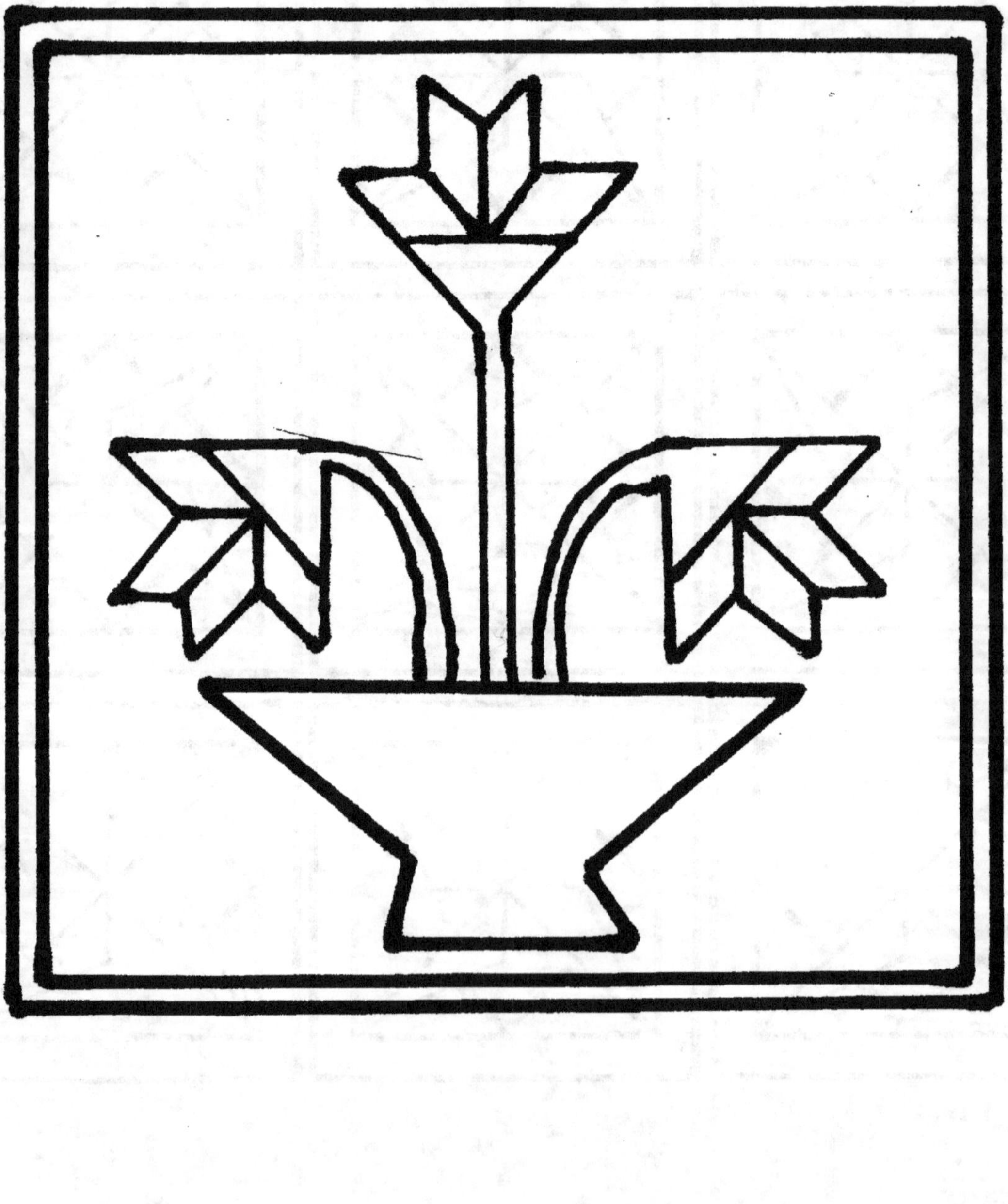

Gibson County Barn Potted Flowers

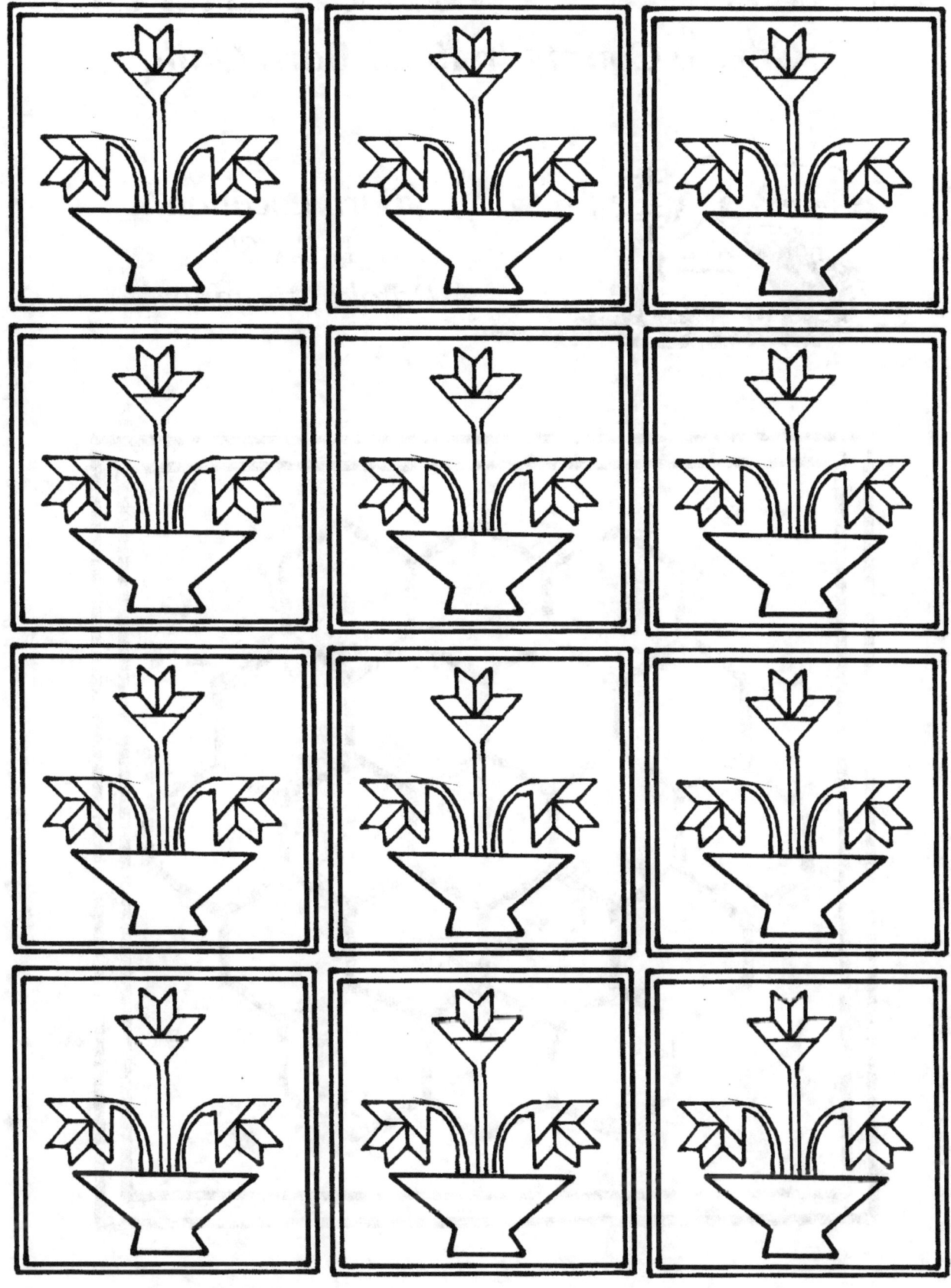

Grandma's Flower Garden

Gibson County Indiana Barn Quilt

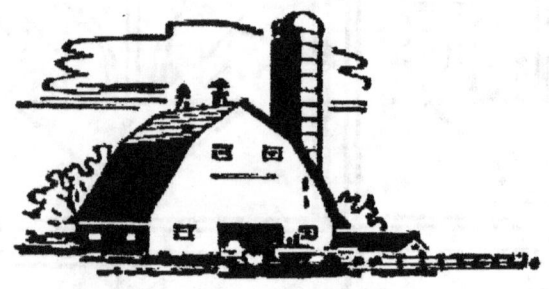

Barn Location
N SR 65
Patoka, Indiana

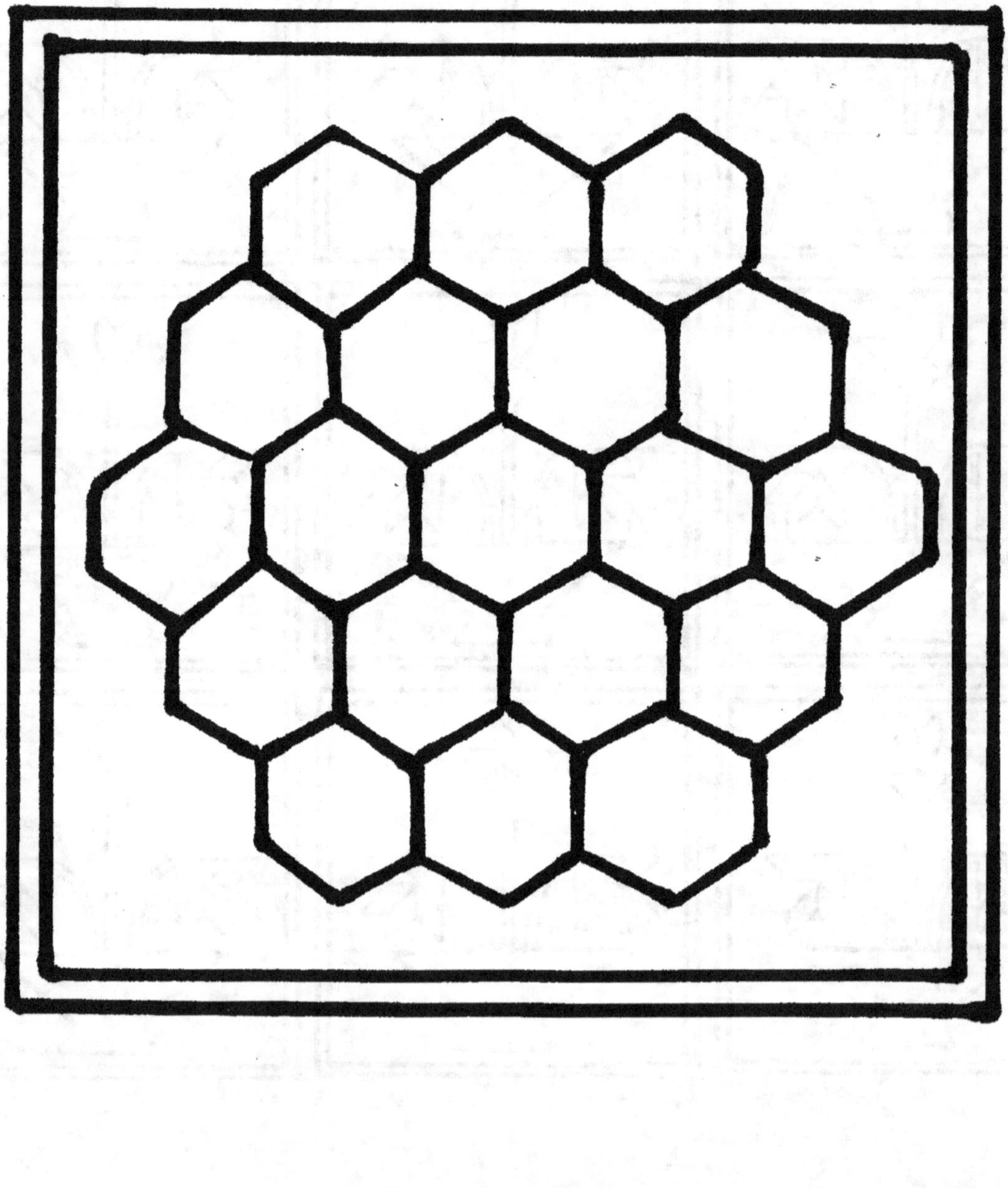

Gibson County Barn Grandma's Flower Garden

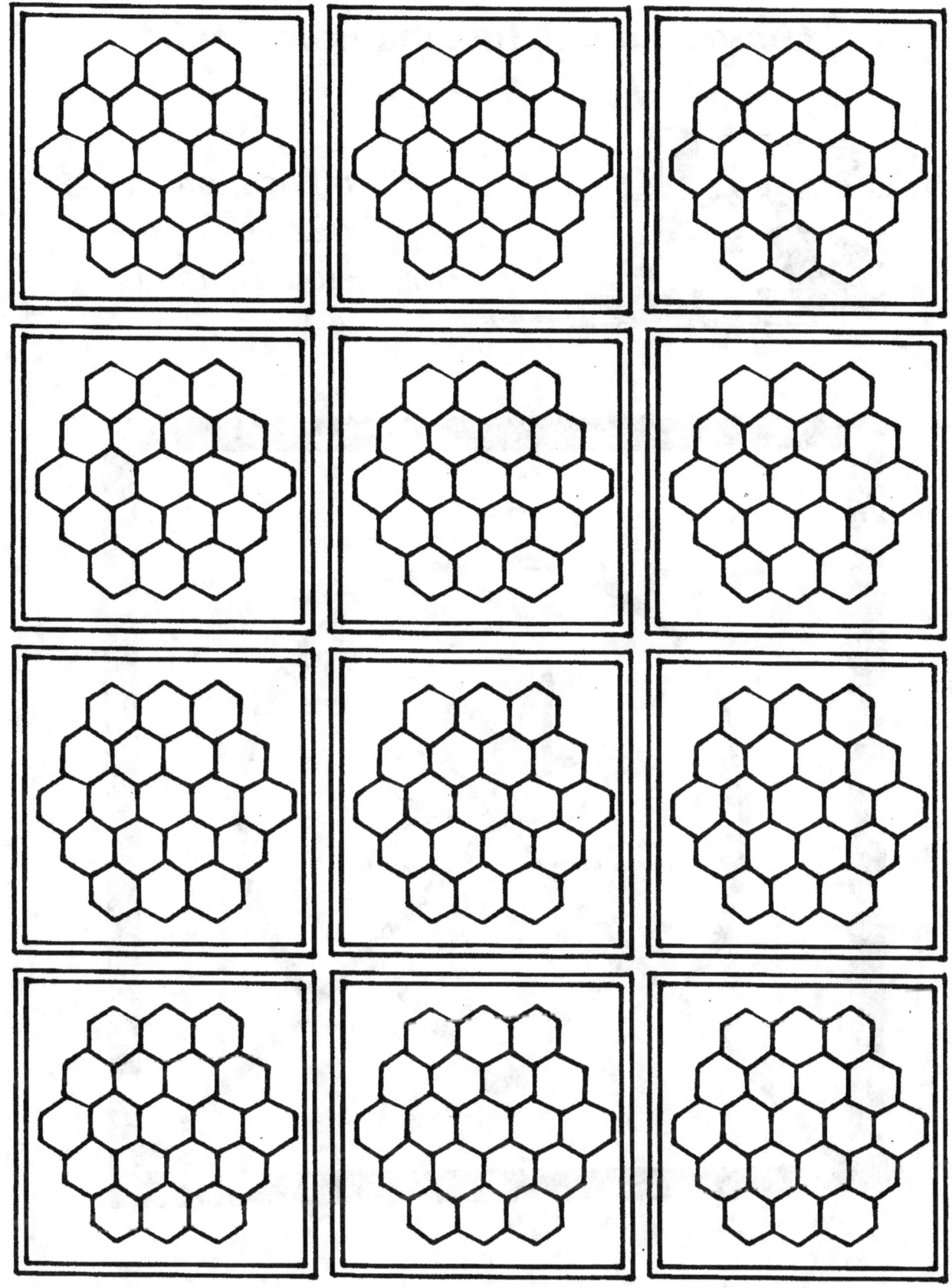

Moon & Stars Over The Mountain

Gibson County Indiana Barn Quilt

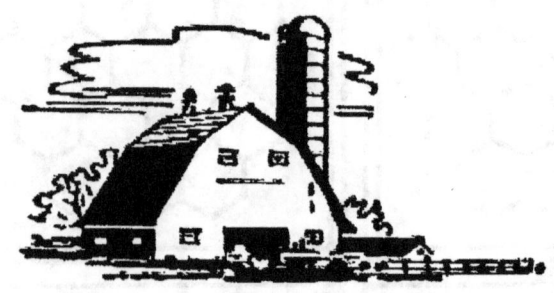

Barn Location
W 225 N
Princeton, Indiana

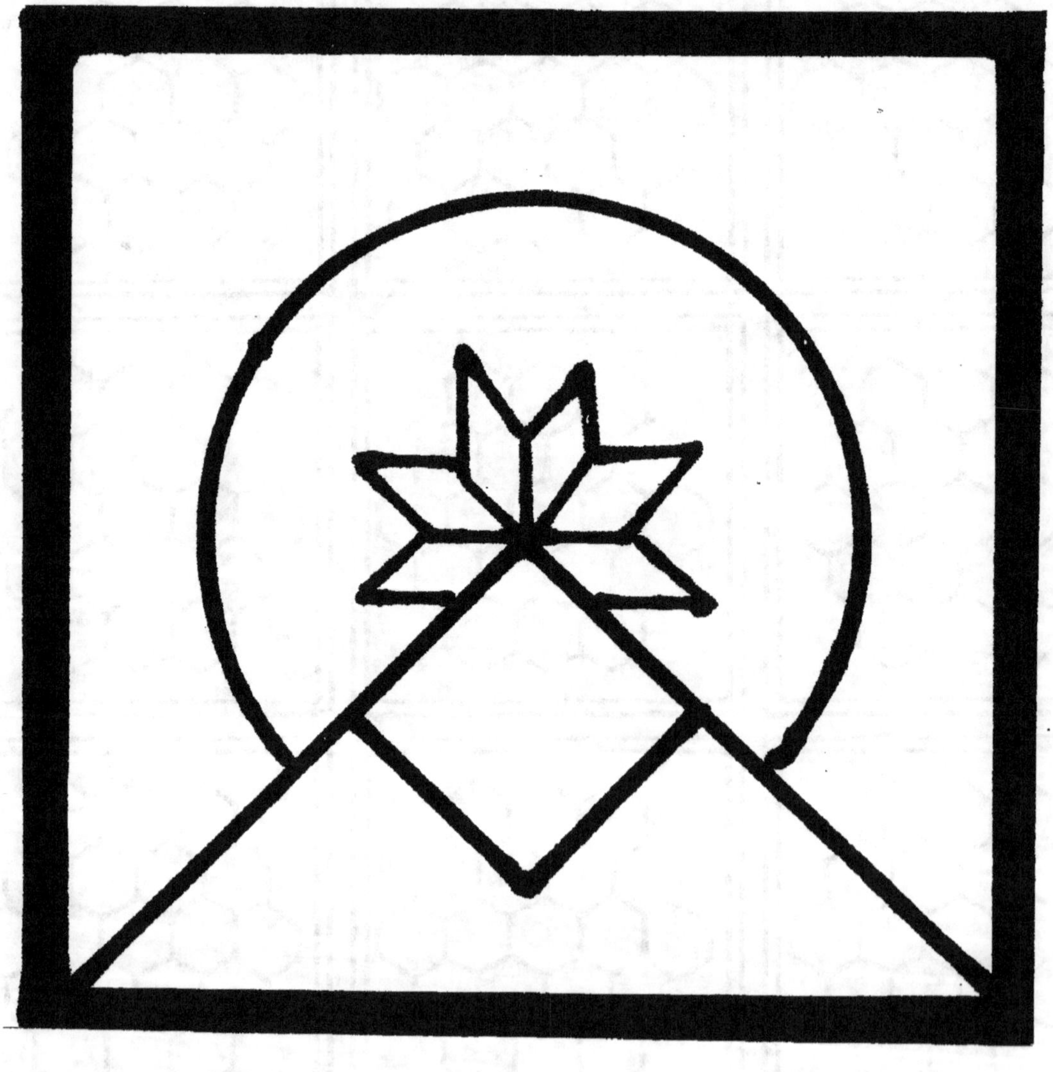

Gibson County Barn Moon & Stars Over The Mountain

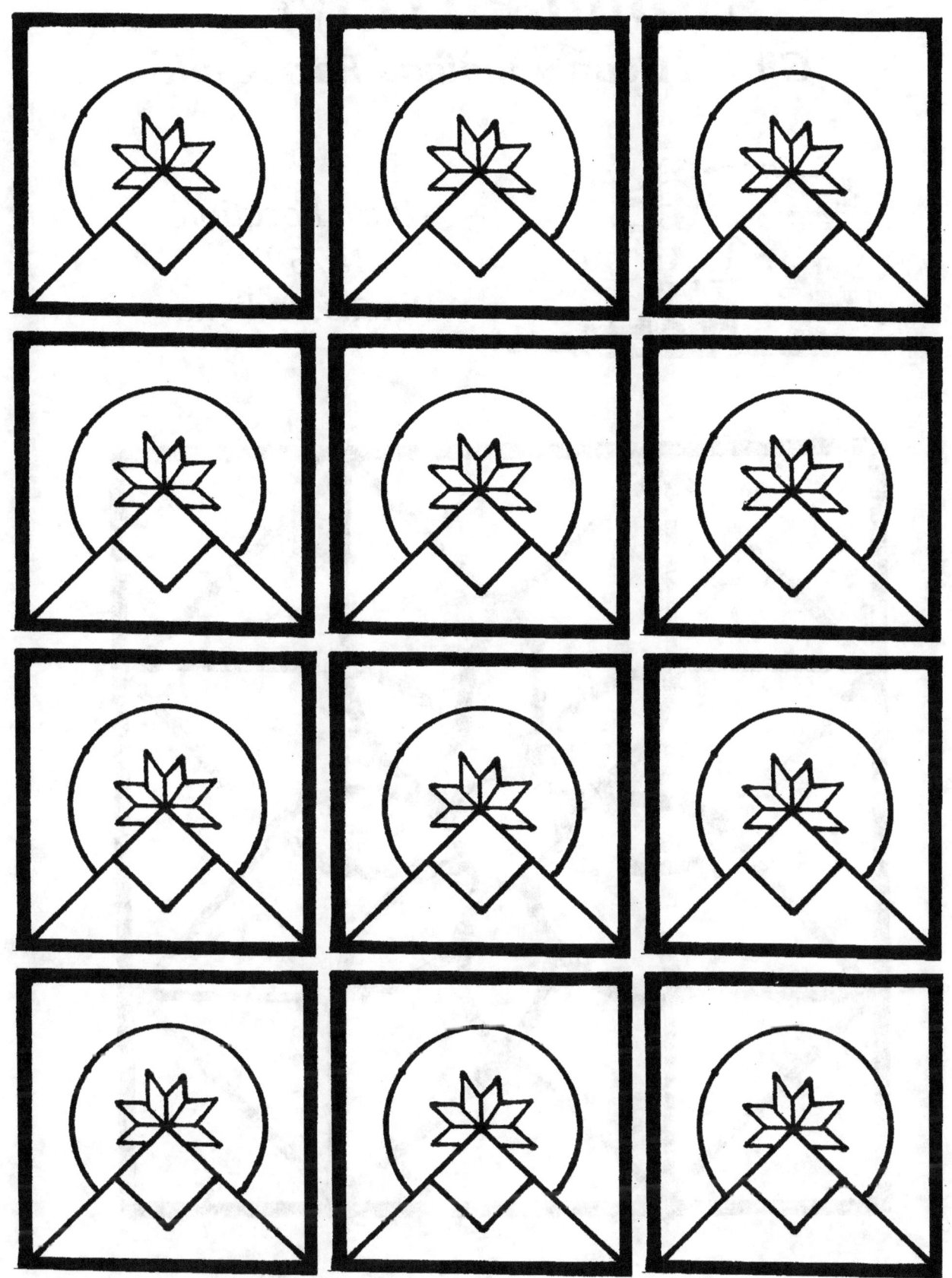

Summer Dayz
Gibson County Indiana Barn Quilt

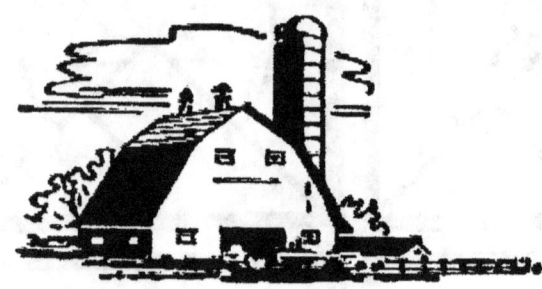

Barn Location
N 75 E
Patoka, Indiana

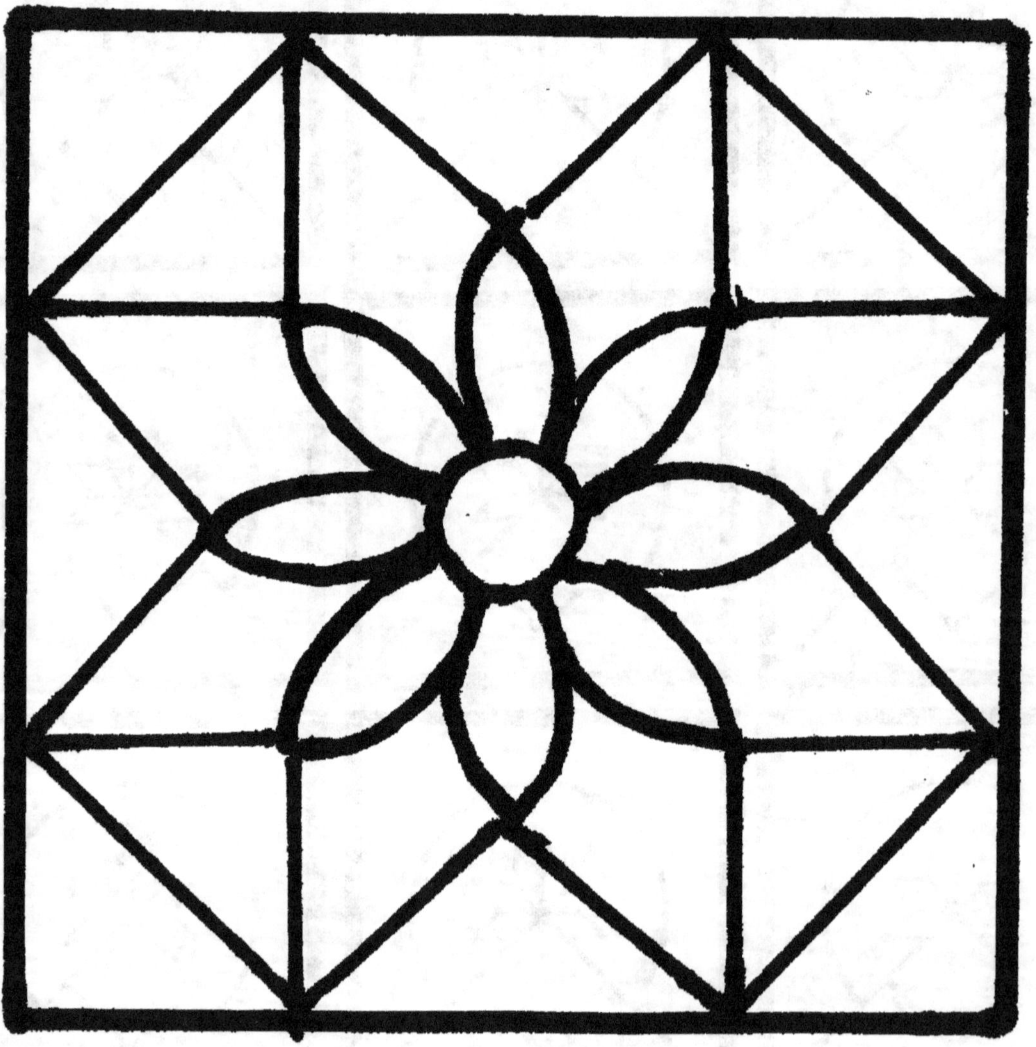

Gibson County Barn Summer Dayz

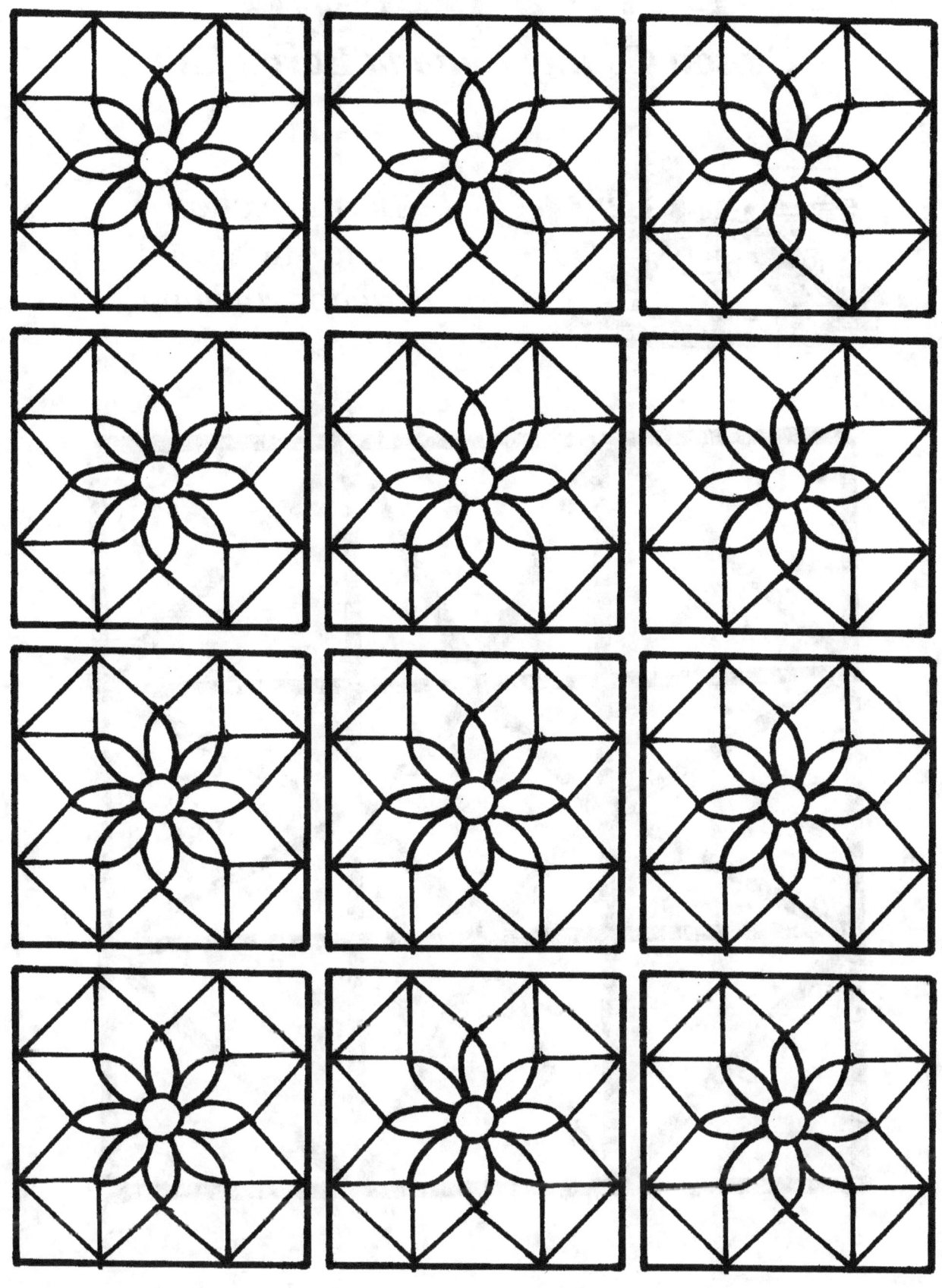

Dora's Delight
Gibson County Indiana Barn Quilt

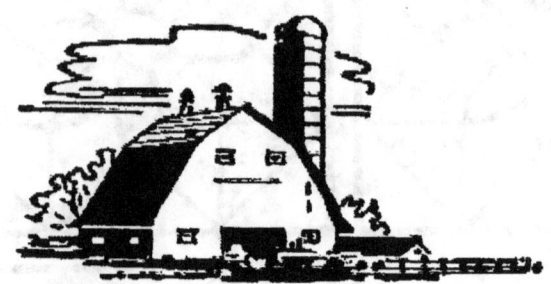

Barn Location
Old Hwy 41
Hazelton, Indiana

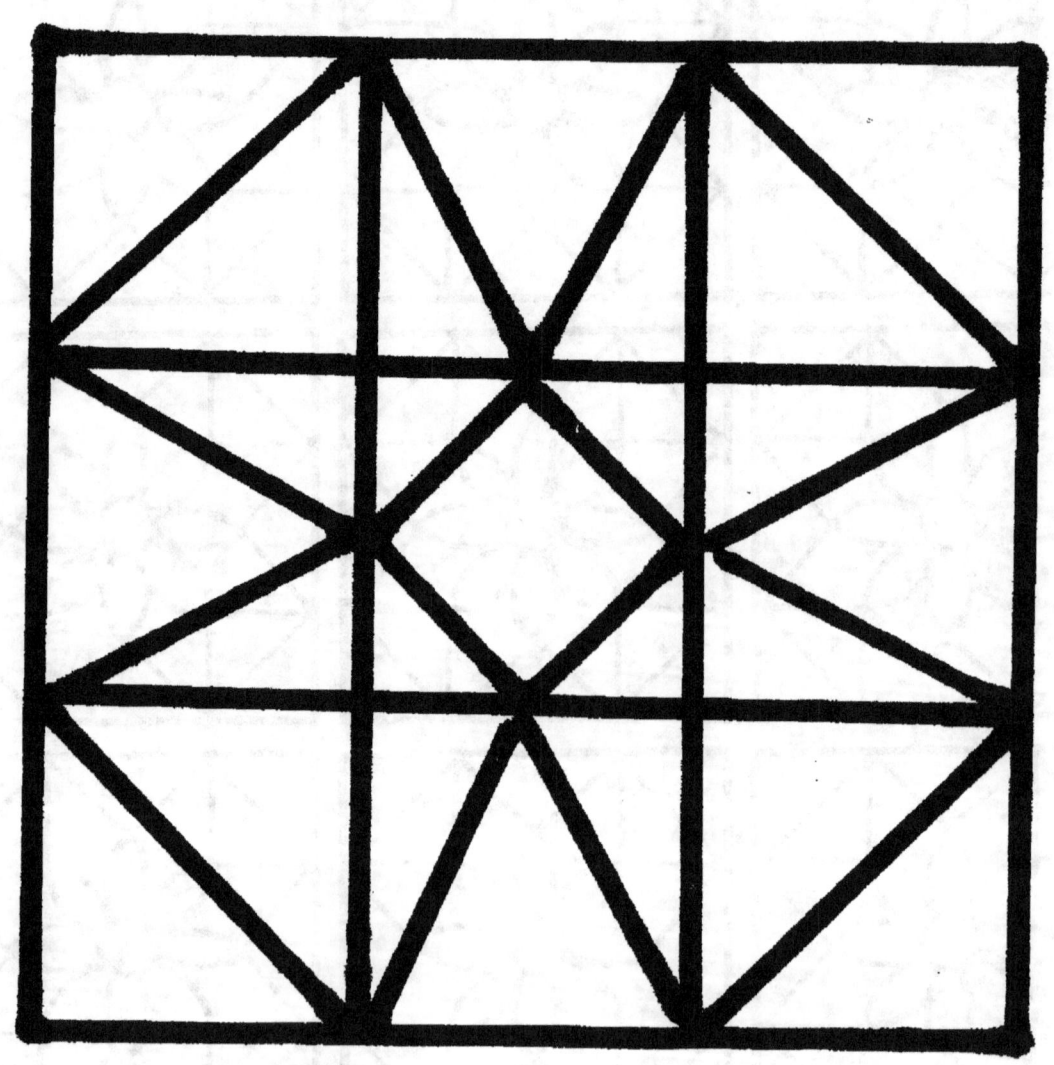

Gibson County Barn Dora's Delight

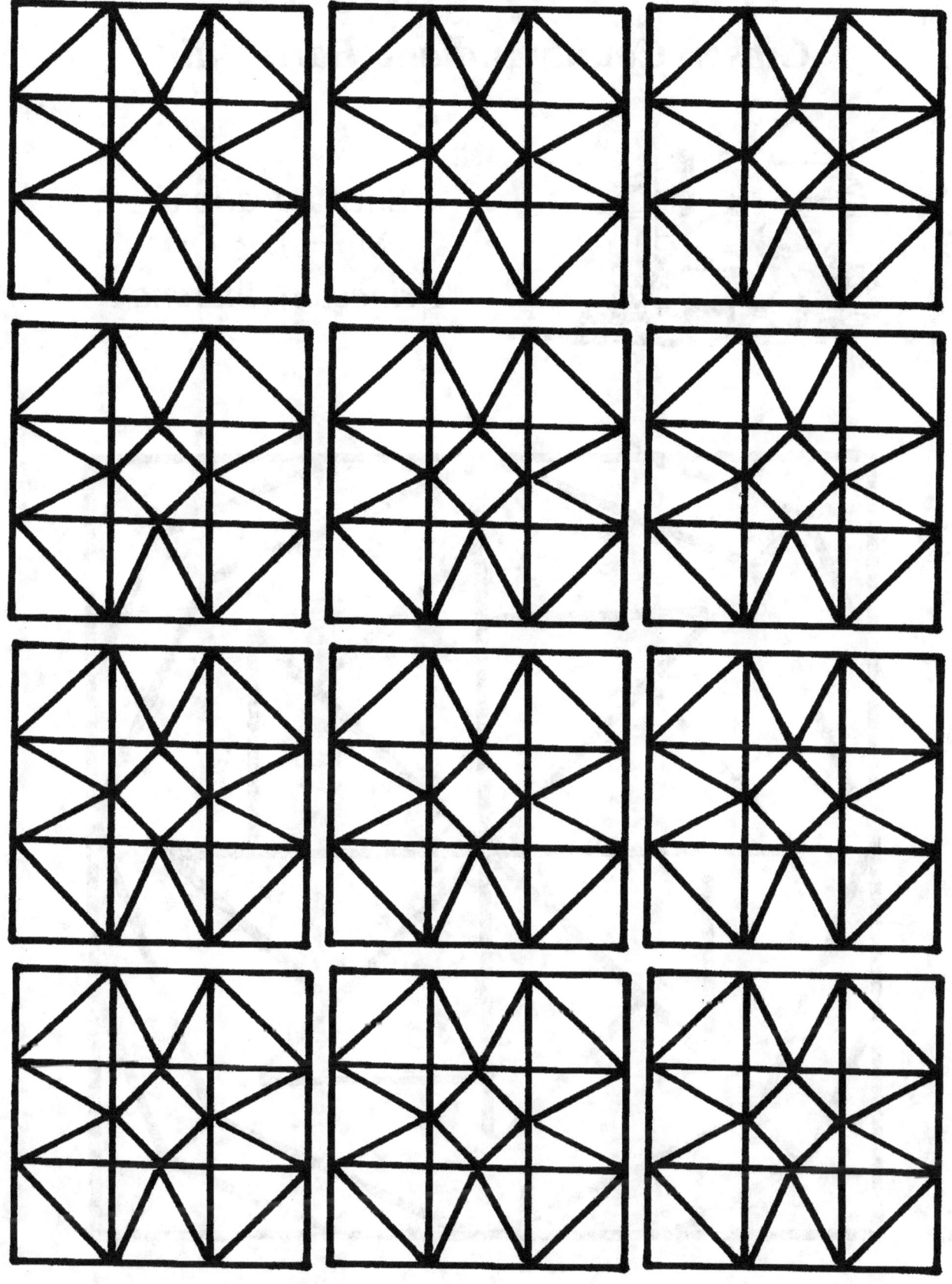

Wheel of Fortune
Gibson County Indiana Barn Quilt

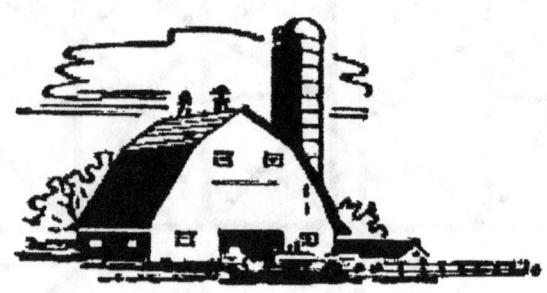

Barn Location
Mary Lee Dr
Princeton, Indiana

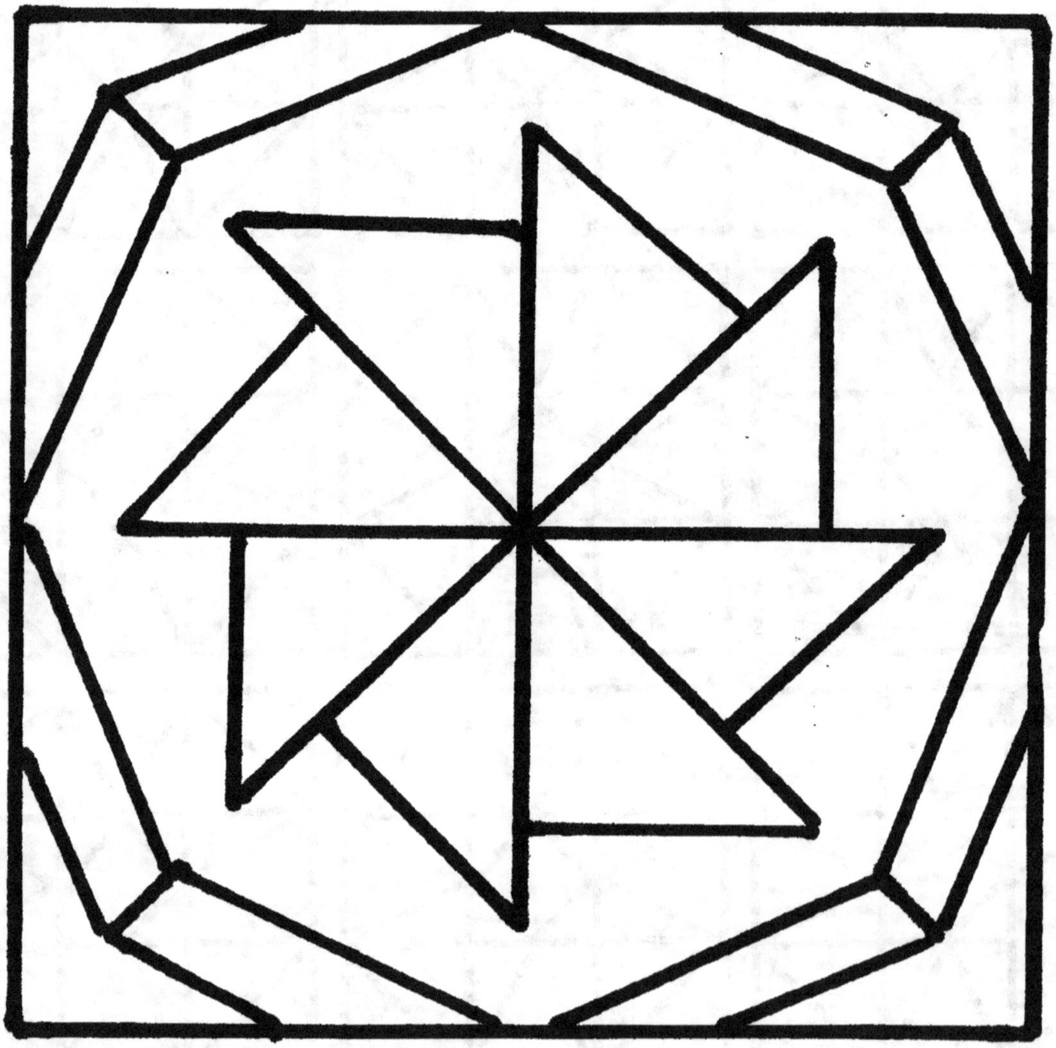

Gibson County Barn Quilt Wheel of Fortune

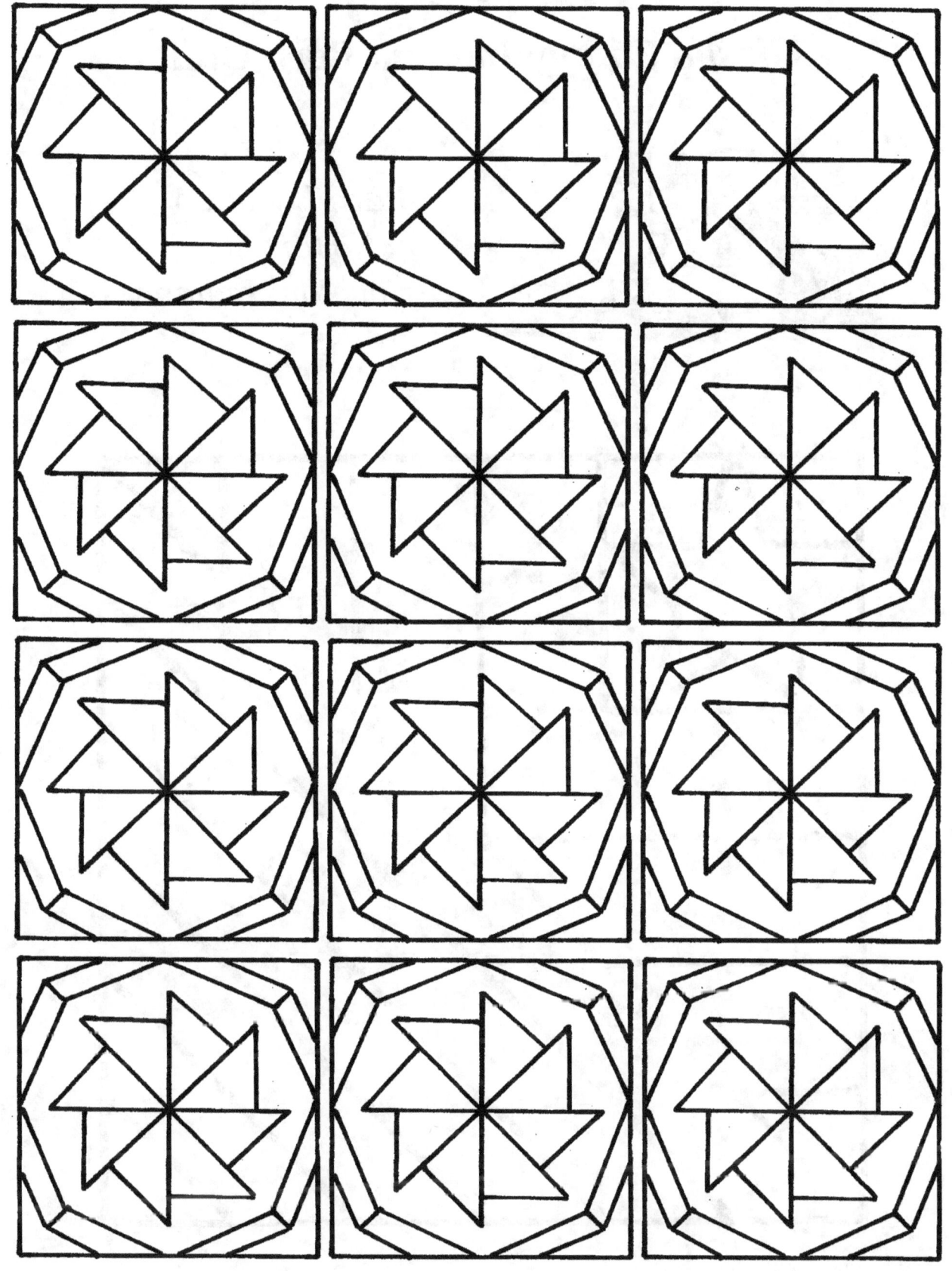

The Flag
Gibson County Indiana Barn Quilt

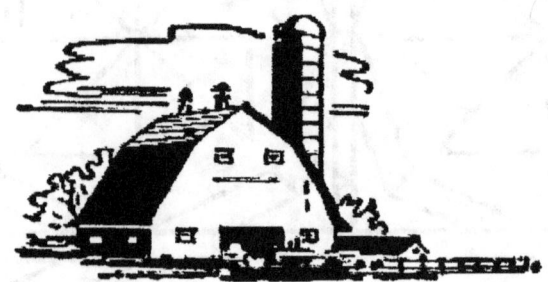

Barn Location
N Hart St
Princeton, Indiana

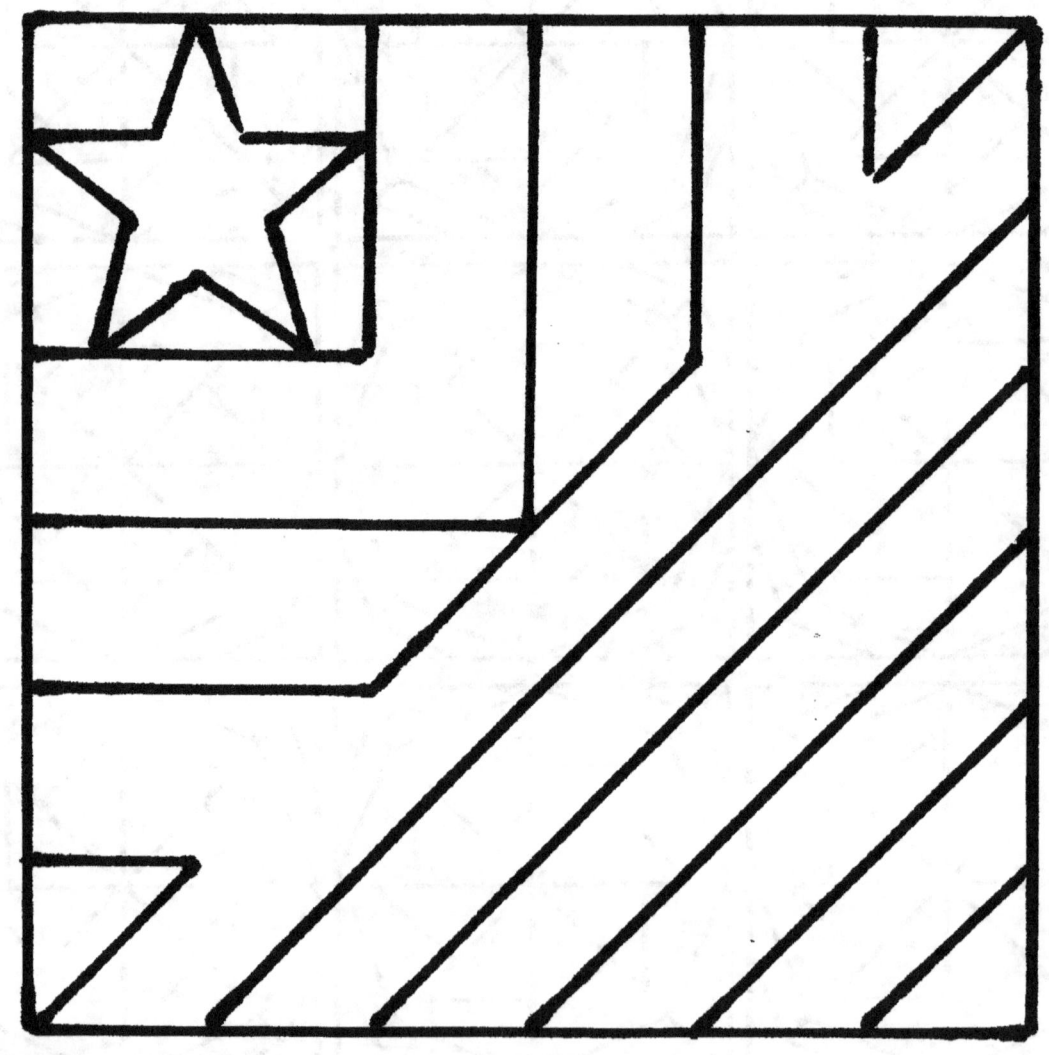

Gibson County Barn Quilt The Flag

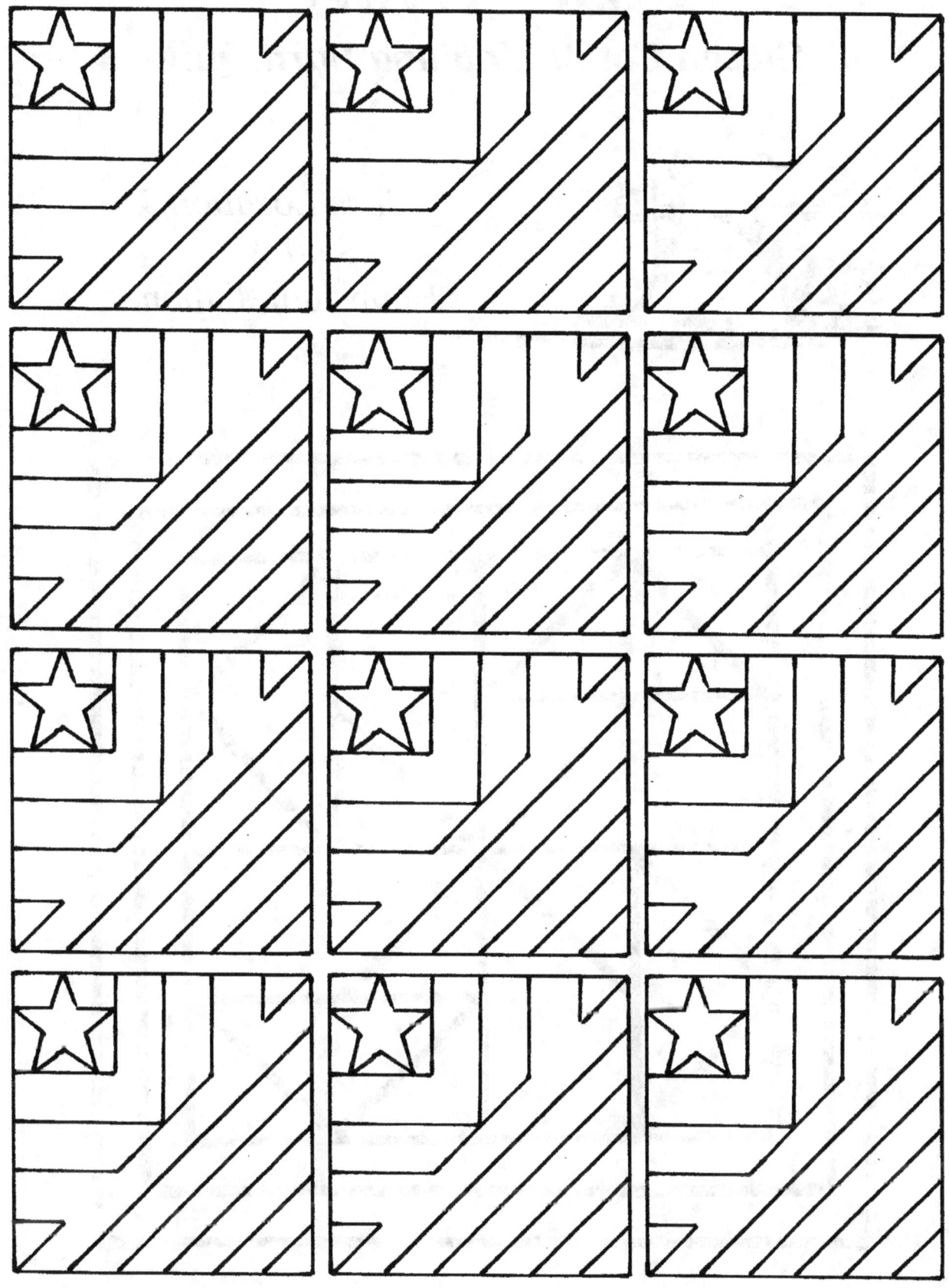

Posie Whirl
Gibson County Indiana Barn Quilt

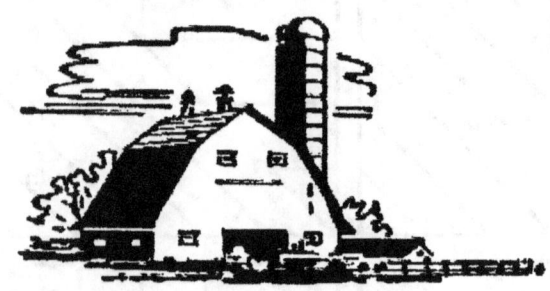

Barn Location
S 40 W
Haubstadt, Indiana

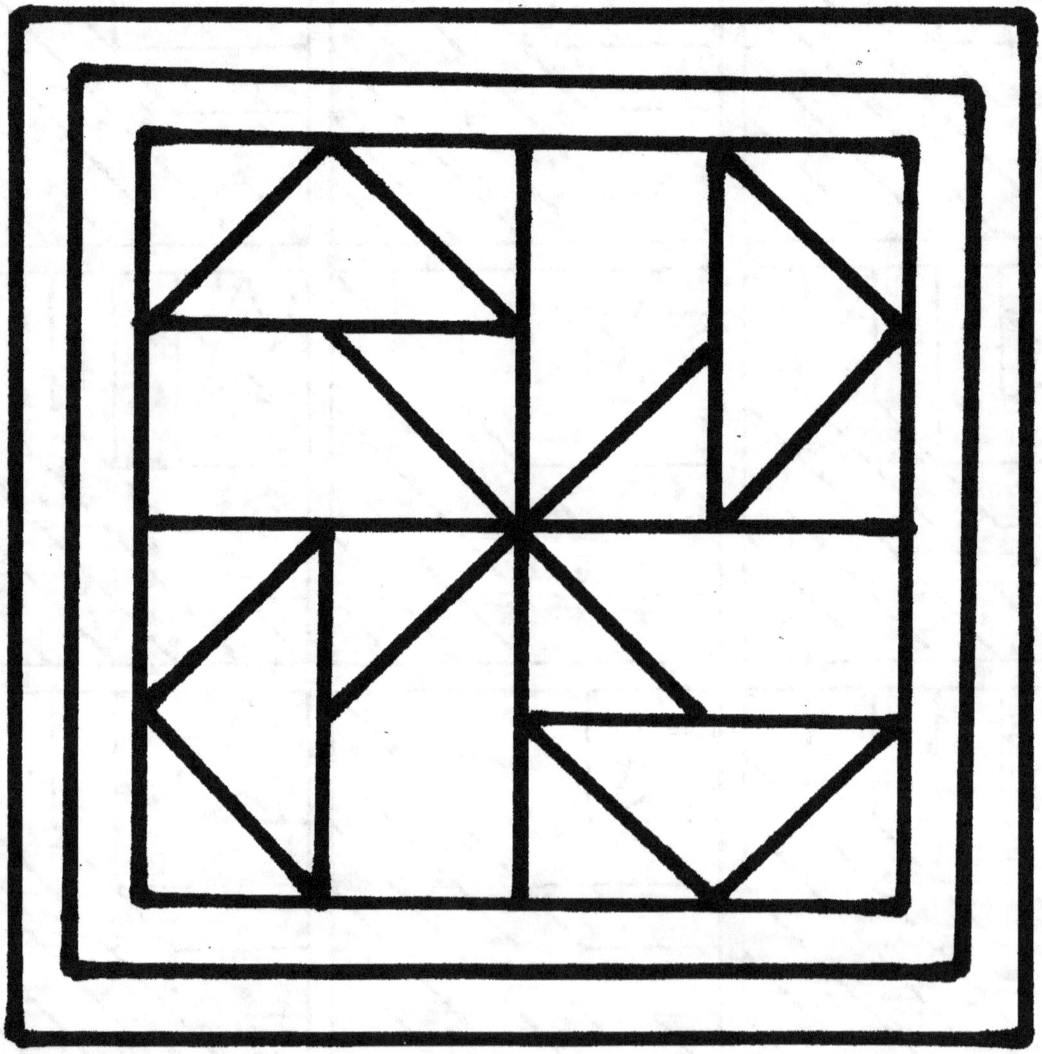

Gibson County Barn Quilt Posie Whirl

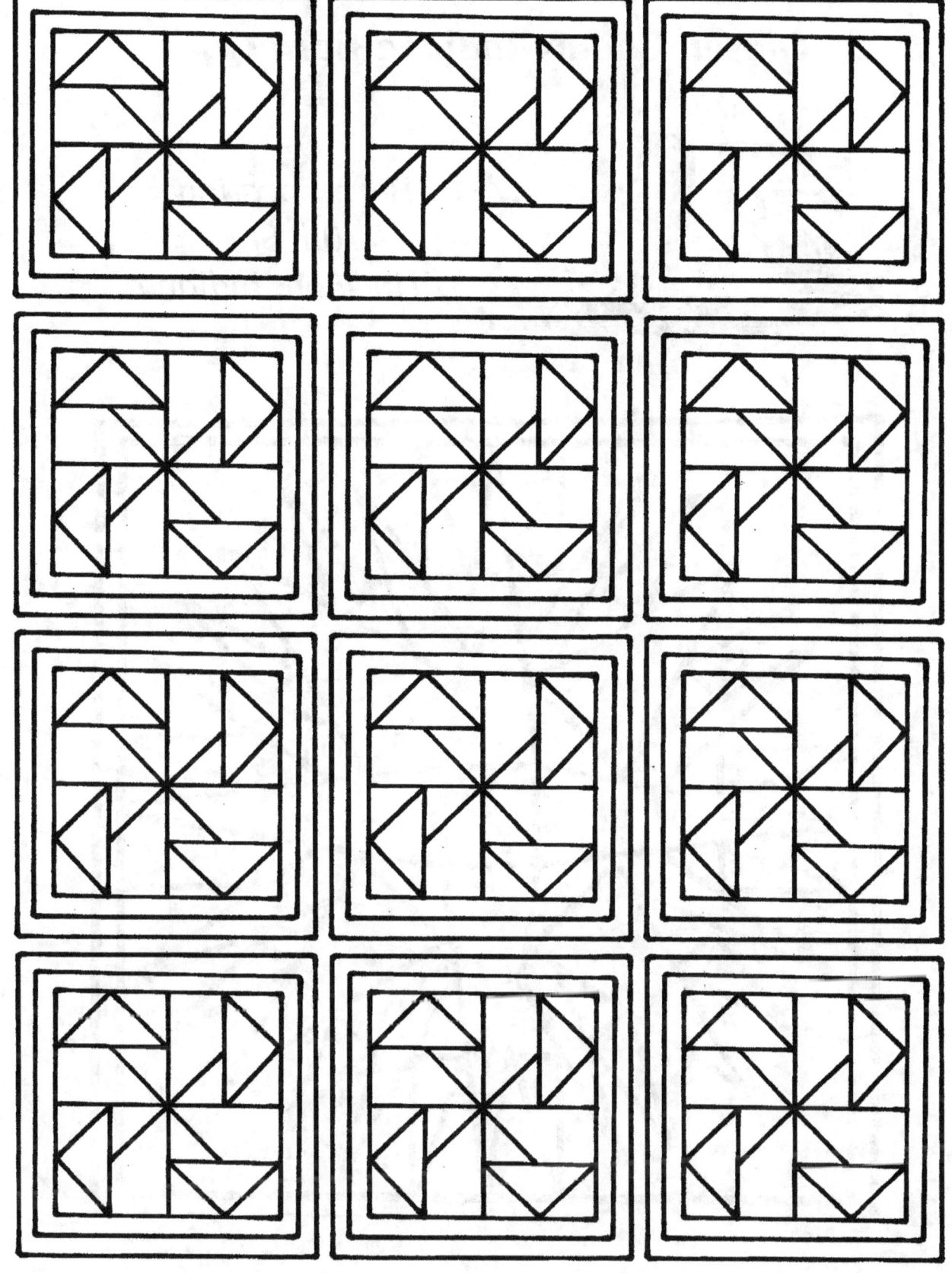

Mariner's Compass
Gibson County Indiana Barn Quilt

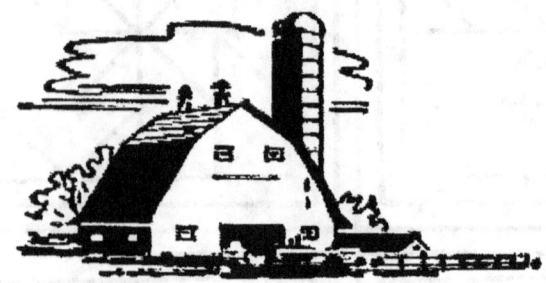

Barn Location
10th St
Princeton, Indiana

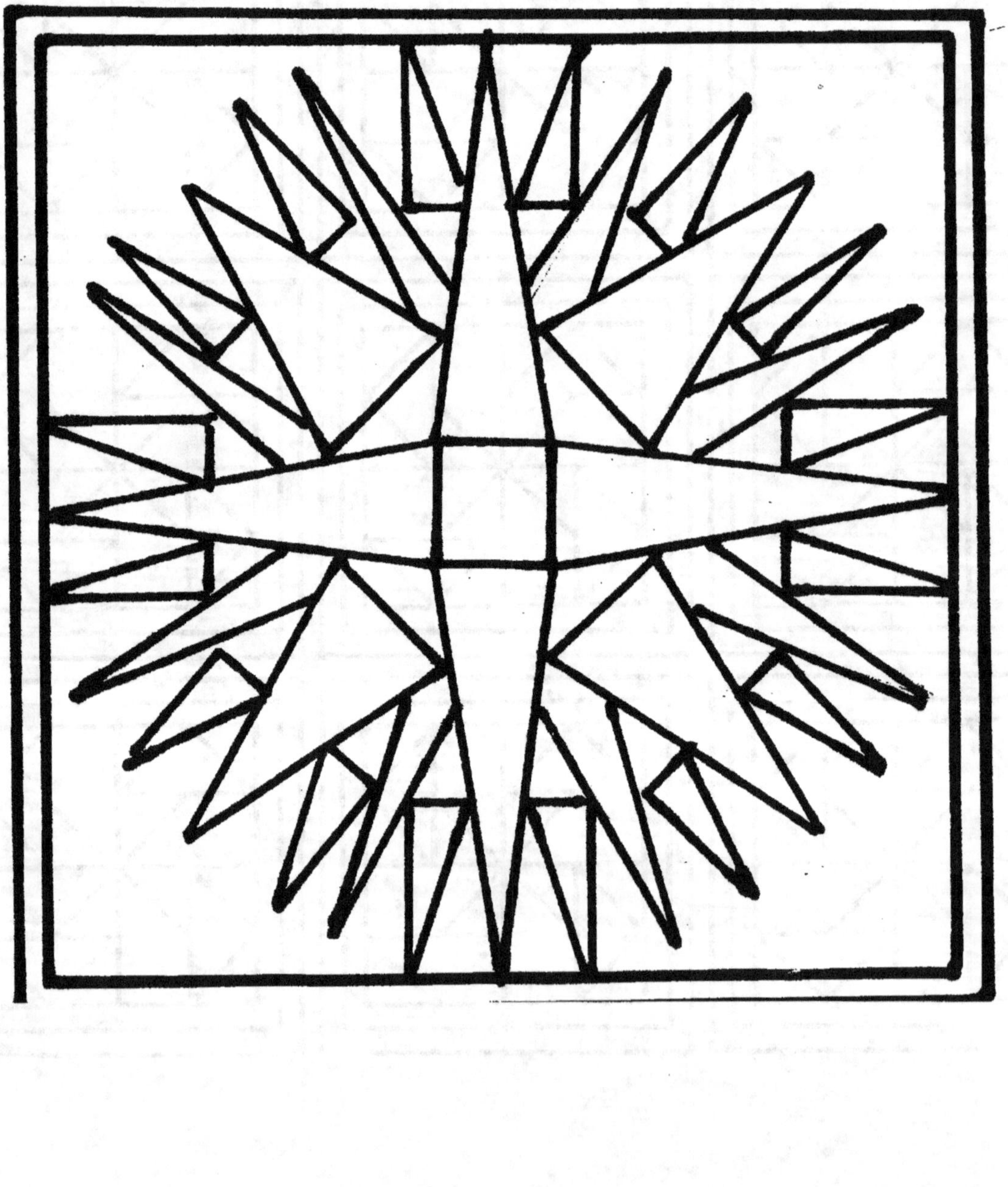

Gibson County Barn Quilt Mariner's Compass

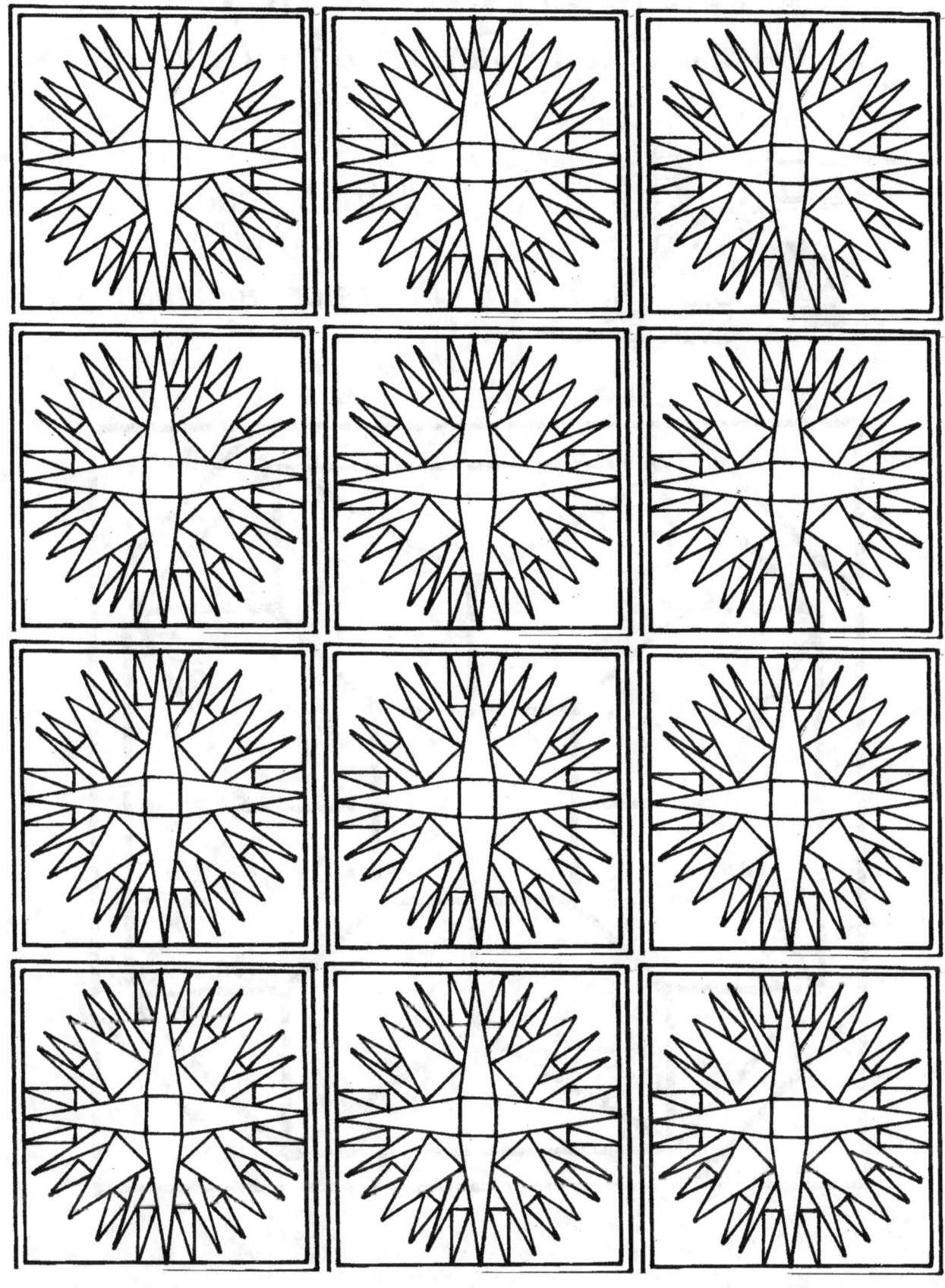

Black Eyed Susan
Gibson County Indiana Barn Quilt

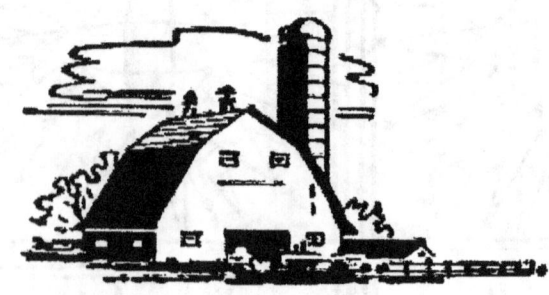

Barn Location
S 100 W
Princeton, Indiana

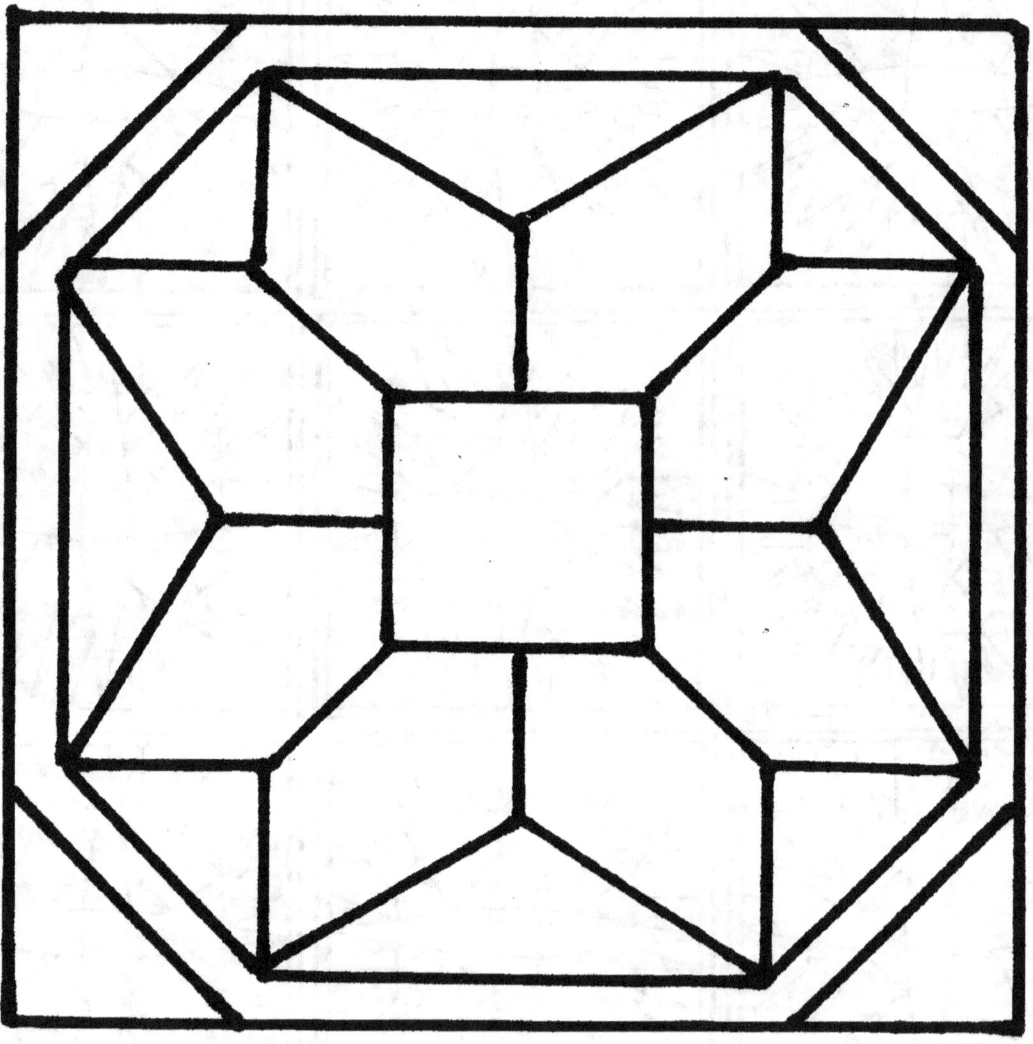

Gibson County Barn Quilt Black Eyed Susan

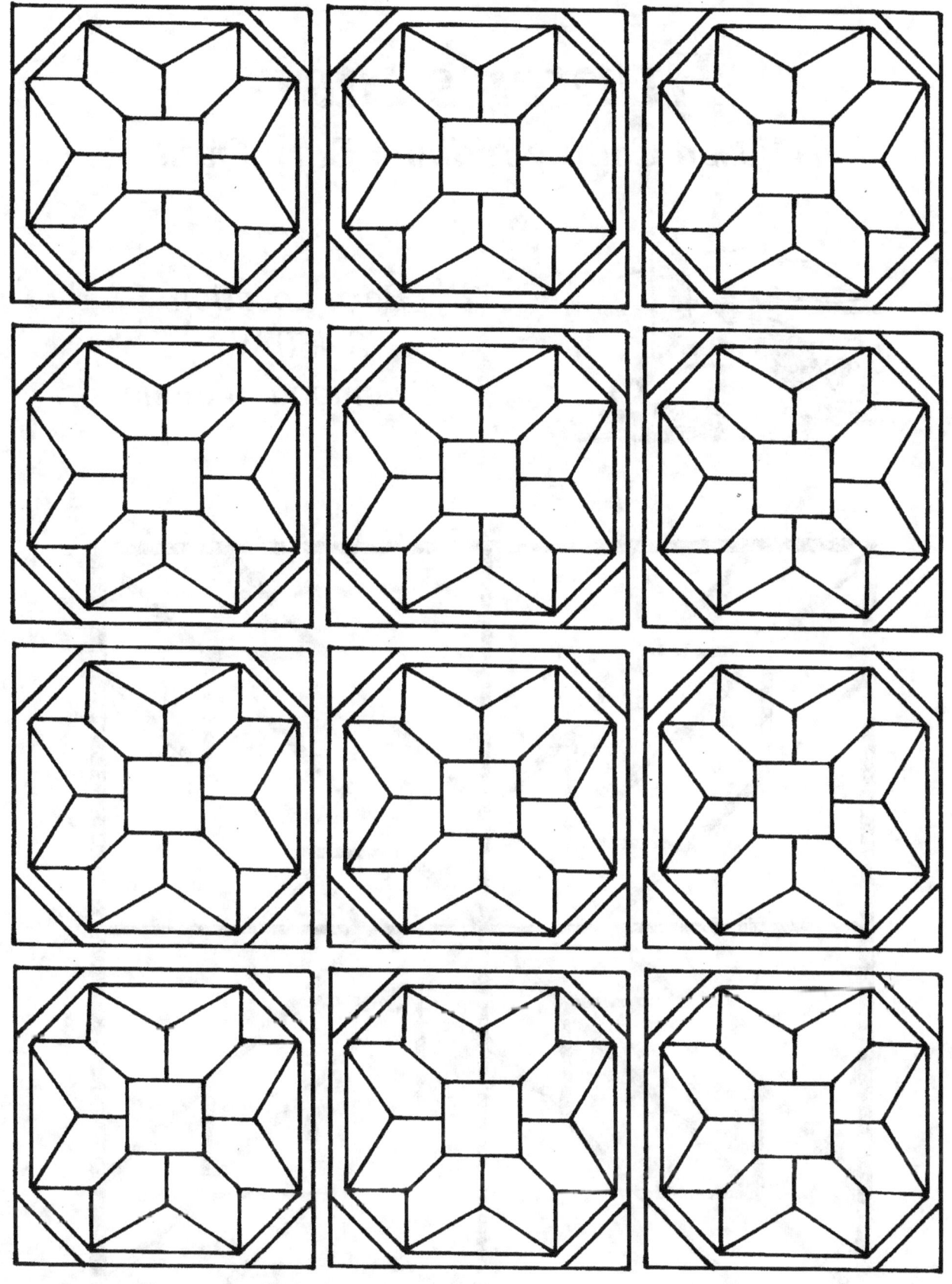

Hunter's Star
Gibson County Indiana Barn Quilt

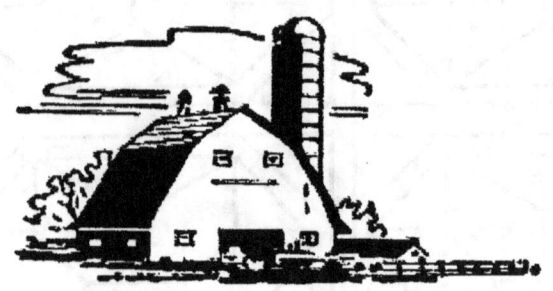

Barn Location
S 450 W
Cynthiana, Indiana

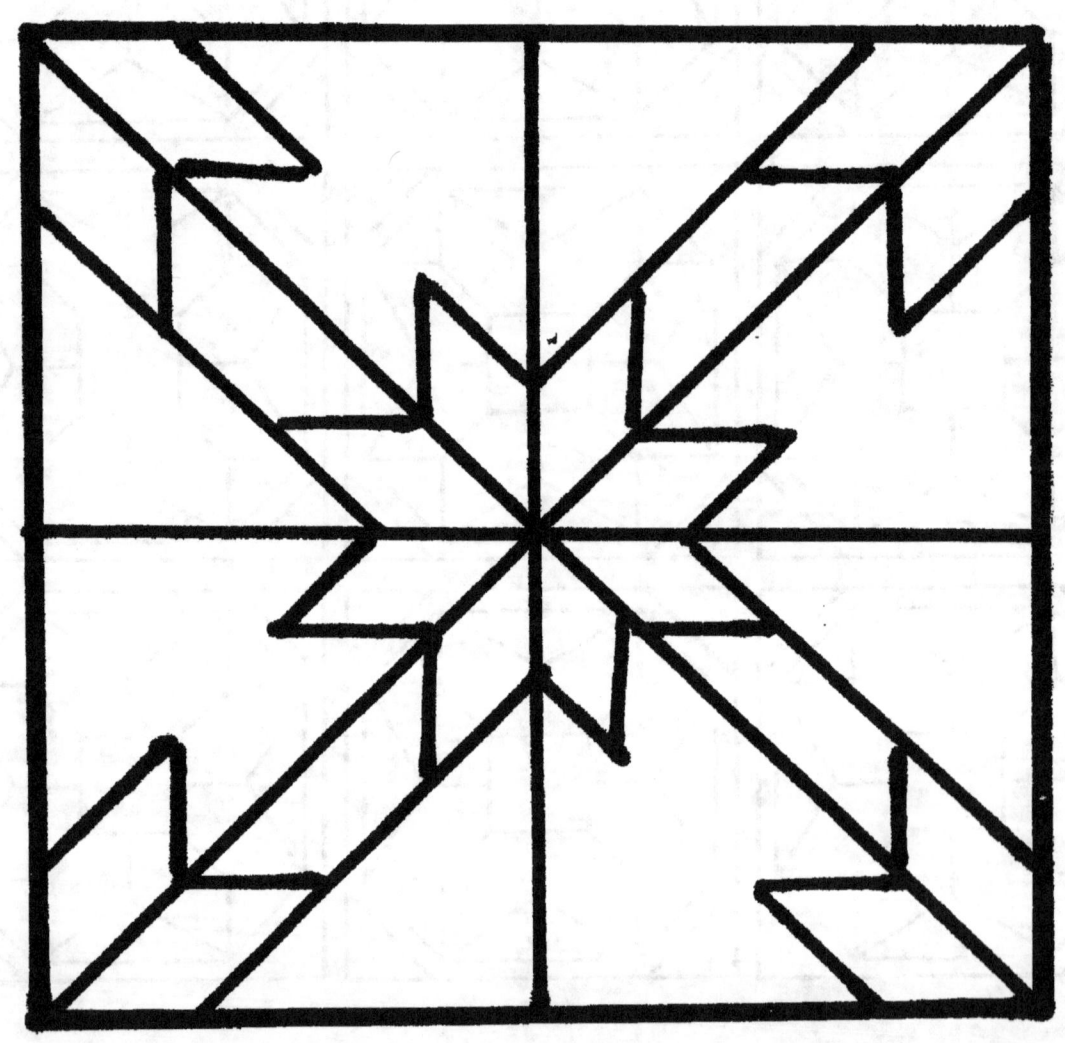

Gibson County Barn Quilt Hunter's Star

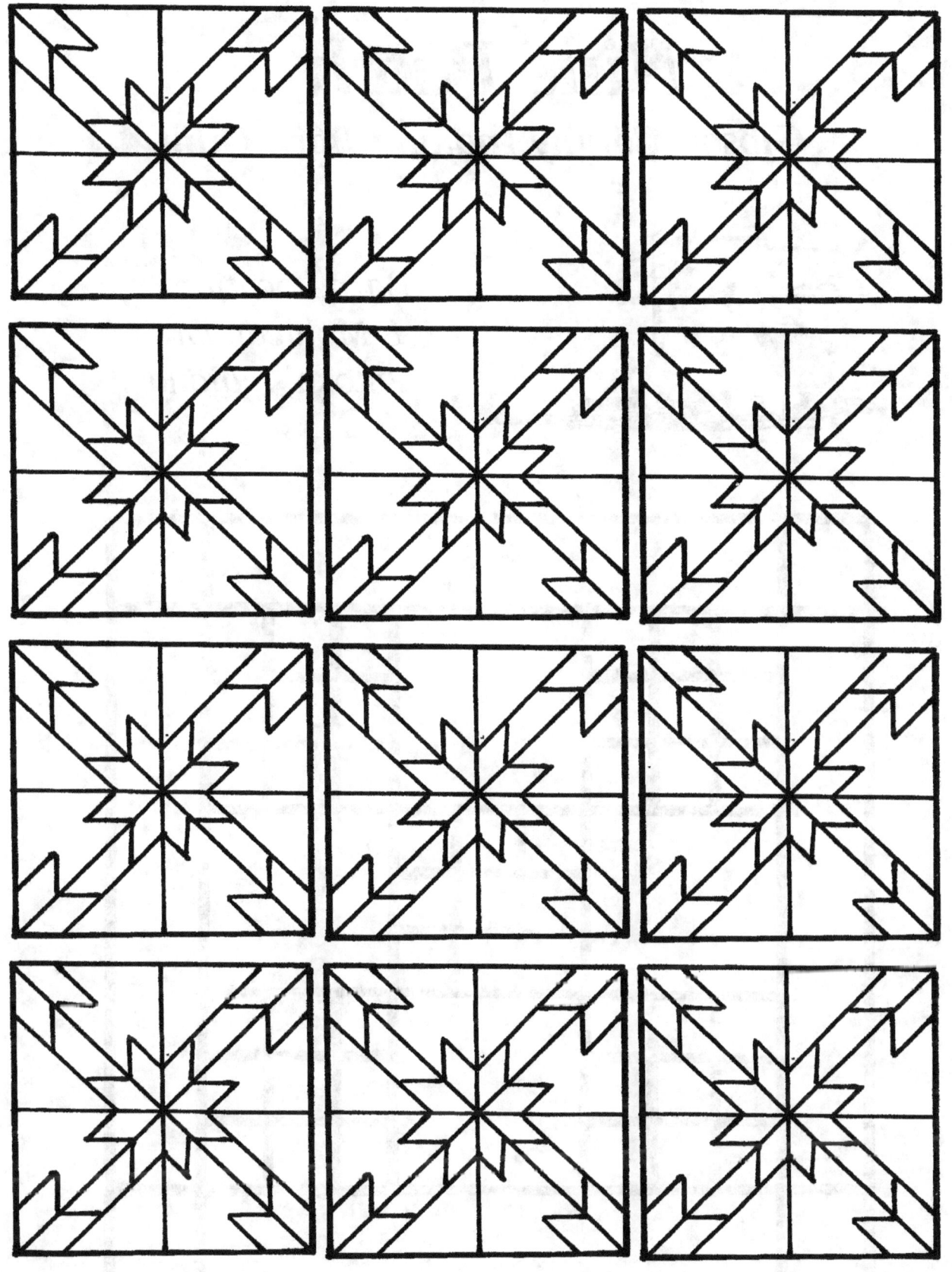

Nine Patch

Gibson County Indiana Barn Quilt

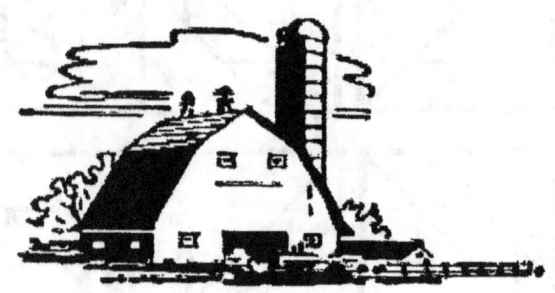

Barn Location
S Mohican Dr
Patoka, Indiana

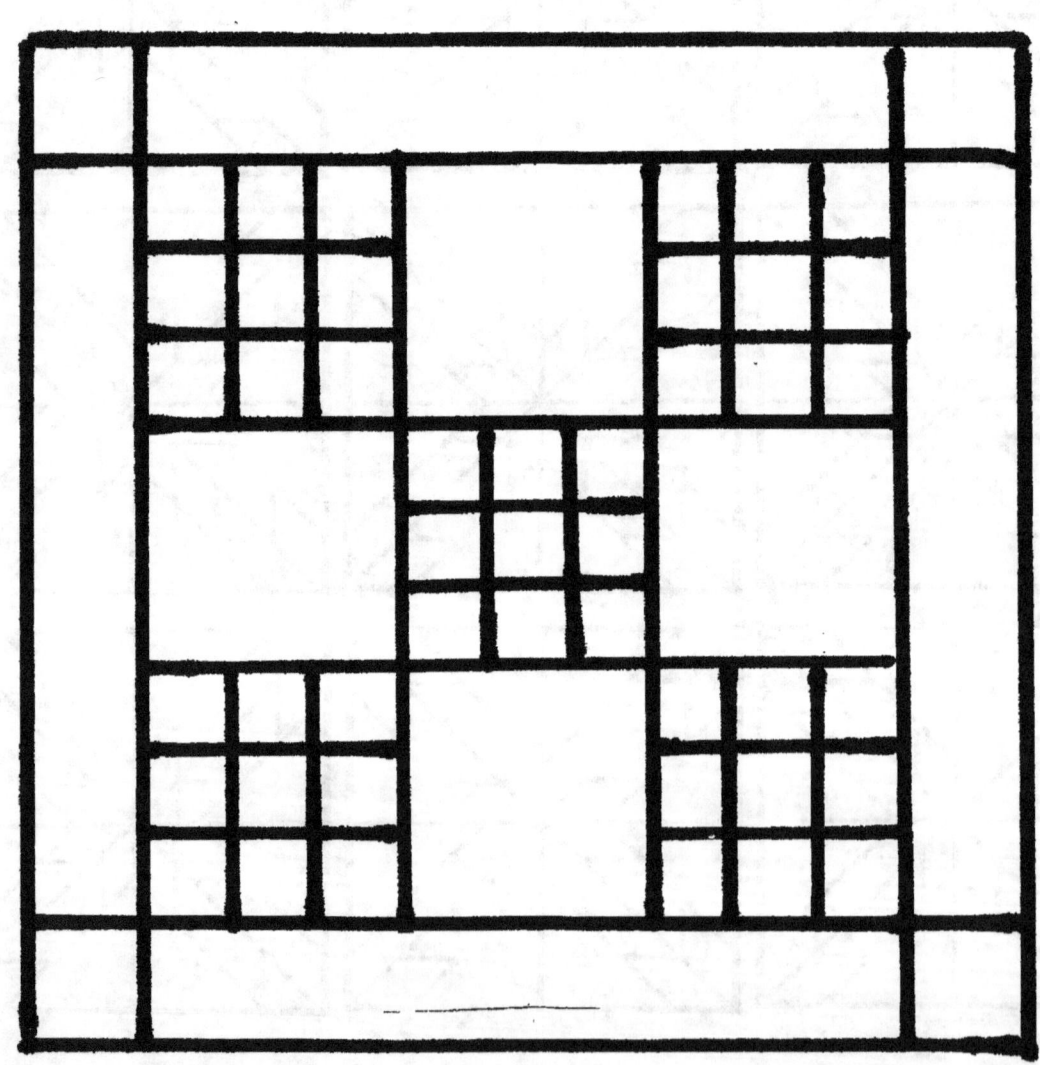

Gibson County Barn Quilt Nine Patch

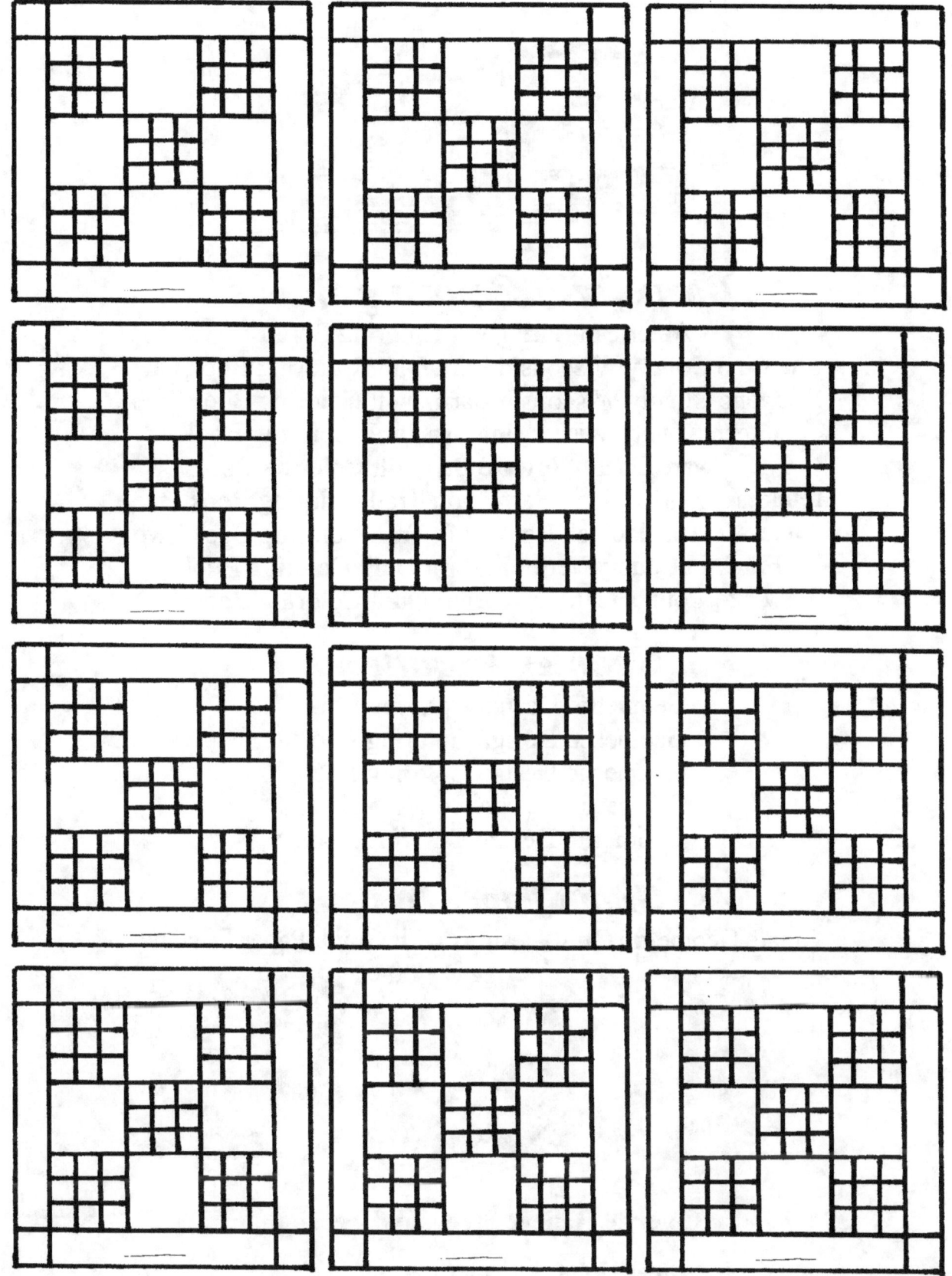

John Lettau Coloring Books

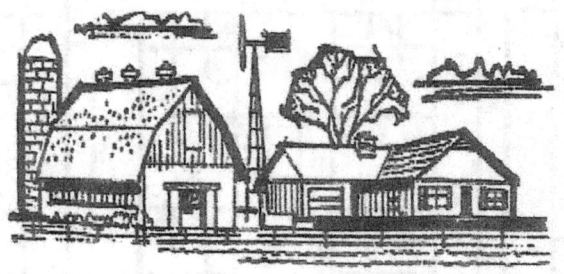

Barn Quilt Coloring Books

American Barn Quilt Coloring Book
Shawano County Wisconsin Barn Quilt Coloring Book One
Shawano County Wisconsin Barn Quilt Coloring Book Two
Green County Wisconsin Barn Quilt Coloring Book
Delaware County Iowa Barn Quilt Coloring Book
Tennessee Appalachian Barn Quilt Trail Coloring Book One
Tennessee Appalachian Barn Quilt Trail Coloring Book Two
Franklin County Vermont Barn Quilt Coloring Book
Lake County California Barn Quilt Coloring Book

Geometric Patterns

Geometric Design Coloring Book 1
Geometric Design Coloring Book 2
Geometric Design Coloring Book 3
Geometric Design Coloring Book 4
Geometric Design Coloring Book 5

Graph Paper Designs

Create Geometric Quilt Designs with Graph Paper Designs

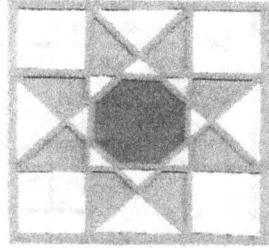 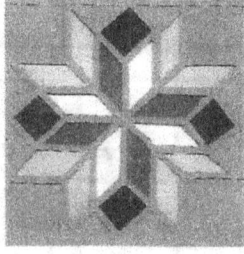 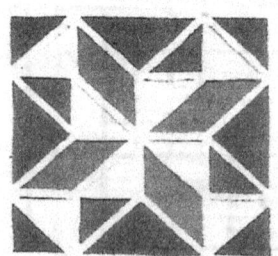

Color to Relieve Stress and Tension

Order...John H. Lettau at Amazon.com

READING & MATH BOOKS by JOHN H. LETTAU

1st Dimension	Grades 3-6
2nd Dimension	Grades 3-6
Primary Dimension	Grades 1-4
Aztec Math Primary Book One	Grades 1-3
Aztec Math Primary Book Two	Grades 1-3
Aztec Math Intermediate Book One	Grades 3-6
Aztec Math Intermediate Book Two	Grades 3-6
Aztec Math Jr. High Book One	Grades 5-8
Aztec Math Jr. High Book Two	Grades 5-8
Aztec Math Decimal Book	Grades 4-8
Aztec Math Fraction Book	Grades 4-8
Sum-Action Number Puzzle Book One	Grades 3-6
Sum-Action Number Puzzle Book Two	Grades 3-6
Sum-Action Number Puzzle Primary Book One	Grades 1-3
Sum-Action Number Puzzle Primary Book Two	Grades 1-3
Multiplication Number Puzzles	Grades 3-6
Geometric Design Puzzle Book One	Grades 3-6
Geometric Design Puzzle Book Two	Grades 3-6
Aztec Reading Primary Book One	Grades 1-3
Aztec Reading Primary Book Two	Grades 1-3
Math in Action	Grades 3-6
A-Maze-ing Number Puzzles	Grades 3-6
Graph Paper Designs	Grades 2-6
Pick-A-Dilly Papers	Grades 3-6
Awards for All Reasons	Grades 1-6
Time Marches On	Grades 1-3
Pennies, Nickels & Dimes	Grades 1-3
Super-Sum Activity Cards	Grades 3-6
Learning Center Game Boards	Grades 1-3
Aztec Design Coloring Book	Grades 1-6

www.ingramcontent.com/pod-product-compliance
Lightning Source LLC
Chambersburg PA
CBHW081735220526
45468CB00008B/2112